A Descartes Dictionary

THE
BLACKWELL PHILOSOPHER DICTIONARIES

A Descartes Dictionary

John Cottingham

BLACKWELL
Reference

First published 1993

First published USA 1993

Blackwell Publishers
108 Cowley Road
Oxford   OX4 1JF
UK

238 Main Street, Suite 501, Cambridge, Massachusetts 02142
USA

British Library Cataloguing in Publication Data

A CIP catalogue record for this book is available from the British Library.

Library of Congress Cataloging-in-Publication Data

Cottingham, John, 1943–
    A Descartes dictionary / John Cottingham.
        p.   cm. –– (The Blackwell philosopher dictionaries)
    Includes bibliographical references and index.
    ISBN 0-631-17683-7 (acid-free paper) : £37.50. –– ISBN
0-631-18538-0 (pbk. : acid-free paper) : £14.95
        1. Descartes, René, 1596–1650––Dictionaries, indexes, etc.
I. Title.   II. Series.
B1831.C67   1993
194––dc20
                                                                92-39483
                                                                CIP

Typeset in Baskerville 10/11pt by Acorn Bookwork, Salisbury, Wilts
Printed in Great Britain by T. J. Press (Padstow) Ltd, Padstow, Cornwall

This book is printed on acid-free paper

Contents

Preface

I should like to record my grateful thanks to Enrique Chávez-Arvizo for invaluable editorial assistance in the final stage of compiling this Dictionary.

J.C.
University of Reading, England
June 1992

Note on the use of this book

The secondary literature on Descartes is gigantic. Since almost all the topics covered in the entries that follow have been the subject of scores of learned articles, if not entire books, any attempt to aim for completeness in discussing the issues involved would be self-defeating. In what follows I have tried to trace out the main outlines of Descartes' thought, attempting as far as possible to let the Cartesian texts speak for themselves (though specialist readers will be well aware of the compression and selectivity that the demands of concision have inevitably required). Although Descartes is an astonishingly lucid writer, that very lucidity can be a pitfall, since terms whose sense at first appears transparent may in fact carry connotations or presuppositions whose import is far from straightforward; in such cases I have tried to show something of the intellectual background which shaped Descartes' ideas, despite his claim to be 'starting afresh'. Apart from citations from such early sources, and some writings from contemporaries or near contemporaries of Descartes, individual entries have been kept clear of references to the works of commentators and critics; a selection of some of the most important of these secondary works will be found in the Bibliography.

Abbreviations

In this book, the following standard abbreviations are used to refer to editions of Descartes:

AT: C. Adam and P. Tannery (eds.), *Œuvres de Descartes* (revised edn., 12 vols., Paris: Vrin/CNRS, 1964–76). References are by volume number (in roman) and page number (in arabic).

CSM: J. Cottingham, R. Stoothoff and D. Murdoch (eds.), *The Philosophical Writings of Descartes* (2 vols., Cambridge: Cambridge University Press, 1985). References by volume number (in roman) and page number (in arabic).

CSMK: Volume III of the preceding, by the same translators and Anthony Kenny (Cambridge: Cambridge University Press, 1991). References by page number.

It should be noted that, while passages are generally quoted verbatim from the translations in CSM and CSMK, I have occasionally introduced minor modifications in style and phrasing for the purposes of the present volume.

In addition to the editions mentioned above, citations from the *Principles of Philosophy* and the *Passions of the Soul* are sometimes made by reference to the original Part and article numbers, which are to be found in all editions and translations of these works.

Details of all other editions of Descartes, and of other primary and secondary sources, are to be found in the Bibliography.

Introduction:
Descartes' Life and Works

'An unending task, beyond the scope of a single person' (AT X 157: CSMK 43). So Descartes, writing as a young man of twenty-three, described the daunting intellectual project on which he had embarked. During the following three decades, until his untimely death at the age of fifty-three, he developed a philosophical and scientific system of the most extraordinary range and power. In a way which has long since ceased to be possible in our modern specialized age, he tackled the major structural problems of metaphysics and epistemology, devised a general theory of the nature and origins of the physical world, did detailed work on pure and applied mathematics, composed treatises on mechanics and physiology, examined the nature of man and the relationship between mind and body, and published extensive reflections on psychology and ethics. Perhaps no other philosophical system provides such an impressively integrated conception of the scope of human knowledge, and perhaps no other writer has succeeded in communicating his central ideas so vividly or so directly. To confront the Cartesian system is to contemplate a magnificently laid out map of human cognitive endeavour – finely detailed, yet one whose general outlines are remarkably clear and easy to grasp; to follow Descartes' arguments is to be drawn into some of the most fundamental and challenging issues in philosophy, many of which are still vigorously alive today.

Descartes is often called the 'father of modern philosophy', but the concept of modernity is a slippery one. It is certainly true that, along with other giants of the intellectual 'revolution' of the seventeenth century such as Galileo, Descartes articulated some of the most central presuppositions of what we now think of as the modern 'scientific' outlook; by the end of his life he had, if not demolished, at least seriously undermined, many of the hallowed tenets of traditional medieval and scholastic philosophy. But it is also true (as some of the entries in this book should help to make clear) that his ways of thinking, particularly in metaphysics, were often heavily indebted to the ideas of the traditionalists whom he claimed to supplant. Revolutions in thought are seldom instant affairs; part of the fascination of the study of Descartes, along with the other major philosophers of the seventeenth century, is the sense of continuous struggle which emerges as the old categories of thought are systematically re-examined. Descartes self-consciously presented himself as an innovator: 'I realized that it was necessary, once in the course of my life, to demolish everything completely and start again right from the foundations, if I wanted to establish anything at all in the sciences that was stable and likely to last' (AT VII 17: CSM II 12). Although the 'demolition' job was not, perhaps, as radical as Descartes advertised it as being, the central Cartesian texts none the less draw the reader along with a sense of excitement, as one after another of our preconceptions is critically scrutinized. It is above all this sense of challenge, of being forbidden to take anything for granted and being thrown back on our own individual resources, that makes the central Cartesian texts so gripping. But beyond this, the issues that Descartes tackles – the search for reliable foundations for science, the transition from subjective awareness to objective knowledge, the place of man in the universe, the nature of mental states and their relationship with the body – still remain at the very heart of philosophical inquiry. Though the Cartesian solutions seldom command assent among today's philosophers, few would deny that the conceptual landscape within which the problems arise has been largely shaped, for better or worse, by the philosophy of Descartes.

René Descartes was born in France on 31 March 1596 in the small town of La Haye (now renamed 'Descartes') between Tours and Poitiers. The house where he was born still stands, and is now a small museum. He was brought up by his maternal grandmother (his mother having died soon after his birth), and at the age of ten he was sent to the recently founded Jesuit college of La Flèche in Anjou, where he remained as a boarding pupil for nine years. At La Flèche he studied classical literature, and traditional classics-based subjects such as history and rhetoric, as well as taking extended courses in natural philosophy (based on the Aristotelian system) and theology. He later wrote of La Flèche that he considered it 'one of the best schools in Europe', but that, as regards the philosophy he had learned there, he saw that 'despite being cultivated for many centuries by the best minds', it contained 'no point which was not disputed and hence doubtful' (AT VI 8; CSM I 115).

At the age of twenty-two, having taken a law degree at Poitiers, Descartes set out on a series of travels in Europe 'resolving', as he later put it, 'to seek no knowledge other than that which could be found either in myself or the great book of the world' (AT VI 9: CSM I 115). The most important influence of this early period was Descartes' friendship with the Dutchman Isaac Beeckman, who awakened his lifelong interest in mathematics – a science in which he discerned precision and certainty of the kind which truly merited the title of *scientia* (Descartes' term for genuine systematic knowledge based on reliable principles). A considerable portion of Descartes' energies as a young man was devoted to pure mathematics: his essay on *Geometry* (published in 1637) incorporated results discovered during the 1620s. But he also saw mathematics as the key to making progress in the applied sciences; his earliest work, the *Compendium Musicae* ('Compendium of Music'), written in 1618 and dedicated to Beeckman, applied quantitative principles to the study of musical harmony and dissonance. More generally, mathematics was seen by Descartes as a kind of paradigm for all human understanding: 'those long chains composed of very simple and easy reasonings, which geometers customarily use to arrive at their most difficult demonstrations, gave me occasion to suppose that all the things which fall within the scope of human knowledge are interconnected in the same way' (AT VI 19: CSM I 120).

In the course of his travels, Descartes found himself closeted, on 10 November 1619, in a 'stove-heated room' in a town in southern Germany, where after a day of intense meditation, he had a series of vivid dreams which convinced him of his mission to found a new scientific and philosophical system. The general outlines of that system are expounded in an unfinished work composed during the late 1620s, the *Regulae ad directionem ingenii* (*Rules for the Direction of our Native Intelligence*). Here Descartes defines 'knowledge' (*scientia*) as 'certain and evident cognition', based either on the direct mental apprehension of self-evident truths (what Descartes calls 'intuition'), or else on what can be deduced from such truths in an unbroken chain of inference. He also outlines the plan for a 'universal science' which will encompass all the branches of human knowledge: 'I came to see that the exclusive concern of mathematics is with questions of order or measure, and that it is irrelevant whether the measure in question involves numbers, shapes, stars, sounds, or any other object whatsoever; this made me realize that there must be a general science which explains all the points that can be raised concerning order and measure, irrespective of subject matter' (AT X 378: CSM I 19).

Descartes emigrated to Holland in 1628, where he was to live (though with frequent changes of address) for most of the rest of his life. In the early 1630s, he formed a liaison with his serving woman Hélène, and the result of this involvement was a daughter, Francine, born on 19 July 1635; the girl died tragically of a fever, five years later. In general, Descartes seems to have shunned company, and he wrote later to Mersenne that the quiet of north Holland was far better suited to his work than the 'air of Paris with its innumerable distractions' (AT II 152). In 1633, he had ready a treatise on cosmology and physics, *Le Monde* ('The World' or 'The Universe'), but he cautiously withdrew the work from publication when he heard of the condemnation of Galileo by the Inquisition for rejecting (as Descartes himself did) the traditional geocentric theory of the universe. *Le Monde* also contained a section (now known as *Le Traité de l'Homme* or 'Treatise on Man') which attempted to explain the workings of the human body in strictly physical and mechanical terms, by reference to the same laws of matter in motion that Descartes saw as operating throughout the universe.

In 1637, Descartes overcame his caution sufficiently to release for publication, in French, a sample of his scientific work, the three essays entitled the *Optics, Meteorology* and *Geometry* (*La Dioptrique, Les Météores, La Géométrie*). Prefaced to that selection was an autobiographical introduction entitled *Discourse on the Method of rightly conducting one's reason and reaching the truth in the sciences* (*Discourse de la Méthode pour bien conduire sa raison et chercher la vérité dans les sciences*). The *Discourse*, which includes discussion of a number of scientific issues such as the circulation of the blood, contains (in Part IV) a summary of Descartes' views on knowledge, certainty, and the metaphysical foundations of science. Criticisms of his arguments here led Descartes to compose his philosophical masterpiece, the *Meditations on First Philosophy* (*Meditationes de Prima Philosophia*), written in Latin and published in Paris in 1641 – a dramatic account of the voyage of discovery from universal doubt to certainty of one's own existence, and the subsequent struggle to establish the existence of God, the nature and existence of the external world, and the relation between mind and body. In the Sixth and last Meditation, Descartes advances his famous dualistic thesis that there is a 'real' or substantial distinction between unextended thinking substance, or mind, and extended substance, or body. The *Meditations* aroused enormous interest among Descartes' contemporaries, and six sets of objections by celebrated philosophers and theologians (including Marin Mersenne, Thomas Hobbes, Antoine Arnauld and Pierre Gassendi) were published, along with Descartes' replies, in the same volume as the first edition; a seventh set of objections, by the Jesuit Pierre Bourdin, was included, with Descartes' replies, in the second edition, which appeared in Amsterdam in 1642.

A few years later, Descartes published, in Latin, a mammoth compendium of his metaphysical and scientific views, the *Principia Philosophiae* (*Principles of Philosophy*, 1644; a slightly augmented French version, produced, with Descartes' approval, by the Abbé Picot, appeared in 1647). Descartes hoped that his *Principles* would become a university textbook to rival the standard texts based on Aristotle; he had written earlier to his friend and literary editor Marin Mersenne that his plan was to make the results of his *Le Monde* more acceptable to the scholastics (AT III 523: CSMK 210). The work comprises four parts, each divided into a number of short sections or 'articles' (there are 504 in all). Part I lays out Descartes' principal metaphysical doctrines regarding knowledge, God, mind and body; Part II expounds the principles of Cartesian physics; Part III gives a detailed explanation, in accordance with those principles, of the nature of the universe; and Part IV deals similarly with the origins of the earth and a wide variety of terrestrial phenomena, including 'gravity', the tides, fire, the making of glass and of steel, and magnetism. A further two parts were planned, covering plants and animals, and man, but these were never completed. Descartes did, however, resume his study of human physiology in the late 1640s, the resulting (unfinished) treatise (known as *La Description du Corps Humain* – 'Description of the Human Body'), deals with the circulation of the blood and the formation of the foetus. Taking up the theme of his earlier *Treatise on Man*, Descartes argues that, if we leave aside the intellectual and volitional activities of the 'rational soul', the workings of 'the entire bodily machine' can be explained on purely mechanical principles (AT XI 226: CSM I 315).

A source of constant worry to Descartes during the 1640s was the hostility his work aroused among the theologians. His correspondence contains many of his replies – sometimes cautiously polite, sometimes testy and impatient – to a wide spread of objections, ranging from minor quibbles to major broadsides, both from his co-religionists in Catholic France and also from Dutch Protestant ministers in his country of exile. Among the most implacable of his opponents was the Professor of Theology and Rector at the University of Utrecht, Gisbert Voët (or Voetius), and after Voetius persuaded the Senate at Utrecht to issue a formal condemnation of the Cartesian philosophy, Descartes published, in May 1643, a long open letter of self-defence, the *Epistula ad Voetium* ('Letter to Voetius'). Part of Voetius' hostility was directed against the work of an eager pupil of Descartes, Henri Le Roy (Regius), whom Descartes had at first encouraged (though often cautioning him about the most prudent way of avoiding needless controversy). Eventually, however, Regius published, in 1646, a work called the 'Foundations of Physics' (*Fundamenta physices*), which not only plagiarized many of Descartes' published and unpublished ideas, but also (so Descartes felt) systematically distorted his views on the nature of man and the relation between mind and body. Descartes published a short refutation of Regius' views, the 'Comments on a Certain Broadsheet' (*Notae in Programma quoddam*) early in 1648. In April of the same year he was interviewed, at his home in Egmond-Binnen, by a young Dutchman, Frans Burman, who questioned him in detail about many problematic passages in the *Meditations, Principles* and *Discourse*. Burman's notes of the interview have survived in manuscript, and the resulting document (now known as the *Conversation with Burman*) throws light on several important aspects of Cartesian metaphysics, as well as indicating Descartes' impatience with the theological disputes into which he was so often unwillingly drawn.

In the later 1640s, Descartes became interested in questions of ethics and psychology, partly as a result of acute questions about the implications of his system raised by Princess Elizabeth of Bohemia in a long and fruitful correspondence. The results of this interest were published in 1649 in a lengthy French treatise entitled *Les Passions de l'âme* (*The Passions of the Soul*). This work provides a wealth of detail on the 'substantial union' between mind and body, which Descartes took to be definitive of the human condition, and explains, or at any rate describes, the physiological basis for the wide range of emotions and feelings which 'arise in the soul' when our brains are stimulated in various ways. The book also contains Descartes' recipe for the good life; he had earlier observed to Elizabeth that 'the supreme felicity of man depends on the right use of reason' (AT IV 267: CSMK 258), and he now set out the means whereby that reason can be used to channel and regulate the passions, on whose well-moderated flow depend 'the sweetest pleasures of which we are capable in this life' (AT XI 488: CSM I 404).

In the same year as the publication of the *Passions*, Descartes accepted (after much hesitation) an invitation to go to Stockholm to give philosophical instruction to Queen Christina of Sweden. He was required to provide tutorials at the royal palace at five o'clock in the morning, and the strain of this break in his habits (he had maintained a lifelong custom of lying in bed late into the morning) led to his catching pneumonia. He died on 11 February 1650, just short of his fifty-fourth birthday. Among the materials found in his papers on his death was an unfinished dialogue, *La Recherche de la Vérité* (*The Search for Truth*), which describes how 'Polyander' (or 'Everyman'), the untutored person of ordinary common sense, can, 'without any help from religion or philosophy', learn to be guided simply by the inner 'natural light', so as to 'penetrate into the secrets of the most recondite sciences' (AT X 495: CSM II 400).

The appeal to the light of truth within each individual is an enduring theme of Descartes' philosophy. He was not a rigid 'apriorist' – his work on science shows the indispensable role of empirical observation for reaching decisions when rival hypotheses conflict (AT VI 64–5: CSM I 144). But he did believe that the general outlines of science could be derived from the 'laws of nature which God has implanted in each soul' (AT VI 41: CSM I 131), and, more fundamentally still, that the metaphysical foundations for science could be securely established by the careful introspective reflections of the isolated individual meditator. The resulting vision of a unified, reliably grounded philosophical and scientific system was one that Descartes never lost sight of, from the time when, as a young traveller in Germany, he had written of his plan to 'unmask the sciences' and reveal them linked together 'in all their beauty' (AT X 215: CSM I 3). A principal motive for philosophizing has always been to see how far the various areas of human cognitive endeavour fit (or fail to fit) together. This project, and the way in which it was conceived and developed by its most famous and articulate exponent, will continue to fascinate for as long as philosophy is studied.

A

---

analogies　In the opening section of the *Optics*, Descartes argues that 'the light in the bodies we call "luminous" is nothing other than a certain movement or very rapid and lively action, which passes to our eyes through the medium of the air and other transparent bodies, just as the movement or resistance of the bodies encountered by a blind man passes to his hand by means of his stick' (AT VI 84: CSM I 153; later in the same passage, he switches to a different model – that of grapes in a wine-press). The use of analogies like those of the walking stick or the wine-press in order to explain the transmission of light is fairly typical of Descartes' procedure when presenting his scientific views, and he emphatically defended their use on several occasions (see letter to Plempius of 3 October 1637: AT I 416: CSMK 63). In each case, what Descartes invokes is a relatively commonplace and familiar example, drawn from everyday experience, which is then used to support the plausibility of the micro-mechanical explanation which he is offering for a given phenomenon. It has to be said that despite the 'empirical' flavour of Descartes' scientific analogies, there is very little empirical research, in the modern sense, to support his claims that the phenomena of light, or heat, or the motion of the solar system (where the famous VORTEX analogy is used) actually operate analogously to the models invoked. Rather, Descartes seems content to have put forward a general explanatory programme for physics (based on a few fundamental laws of mechanics), and then to have tried to underscore the simplicity and self-evidence of the type of explanation offered by drawing as many comparisons as possible with ordinary 'middle-sized' mechanical examples. 'In the analogies (*les comparaisons*) which I employ', he wrote to Morin on 12 September 1638, 'I compare movements only with other movements, or shapes with other shapes; that is, I compare things that are too small to be perceived by the sense with other things that can be so perceived, the latter differing from the former simply as a large circle differs from a small one. I maintain therefore, that analogies of this sort are the most appropriate means available to the human mind for laying bare the truth in problems of physics' (AT II 368: CSMK 122).

analysis, method of In many of his writings, Descartes claimed to be following a new 'method' of inquiry, and the general features of this are tolerably clear (*see* METHOD). The more specific term 'the method of analysis' is, however, also used in a number of contexts, and it was a label which Descartes' critics sometimes employed to refer to his philosophical approach (cf. Sixth Replies, AT VII 413: CSM II 278). In the *Regulae*, Descartes had referred to 'the geometers of antiquity who employed a sort of analysis which they went on to apply to the solution of every problem, though they begrudged revealing it to posterity' (AT X 373: CSM I 17; cf. Dedicatory Letter to *Meditations*, AT VII 4: CSM II 5). In the Second Replies, published with the *Meditations*, Descartes is more explicit, contrasting the 'method of synthesis', where conclusions are deduced from axioms, and 'each step is contained in what has gone before', with his own 'method of analysis'. The former is suited to formal demonstrations in geometry, relying on 'a long series of definitions, postulates, axioms and theorems', but the latter 'shows the true way by means of which [things] are discovered methodically ... so that if the reader is willing to follow, he will make the thing his own, and understand it just as perfectly as if he had discovered it himself' (AT VII 155: CSM II 110). Although Descartes did accept the invitation of Mersenne to provide a 'geometrical exposition' of his metaphysical arguments (AT VII 160ff: CSM II 113ff.), he clearly believed that the dynamic 'order of discovery', which he had in fact followed in the *Meditations*, was better suited to the subject matter (cf. AT VII 159: CSM II 113; cf. *Conversation with Burman*, AT V 153: CSMK 337–8: 'the method and order of discovery is one thing, that of exposition another'). 'The primary notions which are presupposed for the demonstration of geometrical truths are readily accepted by anyone, since they accord with the use of our senses. . . . In metaphysics, by contrast, there is nothing which causes so much effort as making our perception of the primary notions clear and distinct . . . since they conflict with the preconceived opinions derived from the senses which we have got into the habit of holding from our earliest years' (AT VII 157: CSM II 111). It emerges from this that the chief feature of the 'method of analysis' is that it starts from scratch, by demolishing the preconceived opinions of the past, and then proceeds to follow the reflections of an individual meditator, struggling to achieve self-evident starting points for subsequent construction of a body of reliable knowledge. 'This is why', Descartes observed in the Second Replies, 'I wrote "Meditations" rather than "Disputations", as the philosophers would have done, or "Theorems and Problems" as the geometers would have done, for I wanted to make it clear that I would have nothing to do with anyone who was not willing to join me in meditating, and giving the subject matter attentive consideration' (AT VII 157: CSM II 112).

For more on the special character of Descartes' metaphysical inquiries, *see* MEDITATIONS. For the contrast between his approach, and the formal techniques of traditional philosophical method, *see* SYLLOGISM.

angel Traditionally conceived, an angel is a spirit, an incorporeal being which (in Descartes' words) 'though it can act upon an extended thing, is not itself extended' (AT V 270: CSMK 361). Since this is precisely how Descartes conceives of the human mind, there would appear to be a close analogy between an angel temporarily assigned to a body and a human being; in both cases, what seems to be involved is that a pure incorporeal spirit makes use of a bodily mechanism which is alien to its true nature.

This interpretation of Descartes' views led his disciple Regius to present the Cartesian position as asserting that man is an *ens per accidens*, that is, that a human being is not a true entity in its own right, but is composed of two distinct substances, soul and body, which may happen to be joined (e.g. during our earthly life), but which do not make up an essential unity. In his reply to Regius, Descartes tried to distance himself from this interpretation: it is better, he wrote, to say that man is an *ens per se* (an entity in its own right), and 'that the human mind is united in a real and substantial manner to the body' (AT III 493: CSMK 206). But this in turn requires Descartes to explain how a human being differs, in respect of the mind–body relation, from an angel making use of a body. His answer is that 'if an angel were in a human body, he would not have sensations (*sentire*) as we do, but would simply perceive (*percipere*, i.e. be intellectually aware of) the motions which are caused by external objects, and in this way would differ from a real man' (ibid., cf. AT VII 81: CSM II 56). It is thus the sensory dimension which, for Descartes, distinguishes our human mental life from the mental life of an angel, or pure spirit, and an investigation of the nature of sensation thus turns out to be the key to understanding the 'substantial union' of mind and body that constitutes a true human being.

See also HUMAN BEING and SENSATION.

animal spirits Despite the somewhat misleading name, Descartes' 'animal spirits' are purely physical items. In his physiology, they play the role which is today filled by neuro-electrical impulses: they are the medium for the transmission of information throughout the nervous system. 'All the movements of the muscles', Descartes wrote in *The Passions of the Soul*, 'and likewise all sensations, depend on the nerves, which are like little threads or tubes coming from the brain, and containing, like the brain itself, a certain very fine air or wind, which is called the "animal spirits" (*les esprits animaux*)' (*Passions*, Part. I, art. 7, AT XI 332: CSM I 330).

Descartes saw as the principal advantage of his 'pneumatic' account of the

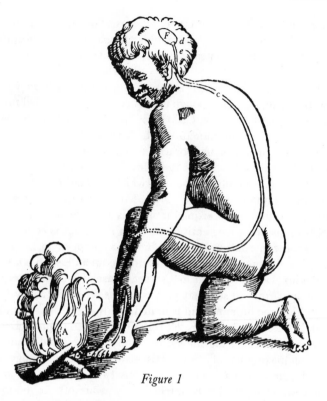

Figure 1

operation of the nervous system that it avoided any reference to occult powers. In place of the scholastic notion of the 'locomotive soul' responsible for movement in humans and other animals, the Cartesian account invokes nothing more than mechanical micro-events, explicable on exactly the same principles as any other physical phenomenon. 'What I am calling "spirits" here are merely bodies: they have no property other than that of being extremely small bodies which move very quickly, like the jets of flame that come from a torch' (*Passions*, Part I, art. 10). In his earlier work, the *Treatise on Man*, Descartes had provided a detailed account of how muscle contractions (e.g. those involved in breathing and swallowing) are brought about by means of the spirits, and he sketched out, in effect, the basis for a theory of reflex actions: 'If fire A is close to foot B, the tiny parts of the fire have the power to move the area of skin which they touch, thus pulling the tiny fibre cc attached to it, and simultaneously opening the entrance to the pore de located by the point where this fibre terminates, just as when you pull one end of string you cause a bell hanging at the other end to ring. When the entrance to the tube de is opened in this way, the animal spirits from cavity F enter and are transmitted, some to the muscles which serve to pull the foot away from the fire, some to the muscles which turn the eyes and head to look at it . . .' In such a process (closely similar whether in human or in animal movements) conscious awareness is not involved at all. Only if God unites a soul to the body will there be 'sensations corresponding to the different ways in which the entrances to the pores in the internal surface of the brain are opened by means of the nerves' (*Treatise on Man*, AT XI 142–3: CSM I 101–2; *see* ANIMALS; MIND AND BODY; SENSATION).

In the final part of the *Passions of the Soul*, Descartes explores the role of the animal spirits in underpinning those habits of thought and feeling that constitute human virtue (Part III, art. 161ff).

See PASSIONS.

animals   The term 'animal' is etymologically connected with the Latin *anima* ('soul'), and hence bears traces of the scholastic idea that living creatures differ from non-living things in virtue of their being 'animated' or 'ensouled'; this notion partly has its roots in the biblical conception of living things as animated with 'the breath of life', and partly derives from Aristotelian biology, which attributed to living things a hierarchy of faculties, often called various kinds of 'soul' – 'vegetative', 'locomotive', 'sensory' and (in the case of man) 'rational'.

Descartes follows tradition only in one respect – the attribution of a rational soul to man (AT XI 143: CSM I 102; AT VI 59: CSM I 141). But in the case of non-human animals (and non-conscious functions in man), he insists that all the relevant behaviour can be explained purely mechanically, without the need to posit any 'animating' principle. Typically, indeed, he avoids the word *animal* to describe creatures like dogs, cats and monkeys, preferring the more down-to-earth label *bête* ('beast'), or in Latin *brutum* ('brute'). The fact that the beasts appear to exhibit complex purposive behaviour (seeking food, running away from danger) did not seem to Descartes to be a decisive objection against his radically reductionistic view of them as mere mechanical automata: if the skill of man is able to construct self-moving machines with the use of a very few parts, why do we not similarly regard a biological body simply as 'a machine which, having been made by the hand of God, is incomparably better ordered than any machine that can be devised by man'? (*Discourse*, Part V: AT VI 56: CSM I 139).

When Descartes' account of animals as mechanical automata is combined with his dualistic ontology (which assigns all things to one of two incompatible realms, the realm of thought and the realm of extension), the implications for our attitude to the beasts become distinctly disturbing. A thinking thing (*res cogitans*) is for Descartes a self-conscious, language-using being, capable in principle of reflecting on its own nature and existence; an extended thing (*res extensa*), by contrast, is characterizable merely in terms of the interactions of its parts, all ultimately reducible to descriptions in terms of size, shape and motion alone. It seems to follow that, since animals are not thinking things, they are mere lumps of extended stuff – complex enough in the organization of their parts, but utterly devoid of anything that could qualify as consciousness. The importance of language, as the 'only sure sign of thought within' (AT V 278: CSMK 366), was seized on by Descartes as crucial evidence that animals were wholly devoid of thought: 'It is quite remarkable that there are no men so dull-witted or stupid – and this includes even madmen – that they are incapable of arranging various words together and forming an utterance from them in order to make their thoughts understood, whereas there is no other animal . . . that can do the like. This is not because they lack the necessary organs, for we see that magpies and parrots can utter words as we do, and yet they cannot speak as we do, that is, they cannot show that they are thinking what they are saying. On the other hand, men born deaf and dumb, and thus deprived of speech organs as much as the beasts or even more so, normally invent their own signs to make themselves understood. . . . This shows not merely that the beasts have less reason than men, but that they have no reason at all' (AT VI 57–8: CSM I 140).

Descartes has interesting arguments to show why the utterances of animals cannot count as genuine language: the sounds that they utter (even in the case of 'talking' animals like parrots) are merely behaviour that is elicited by a particular stimulus. Genuine language-use, on the other hand, involves the ability to respond appropriately to an indefinitely large range of utterances, and this is something that Descartes maintained could not possibly be duplicated by a mere stimulus–response device, whether artificial machine or beast-machine (*see* LANGUAGE).

To deny thought to animals is not *eo ipso* to deny that they *feel*; and Descartes sometimes talked in a way which suggested that animals might have sensations like hunger, or passions like fear, hope and joy (letter to Newcastle of 23 November 1646, AT IV 574: CSMK 303). Descartes' account of the nature of SENSATION is, however, highly problematic. His settled view seems to have been that sensory phenomena arise when mind and body are united; but since animals, on his account, lack minds, it seems to follow that in their case there is, and can be, no psycho-physical union of the kind that could support sensation. And this in turn leaves animals no place in the Cartesian scheme of things except as mere insensible lumps of extended stuff. Certainly, in the century following Descartes' death, his followers became notorious for their ruthless treatment of animals in the course of experimental research in physiology; and we know that Descartes himself practised vivisection with apparent equanimity (AT XI 241–2; CSM I 317). Descartes' own position on the status of animals, however, remains ambiguous: he was adamant in his denial that they have genuine thought/

language, but was content to fudge the issue of what kind of sensory experience, if any, might be attributed to them. 'Please note', he wrote to More on 5 February 1649, 'that I am speaking of thought, not of life or sensation. I do not deny life to animals, since I regard it as consisting simply in the heat of the heart, and I do not even deny sensation, in so far as it depends on a bodily organ. Thus my views are not so much cruel to animals as indulgent to human beings . . . since it absolves them from the suspicion of crime when they kill or eat animals' (AT V 278: CSMK 366).

assumption   Despite the still occasionally found caricature of the Cartesian system as a rigid deductivist one, there are many places where Descartes acknowledges that his scientific system rests on assumptions which may not be rigorously demonstrable. He did not claim that his approach to science eliminated the need for assumptions, only that his assumptions were far more economical, and more fertile, than those of his predecessors: 'Compare my assumptions [French, *suppositions*] with those of others. Compare all their *real qualities*, their *substantial forms*, their *elements* and countless other such things with my single assumption that all bodies are composed of parts. . . . Compare the deductions I have made from my assumption – about vision, salt, winds, clouds, snow, thunder, the rainbow and so on – with what others have derived from their assumptions on the same topics. I hope that this will be enough to convince anyone unbiased that the effects which I explain have no other causes than the ones from which I have deduced them' (letter to Morin of 13 July 1638, AT II 200: CSMK 107).

In the passage just quoted, Descartes goes on nevertheless to reserve the right one day to provide a deductive demonstration of his assumption. There are other passages, however, where he is quite clear that there are limits even in principle to what pure deductive reason can achieve in the realm of science. Having set out his general laws of motion, in the *Principles of Philosophy*, Descartes goes on to observe that the actual organization of the matter in the universe cannot be determined by reason alone; 'since there are countless configurations which God might have instituted here, experience alone must teach us which configurations he actually selected in preference to the rest. We are thus free to make any assumption we choose on these matters [*quidlibet de illis assumere*], provided that all the consequences of our assumption square with experience' (Part III, art. 46, AT VIIIA 101: CSM I 256).

The term 'assumption' was sometimes used in the seventeenth century interchangeably with 'hypothesis', but this could give rise to confusion, since the latter notion carried the connotation that something was being put forward merely as an expository device, without any claim to represent the actual truth. Descartes uses 'hypothesis' in this sense when he writes that 'there is no difference between the [astronomical] hypotheses of Copernicus and Tycho, if they are considered simply as hypotheses'; he goes on to distinguish a 'hypothesis' that merely 'accounts for the appearances' (*satisfacit phaenomenis*) from an account that 'attempts to unfold the actual truth of things' (*ipsam rei veritatem explicare conatur*) (*Principles*, Part III, art. 17). Such a distinction was sometimes invoked by those attempting to defend the heliocentric view of the solar system in the teeth of ecclesiastical opposition, but the Inquisition ruthlessly closed this door when they condemned Galileo's position as heretical in 1633, insisting that his view was unacceptable 'even though he might pretend to put it forward only hypothetically' (*quamvis hypothetice a se illam proponi simularet*; see Descartes' letter to Mersenne of April 1634, AT I 288: CSMK 43). Descartes was clearly shocked by this outcome, and resolved to avoid similar censure for his own views, telling Mersenne that he desired above all 'to live in peace and to continue the life I have begun under the motto "to live well one must live unseen"' (AT I 286: CSMK 43). By the time he wrote the *Principles of Philosophy*, however, he was confident enough to reject the traditional Ptolemaic view of the universe outright, observing that 'Ptolemy's hypothesis is in conflict with many observations made recently, especially the waxing and waning phases of light which are observed on Venus just as they are on the moon, and is now commonly rejected by all philosophers' (*Principles*, Part III, art. 16. The telescopic discovery of the phases of Venus had first been announced by Galileo in 1610). He none the less remained cautious enough to maintain that he wanted 'all the causes set out here to be regarded simply as hypotheses' (Part III, art. 44). This apparent concession is, however, somewhat qualified later by a passage asserting that 'it makes very little difference what initial assumptions are made, since all subsequent changes must occur in accordance with the laws of nature, and there is scarcely any assumption that does not allow the same effects (albeit more laboriously) to be deduced in accordance with the same laws of nature. For by the operation of these laws matter must successively assume all the forms of which it is capable; and if we consider these forms in order, we will eventually be able to arrive at the form which characterizes the universe in its present state. Hence in this connection we need not fear any error that can arise from a false supposition' (Part III, art. 47).

For further reflection by Descartes on the use of the terms 'assumption' and 'hypothesis', see the letter to Morin of 13 July 1638 (AT II 199: CSMK 107).

atheist The curious question 'how much can an atheist know?' came to assume a central importance for seventeenth-century critics and defenders of the Cartesian attempt to base all knowledge on secure metaphysical foundations. In the Fifth Meditation, Descartes summarizes the results of his metaphysical inquiries: 'now I have perceived that God exists, and . . . that everything else depends on him, and that he is no deceiver, and I have drawn the conclusion that everything which I clearly and distinctly perceive is of necessity true . . . . Thus I see plainly that the certainty and truth of all knowledge depends uniquely on my awareness of the true God, to such an extent that I was incapable of perfect knowledge about anything else until I became aware of him' (AT VII 70–1: CSM II 48–9). Descartes' critics objected that to take this literally would imply – absurdly – that an atheist (one who lacks 'awareness of the true God') could not know even a simple truth of geometry such as that the angles of a triangle equal two right angles. Descartes admitted in reply that an atheist could indeed be clearly aware (*clare cognoscere*) that the angles of a triangle equal two right angles; but he went on to argue that 'this awareness [*cognitio*] of his is not true knowledge [*vera scientia*], since no act of awareness that can be rendered doubtful seems fit to be called knowledge' (Second Replies, AT VII 141: CSM II 101). The argument appears to rest on a distinction between an isolated act of cognition or awareness and a systematic and well-grounded body of knowledge. The atheist cannot attain the latter, since he does not have at his disposal a systematic validation of the reliability of the human mind: 'the less power the atheist attributes to the author of his being, the more reason he will have to suspect that his nature may be so imperfect as to allow him to be deceived even in matters which seem utterly evident to him, and he will never be able to be free of this doubt until he recognizes that he has been created by a true God, who cannot be a deceiver' (Sixth Replies, AT VII 428: CSM II 289).

See also CIRCLE, CARTESIAN.

atoms Descartes, in common with a number of other innovative philosopher-scientists of the seventeenth century, sought a mechanistic framework which would explain all physical phenomena by reference to the interactions between particles. One readily available option for those adopting such a mechanistic approach was to follow the lead given by Democritus and Epicurus in classical antiquity, and suppose that all matter was ultimately composed of atoms moving in a void; this was the route taken by several of Descartes' contemporaries, notably Pierre Gassendi (1592–1655). Throughout his working life, however, Descartes himself firmly and consistently dissociated himself from the atomists. In a letter to Mersenne from as early as 1630, he insisted that the 'particles' or 'corpuscles' invoked in the physics which he had begun to construct were not to be thought of as atoms (AT I 140: CSMK 21). It is important for the modern reader, familiar with the idea of 'splitting the atom', to remember that until comparatively recently an atom was thought of as something that was by definition indivisible (Greek ἄτομος, 'not able to be cut'). In the *Principles of Philosophy* (1644), Descartes explicitly argues that 'it is impossible that there should exist atoms, that is, pieces of matter that are by their very nature indivisible; for if there were any atoms, then no matter how small we imagined them to be, they would necessarily have to be extended, and hence we could ... recognize their divisibility' (AT VIIIA 51: CSM I 231). The notion of an atom in the strict sense is thus inconsistent with the Cartesian 'geometrical' account of matter as that which has dimensions, and which is therefore indefinitely divisible (see Sixth Meditation, AT VII 86: CSM II 59).

Though firmly anti-atomist, Cartesian physics may properly be described as 'corpuscularian'. At the end of the *Principles of Philosophy*, Descartes frankly acknowledges that his own physics has a number of general features in common with that of Democritus and the atomists: both systems 'imagine certain small bodies having various sizes, shapes and motions, and suppose that all the bodies that can be perceived by the senses arise from the conglomeration and mutual interaction of these corpuscles' (Part IV, art. 202). But Descartes goes on to explain a number of crucial differences, notably on the question of whether there can be indivisible particles, and with respect to the void (which Cartesian physics rules out; *see* SPACE).

attribute   *see* SUBSTANCE

automaton   In seventeenth-century usage an automaton is simply a self-moving thing (that which contains some internal principle of movement, rather than depending on external impulse to move). Thus Leibniz is able to describe the human soul as 'a kind of spiritual automaton' (*Theodicy* [1710], I, 52). Descartes explicitly comments that he uses the term as equivalent to 'moving machine' (*machine mouvante*, AT VI 55: CSM I 139). In describing the human or animal body as a machine or natural automaton, Descartes means to stress that its functioning and behavioural responses can be explained merely by the minutely organized structure of its internal parts together with the appropriate external stimuli, without the need to posit any occult internal principle such as a 'locomotive soul'. In the *Treatise on Man*, composed in the early 1630s, a whole range of human activities is ascribed to the operations of a self-moving machine which, like a 'clock or an artificial fountain or mill' (*horlorge, fontaine artificielle, moulin*), has the power (*la force*) to operate purely in accordance with its own internal principles, depending solely on the disposition of the relevant organs (*la disposition des organes*) (AT XI 120; CSM I 99).

See also ANIMALS.

axiom   *see* COMMON NOTION

B

blood, circulation of Descartes devotes a large portion of Part V of the *Discourse* to describing the 'movement of the heart and the arteries'. In effect, he uses this as a test case for his new scientific approach, which aimed to reduce physiology and biology to branches of physics, with all the relevant events being described by means of the general laws of matter in motion: 'I supposed that in the beginning God did not place in the body any rational soul or any other thing to serve as a vegetative or sensitive soul, but rather that he kindled in its heart one of those fires without light . . . whose nature I understand to be no different from that of the fire which heats hay when it has been stored before it is dry, or which causes new wine to seethe when it is left to ferment from the crushed grapes' (AT VI 46: CSM I 134).

Resolutely eliminating any reference to occult forces from his account of the heart and the blood, Descartes has no truck with the traditional attribution of a 'beating power' (*vis pulsans*) to the heart. Instead, he attributes the flow of blood out of the heart and along the arteries to the expansion and rarefaction of the blood when heated. After his account of this process (which incorporates a detailed description of the working of the valves), Descartes firmly declares that 'the movement just explained follows from the mere arrangement of the parts of the heart (which can be seen with the naked eye), from the heat in the heart . . . and the nature of the blood; the movement follows just as necessarily as the movement of a clock follows from the force, position and shape of its counter-weights and wheels' (AT VI 50: CSM I 136). The circulation of the blood is then added almost as an afterthought, to explain 'why the blood in the veins is not used up as it flows continually into the heart'. Descartes here gives due credit to 'the English physician who broke the ice on this subject' (William Harvey, whose *De Motu Cordis* was published in 1628), but in his later essay, the *Description of the Human Body*, he takes issue with Harvey on a number of points, notably by insisting that the blood gushes from the heart into the arteries during the cardiac diastole (expansion) phase, not (as Harvey had – in fact correctly – maintained) during the systole (contraction) phase. Descartes cited a number of observational results which he claimed to support his view (more are cited in the letter to Plempius of 15 February 1638, AT I 527: CSMK 82), but the chief motive for his opposition to Harvey seems to have been that no mechanical explanation was readily available to account for the squeezing or contracting action of the heart posited by Harvey: 'if we suppose that the heart moves in the way Harvey describes, we must imagine some faculty which causes this movement; yet the nature of this faculty is much harder to conceive of than whatever Harvey purports to explain by invoking it' (AT XI 243: CSM I 318).

Descartes is thus a transitional figure in the emergence of the modern theory of the circulatory system. He deserves credit for his influential defence of Harvey against the traditionalists on the matter of the circulation of the blood; but with respect to the movement of the heart itself, the account he put forward was scarcely an advance on the crude Aristotelian view that the heart's motion is caused by processes 'similar to the action of liquid boiled by heat' (*Parva Naturalia* 480a4).

body Since the Latin language lacks both a definite and an indefinite article, great care is needed in translating the crucial term *corpus* ('body'), which occurs so frequently in the *Meditations* and the *Principles*. Sometimes the term refers to 'body in general', that is, matter or 'corporeal substance' – the all-pervasive stuff, indefinitely extended in three dimensions, which makes up the physical universe. This is the sense of the term used in *Principles*, Part II, art. 4, where Descartes asserts that 'the nature of matter, or body considered in general (*corpus in universum spectatum*) . . . consists merely in its being something extended in length, breadth and depth' (AT VIIIA 42: CSM I 224). Descartes is, in effect, an ontological monist about 'body' in this general sense: the physical world consists of just one, indefinitely divisible, substance, and the fact that we conventionally divide the world into individual objects does not mean that there is a genuine substantial plurality. All that is really happening is that portions of universal 'body' are moving at different speeds and in different directions: 'I regard the minute parts of terrestrial bodies as being all composed of one single kind of matter, and believe that each of them could be divided repeatedly in indefinitely many ways, and that there is no more difference between them than there is between stones of various different shapes cut from the same rock' (*Meteorology*, AT VI 239).

In many other places, Descartes uses *corpus* in the more ordinary sense (as a count noun) to mean 'a body' (like a rock or a lump of iron, or a celestial body like a planet); see, for example, *Principles*, Part II, arts 52 and 57. He is clear throughout, however, that talk of 'individual bodies' is simply a convenient *façon de parler*; there is no question of radically distinct things, or types of things, since 'the matter existing in the entire universe is one and the same, and is always recognized as matter simply in virtue of its being extended . . . any variation in matter or diversity in its many forms depends on motion' (*Principles*, Part II, art. 23). In some cases Descartes switches within a single paragraph from using *corpus* in the ordinary sense, to refer to 'a body' and using it in his more technical sense to mean 'corporeal substance in general': compare *Principles*, Part II, art. 11, where he invites us to attend to 'the idea we have of *some body* (*alicujus corporis*) such as a stone, and to leave out everything we know to be non-essential to the *nature of body* (*natura corporis*)'; the result of this process is that we are left with the pure notion of something extended in length, breadth and depth, and the conclusion Descartes draws is that there is in fact no real distinction between extension (or space) and corporeal substance (*see* EXTENSION and SPACE).

Lastly, Descartes sometimes (as often in the Sixth Meditation; cf. AT VII 86: CSM II 59) uses the word *corpus* to refer to the human body. But even within the Sixth Meditation the Latin term quite often leaves scope for ambiguity; thus the title of the Meditation ('the real distinction between mind and body') could be taken to refer to the distinction between myself as a thinking substance and this particular body which I inhabit, or, alternatively, to the distinction between a thinking substance and body in general. The later French translation of 1647 removes the ambiguity by talking of 'the real distinction between the soul and body of man', though it is far from clear that this is an improvement on Descartes' original Latin text. Certainly, it fails to accommodate Descartes' meaning in his main argument, later in the Sixth Meditation, for the 'real distinction' between thinking and extended substance (see AT VII 78 line 18: CSM II 54 n. 2). For Descartes makes his underlying intentions here quite clear in the Synopsis to the *Meditations*, where it emerges that an individual human body does not qualify for the title of 'extended substance': 'we need to recognize that body taken in the general sense (*corpus in genere sumptum*) is a substance, so that it . . . never perishes . . . but the human body, in so far as it differs from other bodies, is simply made up of a certain configuration of limbs and other accidental properties of this sort . . . [so that] it loses its identity merely as a result of a change in the shape of some of its parts' (AT VII 14: CSM II 10). The upshot is that the corporeal substance or 'extended thing (*res extensa*)' of which I have a clear and distinct idea, and which I can recognize as utterly distinct from myself *qua* thinking substance, is not this particular human body, but body in general.

See also MIND AND BODY.

C

cause Causality plays a central role both in Descartes' metaphysics and in his physics. In the *Meditations*, in the transition from knowledge of his own existence to knowledge of God, Descartes makes celebrated use of a complex causal principle in order to establish that his idea of God must have its origin in God himself. That principle (sometimes termed the 'causal adequacy principle') states that 'there must be at least as much in the efficient and total cause as in the effect of that cause' (Third Meditation, AT VII 40: CSM II 28). In defending the principle to his critics, Descartes sometimes suggested that it was a mere variant on the universally accepted axiom 'nothing comes from nothing' (AT VII 135: CSM II 97). But in fact the argument requires a considerably stronger and more specific principle than the general deterministic assumption that every item must have *some* cause. Descartes' reasoning supposes what may be called the principle of the 'non-inferiority of the cause' – that the cause of some item possessing a given degree of perfection must itself be as perfect as or more perfect than the item in question ('what is more perfect cannot arise from what is less perfect': [*non*] *posse . . . fieri . . . id quod magis perfectum est . . . ab eo quod minus*; AT VII 40: CSM II 28). Why should this principle be true? It appears that Descartes is implicitly presupposing a model of causation according to which causes pass on or transmit properties to effects, which are then said to derive their features from the causes. And this in turn presupposes that certain kinds of similarity relations hold between causes and effects – in the words of the traditional maxim which Descartes is reported to have quoted approvingly, 'the effect is like the cause' (*effectus similis est causae*; AT V 156: CSMK 340). This is what underlies Descartes' explanation of the causal principle in the Third Meditation: 'For where, I ask, could the effect get its reality from if not from the cause? And how could the cause give it to the effect unless it possessed it?' (AT VII 40: CSM II 28).

The scholastic tradition in which Descartes was trained analysed causation in terms of the four categories proposed by Aristotle: formal, material, efficient and final. The last category, which relates to purposive explanation, may be put aside in the present context (*see* CAUSE, FINAL). It is the third category, that of efficient causality, which Descartes invokes in formulating his principle in the Third Meditation. An efficient cause in Aristotle is the productive or motive agency that brings something about – 'that from which the first origin of change proceeds'; for example, the father is the efficient cause of his child (*Metaphysics*, Book Delta, 1013a29; cf. *Physics* II 3, 194b29). Yet if we apply this to Descartes' reasoning in the Third Meditation, it is not immediately clear why the initiator of a change must itself possess the properties found in the resulting effect. As Gassendi objected to Descartes, a builder (who is the efficient cause of a house) does not himself possess the features found in the resulting house; the Cartesian maxim 'nothing in the effect which was not in the cause' seems to apply, if at all, to Aristotle's *material* cause (the ingredients or components which go to make up some item): thus the various features of the house are derived from its materials, which the builder (in Gassendi's words) simply 'takes from some other source and passes on to the house' (AT VII 288: CSM II 201).

In couching his principle in terms of the 'efficient *and total* cause', Descartes seems to have intended an amalgamation of the complete set of explanatory factors involved. The early seventeenth-century scholastic Eustachius a Sancto Paulo (whom Descartes had studied in his youth – AT III 185: CSMK 154) links the Aristotelian categories together when he writes that 'we may speak of an efficient cause with respect both to the matter and to the form: with respect to the matter, it effectively arranges the matter in question and constructs something out of it; with respect to the form, it actualizes the form and draws it forth from the potentiality of the matter, bringing it from darkness to light' (*Summa philosophica quadripartita* [1609] III, 59–61; cited in Gilson, *Index Scolastico—Cartésien*, p. 40). But unfortunately for Descartes' reasoning, the causal maxim which he invokes, even when construed so as to include the total set of explanatory factors, seems vulnerable to counter-examples. 'Flies, and other animals and plants', objected Descartes' friend Marin Mersenne, 'are produced from sun and rain and earth, which lack life . . . and hence it does happen that an effect may derive from its cause some reality which is nevertheless not present in the cause' (Second Objections, AT VII 123: CSM II 88). Descartes remained unimpressed, partly because his own account of living things as mere mechanical automata tried to avoid the need to attribute to them any characteristics not found in purely inanimate objects, but partly, on his own admission, because he refused to allow that such alleged empirical counter-examples could provide a good reason for doubting a principle so luminously self-evident as the maxim 'nothing in the effect that was not in the cause' (see Second Replies, AT VII 134: CSM II 96).

To explain how this principle appeared self-evident to Descartes, we need to look beyond Aristotle, to that other great pillar of classical philosophy which informed so many of the ontological presuppositions of medieval thought, the philosophy of Plato. In the Platonic theory of forms, the forms are like patterns or archetypes which enjoy a superior mode of being; particulars are copies which owe their being, and their essential properties, to the higher realm from which they derive. Platonic influences (often through the medium of Augustine) are to be found in much of Descartes' metaphysics; thus in the Third Meditation he writes that 'although one idea may perhaps originate from another, there cannot be an infinite regress here: eventually one must reach a primary idea, the cause of which will be like an archetype (Latin *archetypum*; the French version says 'model/pattern or original', *un patron ou un original*) which contains in itself formally all the reality which is present representatively in the idea (AT VII 42 and IX 33: CSM II 29). The Platonic undertones remain despite the fact that Descartes' use of the term 'idea' is very different from Plato's; *see also* IDEA. The influence of the Platonic hierarchy of being is also to be found in the principle, to which Descartes subscribed, that the cause is more noble than the effect (*causa nobilior effectu*) (AT VII 242: CSM II 168; this principle is defended in Eustachius, *Summa*, III 56, and Suárez, *Disputationes Metaphysicae* [1609] 26, 1, 2; see Gilson, *Index*, p. 44). When combined with medieval Christian theology, this notion transmutes into the conception of God as the supreme archetype, the source of being itself, from whom all existing things ultimately derive by a kind of emanation from the divine essence. In the *Conversation with Burman*, Descartes is reported to have said in defence of the principle that effects must resemble their causes: 'here we are talking about the total cause, the cause of being itself, and anything produced by this cause must necessarily be like it . . . hence even stones and suchlike have the image and likeness of God, albeit in a very remote and indistinct way, while as for me, God's creation has endowed me with a greater number of attributes, and so his image is in me to a greater extent' (AT V 156: CSMK 340).

If causation operates by a process of diminution or subtraction from the supreme divine nature, then it will indeed be the case that everything found in the effect will be found either literally, or in some higher form ('formally or eminently' in the jargon – *see* CAUSE, FORMAL VS. EMINENT) in its cause. To imagine an object that had some property not derived from the total and supreme cause of its being would be to suppose, blasphemously, that it was independent of God; conversely, since God is the cause of all things, if anything possessed some feature which it did not get from God, this would be a case of its having got that feature from nothing, which would be absurd. To accept that my idea of God comes from God himself, we need to presuppose that causality operates by a process of emanation or infusion from the more real to the less real, from the supreme archetype to its lower-grade copies or instantiations, from the source of all being to the objects of creation. God is the cause of created things as the sun is the cause of light (says Descartes in the Fifth Replies, echoing another famous Platonic simile), not just in the sense that he is the cause of the coming into being of his creatures, but in the sense that he is the cause of their very being (AT VII 369: CSM II 254). The deep paradox in Cartesian metaphysics is that while Descartes purports to sweep away all preconceived opinion and start from self-evident foundations, the basis of his thought remains deeply indebted to an elaborate fusion of Platonic and Christian metaphysics; without this apparatus, the crucial transition from self-knowledge to knowledge of God, and the subsequent validation of science, cannot be effected.

If we move from metaphysics to physics, Descartes' use of the notion of causality becomes in many respects more straightforward. The role of God as supreme cause is still crucial: he is the 'universal and primary cause' of the existence of the extended physical universe; moreover, the laws of motion, which are the basis of Cartesian physics, have their direct source in God, who 'in the beginning created matter, along with its motion and rest, and now merely by his regular concurrence preserves the same amount of motion as he put there in the beginning' (*Principles*, Part II, art. 36). But in the case of particular causal explanations, Descartes wholly discards the Aristotelian–scholastic ontology of substances and essences, of 'substantial forms' and 'real qualities', with properties being transmitted, by a process of infusion from cause to effect. Instead, a particular physical effect is explained merely by reference to the covering laws of mathematics, the values for whose variables are purely quantitative representations of dimension and motion. Thus in the Cartesian 'rules of impact', Descartes provides abstract mathematical principles for determining the result of various possible cases of collision between particles, invoking no more than the abstract principle of the conservation of rectilinear motion (*see* INERTIA), plus the principle that smaller and slower particles are always deflected by larger and faster ones (*Principles*, Part II, arts 45–52). In this attempt to mathematicize physics, we see the beginnings of the 'modern' revolution in the philosophy of science, which discards the medieval structure of qualitative connections between causes and effects, in favour of subsuming particular cases under abstract mathematical covering laws.

cause, efficient *see* CAUSE

cause, final A final cause was defined by scholastic philosophers (following Aristotle) as 'that for the sake of which something comes about'; thus health is the 'final cause' or goal or purpose which leads us to take exercise, or to take medicine when we are ill (the first example comes in Aristotle, *Metaphysics* 1013a32, the second in Eustachius, *Summa philosophica* [1609] III 65, cited in Gilson, *Index*, 39). Final causes were widely employed in the centuries prior to Descartes in a way that tended to make physics subordinate to theology: the benevolent purposes of the creator were the ultimate 'final cause' of everything to be found in the created universe (thus the final cause of the moon was to give light to the world by night). A familiar theme of seventeenth-century philosophy is that such purposive explanations, pious though they might be, are a block to productive scientific inquiry; thus Bacon wrote in *De Augmentiis Scientiarum* [1623] that 'the search for final causes is barren, and like a virgin consecrated to God brings forth no offspring' (Book III, ch. 5).

Descartes, who proposed to explain the entire structure of the physical universe mechanistically, from a few mathematical laws governing the behaviour of matter in motion, was equally adamant that satisfying progress in science must involve abandoning the traditional search for final causes. He adds, moreover, that such a search is not even pious, but on the contrary an impious piece of arrogance. God is by his nature infinite, and thus beyond the comprehension of finite human minds: 'for this reason alone I consider the customary search for final causes to be utterly useless in physics: there is considerable rashness in thinking myself capable of investigating the impenetrable purposes of God' (Fourth Meditation, AT VII 55: CSM II 39).

To this metaphysical point Descartes conjoins a further objection to final causality, drawn from the new cosmology of the post-Copernican era. If the earth is no longer the centre of the universe, and the universe itself is indefinitely large, and contains an infinite plurality of worlds, it can no longer be assumed that all its contents are arranged for the special benefit of mankind. After commenting on the vast immensity of the created universe, Descartes declares in the *Principles* that it is 'wholly improbable that all things were made for our benefit ... and in the study of physics such a supposition would be utterly ridiculous and inept, since there is no doubt that many things exist, or once existed, which have never been seen or thought of by any man' (Part II, art. 3; cf. *Conversation with Burman*, AT V 158: CSMK 341). The 'anti-finalistic' Cartesian approach to physics thus prefigures the deism of the following century, where God is seen as an impersonal creator, remote from the affairs of mankind.

cause, formal vs. eminent   When explicating the principle that 'there must be at least as much in the cause as in the effect' (*see* CAUSE), Descartes observes that 'a stone, for example, which did not previously exist, cannot begin to exist unless it is produced by something which contains, either formally or eminently [*formaliter vel eminenter*] everything to be found in the stone' (AT VII 41: CSM II 28). The later French version adds the following gloss: 'that is, the cause will contain in itself the same things as are in the stone or other more excellent things' (AT IXA 32). In the scholastic terminology which Descartes makes use of here, to possess something 'formally' means to possess it in the literal and strict sense, in accordance with its definition, while to possess something 'eminently' is to possess it in some higher or grander form, in virtue of its enjoyment of a superior degree of perfection. Thus, as Descartes says somewhat enigmatically in the Second Replies: 'Something is said to exist *eminently* in an object when, although it does not exactly correspond to our perception of it, its greatness is such that it can fill the role of that which does so correspond' (AT VII 161: CSM II 114). Compare the following analogy: 'Who can give three coins to a beggar? Either a poor man who has (*formally*) the coins in his purse, or a rich banker who has (*eminently*) far greater assets in his account' (J.-M. Beyssade, 'The idea of God and the proofs of his existence', in J. Cottingham (ed.), *The Cambridge Companion to Descartes*).

The difficulty which Descartes faces in employing this terminology in his proof of God's existence is that, on the one hand, he wants to keep to the relatively simple principle, the cause resembles the effect, to demonstrate that his idea of a perfect being is indeed caused by a really perfect God; he takes it, in other words, that he has a clear idea of the deity, since his idea of God (the effect) is a kind of image or stamp of the divine essence that caused it – the 'mark of the craftsman stamped on his work' (AT VII 51: CSM II 35). But, on the other hand, the notion of 'eminent' causation tells us that there may be many features in an effect which are not in any direct and self-evident sense 'derived' from the essence of the cause: thus God is, on the traditional view, the 'eminent' cause of the extended physical universe, even though he is not himself extended or physical. And this in turn seems to imply that we may not, after all, have a clear and distinct idea of God, since God's causal powers, and indeed his ultimate nature, are of a wholly different order of reality, beyond our comprehension.

For more on these tensions, *see* INFINITE.

certainty Descartes distinguishes two grades of certainty. The first is 'absolute' certainty, which he defined as the kind of certainty which arises 'when we believe that it is wholly impossible that something should be otherwise than we judge it to be' (*Principles*, Part IV, art. 206). This is the kind of certainty which Descartes aims for in the metaphysical foundations of his philosophy – the kind of certainty that will survive even the extreme or 'hyperbolical' doubts raised at the start of the *Meditations* (see First Meditation, AT VII 22: CSM II 15, and Third Meditation, AT VII 36: CSM II 25). It is sometimes suggested that Descartes claimed that all science ought to achieve this kind of certainty; such an impression is no doubt fostered by the passages where Descartes illustrates his conception of scientific knowledge by referring to the watertight logical demonstrations of the mathematicians (cf. AT VI 19: CSM I 120). But elsewhere he allows for a lesser, but none the less acceptable, grade of certainty, namely 'moral' certainty, which is defined as 'certainty sufficient for application to ordinary life' (*Principles*, Part IV, art. 205). The example given in this passage is the cracking of a cipher: if a codebreaker manages to find a substitution scheme for an encoded jumble of letters which yields a meaningful message, then although it is theoretically possible that he has the wrong code and that the true message is different, it is (particularly if the message is a long one) for all practical purposes certain that the code has been cracked. Descartes himself believed that he had cracked the code of the physical universe, and that it was 'morally certain' that the true explanation for all physical phenomena lay in the basic principles of matter in motion which he articulated: 'if people look at all the many properties relating to magnetism, fire and the fabric of the entire universe which I have deduced in this book from just a few principles, then, even if they think that my assumption of these principles was arbitrary, they will perhaps acknowledge that it would *hardly have been possible* for so many items to fit into a coherent pattern if the original principles had been false' (ibid., emphasis supplied). For another important example of a claim by Descartes to have achieved moral certainty, compare his argument about the inability of a purely physical system to produce genuine thought and language (*Discourse*, Part V, AT VI 57: CSM I 140).

circle, Cartesian   This has become the standard label for a major structural problem which besets Descartes' attempt, in the *Meditations*, to establish his new scientific system on a completely secure metaphysical base; the difficulty was first raised by Descartes' own contemporaries, notably Marin Mersenne and Antoine Arnauld (Second and Fourth Objections respectively, AT VII 125: CSM II 89 and AT VII 214: CSM II 150). The problem arises from the fact that Descartes' proof of God's existence is intended to establish the possibility of systematic knowledge. If a perfect God exists, then the intellectual apparatus which he bestowed on me cannot be intrinsically inaccurate. Of course, I may make mistakes from time to time, but this is due (Descartes argues in the Fourth Meditation) to a wilful misuse of the divine gift: I often rashly jump in and give my assent to a proposition when I do not have a clear and distinct perception of it. But if I confine myself to what I clearly and distinctly perceive, I can be sure of avoiding error: 'I shall unquestionably reach the truth if only I give sufficient attention to all the things which I perfectly understand, and separate these from all the cases where my apprehension is more confused and obscure' (AT VII 62; CSM II 43). Provided I keep to this rule, I can achieve knowledge of countless things, including, most importantly, the structure of the physical universe – the 'whole of that corporeal nature which is the subject of pure mathematics'

(Fifth Meditation: AT VII 71: CSM II 49). Now the problem, in a nutshell, is this: if existence of a non-deceiving God has to be established in order for me to have confidence in the clear and distinct perceptions of my intellect, then how, without circularity, can I rely on the intellectual perceptions needed to construct the proof of God's existence in the first place?

When directly challenged on this issue, Descartes is reported to have replied that when proving God's existence, the meditator knows he is not being deceived about the truth of the relevant premises, 'since he is actually paying attention to them; and for as long as he does pay attention he is certain that he is not being deceived' (*Conversation with Burman*, AT V 148: CSMK 334). The claim seems to be that there are some propositions whose truth is so clearly manifest that, so long as we direct our attention towards them, the possibility of our being mistaken is wholly excluded. The 'so long as' clause is crucial here: the epistemic guarantee lasts only so long as the relevant propositions are attended to. (Compare the way Descartes phrases his famous Cogito argument; 'Let the demon deceive me as much as he can, he will never bring it about that I am nothing so long as I think I am something' (AT VII 25: CSM II 17. *See* COGITO ERGO SUM).) The upshot, for Descartes, is that true cognition is not, after all, wholly dependent on knowledge of God: even before God's existence is established isolated cognitive acts can indeed attain to a self-guaranteeing certainty: 'when I said that we can know nothing for certain until we are aware that God exists . . . I was speaking only of knowledge of those conclusions which can be recalled when we are no longer attending to the arguments from which we deduced them' (AT VII 140: CSM II 100. Cf. Fourth Replies, AT VII 246: CSM II 171).

Descartes' reply to the circularity challenge is not wholly satisfying for two reasons. The first is that his strategy rests on the claim that the premises needed to prove God's existence are so simple and transparent that, so long as we attend to them, their certainty is guaranteed. But critical scrutiny of the premises used in the proof of God in Meditation III reveals them to be far from straightforward (*see* CAUSE). Second, Descartes' claim that some simple propositions are so transparent and self-evident that nothing could call them into question sits uneasily with the possibility of extreme or 'hyperbolical' doubt that he himself had raised in the First Meditation. There the meditator had raised the nightmarish doubt that my nature might be such as to 'make me go wrong every time I add two and three or count the sides of a square *or even in some simpler matter, if that is imaginable*' (AT VII 21: CSM II 14; emphasis supplied). The doubt, in short, seems to extend to the possibility that the fundamental processes of human reasoning may be unreliable. Once the existence of a non-deceiving God has been established, that doubt can be laid to rest: 'a reliable mind is God's gift to me' (AT V 148: CSMK 334). But the very process of establishing the existence of God seems itself to presuppose the reliability of the workings of the human mind; and this in turn appears to reintroduce the problem of the circle.

The nearest Descartes comes to addressing this fundamental issue is in the Second Replies, where he seems in effect to admit that reason cannot (on pain of circularity) be used to validate itself, but still maintains that his strategy for establishing reliable knowledge is sound, since it provides us with all the certainty we could reasonably want: 'As soon as we think we correctly perceive something, we are spontaneously convinced that it is true. Now if this conviction is so firm that it is impossible for us ever to have any reason for doubting what we are convinced of, then there are no further questions for us to ask: we have everything that we could reasonably want. What is it to us that someone may make out that the perception whose truth we are so firmly convinced of may appear false to God or an angel, so that it is, absolutely speaking, false? What do we care about this alleged "absolute falsity" since we neither believe in it, nor have even the smallest suspicion of it? For the supposition we are making here is of a conviction so firm that it is quite incapable of being destroyed; and such a conviction is clearly the same as the most perfect certainty' (AT VII 145: CSM II 103). The implications of this passage remain the subject of debate by Cartesian scholars; on the face of it, Descartes is drawing in his horns, and pulling back from the ambitious 'foundationalist' project of supplying absolute guarantees for human know-ledge. Our epistemic credentials, on this account, cannot be 'externally validated'; what the human mind can aim to reach is a defence of knowledge that shows how our cognitive achievements attain to all the certainty that could reasonably be demanded.

clarity and distinctness   In the *Meditations*, having established the cer-tainty of his own existence as a 'thinking thing', Descartes casts around for a general criterion of certain knowledge: 'I am certain that I am a thinking thing; do I not therefore also know what is required for my being certain about anything? In this first discovery, there is simply a clear and distinct perception of what I am asserting; this would not be enough to make me certain of the matter if it could ever turn out that what I perceived with such clarity and distinctness was false. So I now seem to be able to lay it down as a general rule that whatever I very clearly and distinctly perceive is true' (*illud omne est verum quod clare et distincte percipio*, Third Meditation: AT VII 35: CSM II 24).

'Perceive' (*percipio*) is Descartes' standard term for the inner act of direct apprehension by which the mind is aware of simple truths – both about its own nature and about the nature of God and the subject-matter of mathema-tics. And just as external vision operates thanks to sunlight, so the intellec-tual 'perception' of the mind operates in virtue of an inner light (for the 'natural light', *see* INTUITION). Not all of the mind's perceptions, however, are clear and distinct. 'I call a perception clear', Descartes writes in the *Principles*, 'when it is present and accessible to the attentive mind, just as we say that we see something clearly when it is present to the eye's gaze and stimulates it with a sufficient degree of strength and accessibility' (Part I, art. 45). When the mind is focused on such items, they are, as it were, right in front of the mind, plain to see, in a way which allows no possibility of error. Elsewhere, Descartes provides examples of perceptions enjoying this kind of transparency: 'some perceptions are so transparently clear and at the same time so simple that we cannot ever think of them without believing them to be true. The fact that I exist so long as I am thinking, or that what is done cannot be undone, are examples of truths in respect of which we manifestly possess this kind of certainty. For we cannot doubt them unless we think of them; but we cannot think of them without at the same time believing they are true' (AT VII 145–6: CSM II 104).

The examples in the previous paragraph qualify not just as clear but also as distinct. Distinctness is a stricter notion than clarity, and implies that 'as well as being clear, the perception is so sharply separated from all other perceptions that it contains within itself only what is clear' (*Principles*, Part I, art. 45). For Descartes, simple propositions such as 'I am thinking' or 'two and three make five' are entirely transparent: they contain no implications which might subsequently cause us to doubt them. By contrast, a proposition like 'I have a pain in my foot' is, for Descartes, indistinct; the sensation of pain itself may be clear enough, but 'people often confuse this perception with an obscure judgement they make concerning the nature of something which they think exists in the painful spot, and which they suppose to resemble the sensation of pain' (*Principles*, Part I, art. 46).

The paradigm instances of clear and distinct perception in Descartes' philosophy concern the mind's awareness of the SIMPLE NATURES. Our knowledge both of our own nature as thinking things, and of the nature of extension (in so far as it can be analysed in purely mathematical terms) is based on such clear and distinct perceptions (see AT VII 70–1: CSM II 48–9). Clarity and distinctness are thus characteristically found in the perceptions of the intellect, rather than in sensory awareness. Despite Descartes' occasional suggestion that a sensation (such as a feeling or pain) can at least be clear (if not distinct), his standard position is that sensation is an inherently obscure and confused form of awareness (*see* SENSATION).

In ascribing to the intellect the power of clear and distinct perception, Descartes has seemed to some critics to be guilty of trying to solve the problem of the validation of human knowledge by a kind of complacent fiat – a simple declaration that truth is self-manifesting to the human mind. The charge of complacency is, however, misplaced, since Descartes never asserts that the truth is *easy* for the human intellect to discover. On the contrary, the whole procedure of the *Meditations* can be seen as the difficult and laborious task of sorting out what is clear and distinct in our beliefs from what is obscure and confused: 'nothing can be clearly and distinctly perceived without its being just as we perceive it to be, i.e. without its being true; but nevertheless, it requires some care to make a proper distinction between what is clearly and distinctly perceived and what merely seems or appears to be' (AT VII 462: CSM II 310). This last point notwithstanding, it is striking that in both the *Discourse* and the *Meditations* the 'truth rule' ('whatever I clearly and distinctly perceive is true') is confidently asserted *before* the existence of a non-deceiving God has been proved. And this gives rise to the question of how, without circularity, the truth rule itself is to be validated (*see* CIRCLE, CARTESIAN).

Cogito ergo sum   'I am thinking, therefore I exist.' The celebrated phrase, perhaps the most famous in the whole history of philosophy, occurs first in its French form – *je pense donc je suis* – in Part IV of the *Discourse* (1637): 'I noticed, in the course of trying to think that everything was false, that it was necessary that I, who was thinking this, was something. And observing that this truth, *I am thinking, therefore I exist*, was so firm and sure that all the most extravagant suppositions of the sceptics were incapable of shaking it, I decided that I could accept it without scruple as the first principle of the philosophy I was seeking' (AT VI 32: CSM I 127). The Latin formulation occurs in the *Principles of Philosophy* (1644), where *cogito ergo sum* is described as 'the first and most certain discovery to occur to anyone who philosophizes in an orderly way' (Part I, art. 7).

The canonical phrase does not occur in Descartes' fullest treatment of his metaphysics, the *Meditations*, but it is in this work that Descartes nevertheless offers the clearest explanation of why the awareness of one's own existence should be the first secure step in the path to knowledge. The meditator's certainty of his own existence emerges as a direct result of the systematic process of doubt described in the First Meditation, and in particular, from the extreme scenario of a supremely powerful deceiver: 'let him deceive me as much as he can, but he will never bring it about that I am nothing, so long as I think that I am something. . . . So I must finally conclude that this proposition, *I am, I exist* is necessarily true whenever it is put forward by me or conceived in my mind' (AT VII 25: CSM II 17).

The qualifying clause at the end of the sentence just quoted is important. The certainty of my existence is not like the certainty of some timeless necessary truth of logic or mathematics; there is nothing necessary about my existence (quite apart from ordinary contingencies, the omnipotent demon scenario entails that I could be annihilated at any time). But so long as I am actually engaged in the process of thinking, I must exist. Moreover, the very fact of my doubting my existence, the very fact of my raising the possibility of my being deceived, confirms that I do indeed, so long as I am entertaining these reflections, exist. 'Dubito ergo sum' ('I am doubting, therefore I exist') would be an equally valid argument from Descartes' point of view, as would Augustine's 'fallor ergo sum' ('I am being deceived, therefore I exist') (cf. Augustine, *De civitate Dei* xi 26, and AT III 247f: CSMK 159).

Descartes was questioned by contemporary critics as to whether his Cogito argument was syllogistic in form: does not 'I am thinking therefore I exist' have a concealed major premise, 'Everything that thinks exists' (cf. SYLLOG- ISM). Descartes replied that 'when we become aware that we are thinking things, this is a primary notion not derived from any syllogism'. In this passage, Descartes does not deny that one could construct a valid syllogism of the form just outlined, but he insists that the individual meditator does not have to do so; he simply 'recognizes in his own particular case that it is impossible that he should think without existing' (AT VII 140: CSM II 100). It might be objected that even to make the inference in one's own case, one must surely first understand that thought presupposes existence. This much Descartes did in effect concede: the Cogito is the 'first truth' in his system only in the sense that it is the first matter of existence which we can be sure of, but some prior knowledge of the meanings of the terms involved, and their logical implications, must already be presupposed (AT VIIIA 8: CSM I 196). It should be stressed, however, that what is crucial for Descartes in uncovering the certainty of his existence is not the formal validity of an abstract piece of reasoning, but rather an individual *act* of thinking: it is in the performance of this act by each individual meditator that the certainty of his existence becomes manifest, and indubitable.

See also THOUGHT.

colour 'In the bodies we call "coloured", the colours are nothing other than the various ways in which the bodies receive light and reflect it against our eyes' (*Optics*, AT VI 85: CSM I 153). Descartes, in common with other inaugurators of the seventeenth-century scientific revolution, notably Gali- leo, aimed to invoke only quantitative notions in his account of the physical universe: 'I recognize no matter in corporeal things apart from what the geometers call quantity, and take as the object of their demonstrations, i.e. that to which every kind of division, shape and motion is applicable' (AT VIIIA 79: CSM I 247). A qualitative notion such as redness (or any other colour) has no place in this explanatory schema, except in so far as state- ments about its presence in an object can be reduced to statements about that object's size, shape and motion (to this account Descartes adds the further fact that when an object of this kind interacts with our sense organs, we will have a colour-sensation of a characteristic kind). There is thus a sense in which 'redness', understood as a real quality, should not properly be attributed to a physical object at all: 'when we say that we perceive colours in objects, this is really just the same as saying that we perceive something in the objects whose nature we do not know, but which produces in us a certain very clear and vivid sensation which we call the sensation of colour . . . . If we suppose we perceive colours *in objects*, we do not really know what it is that we are calling a colour, and we cannot find any intelligible resemblance between the colour we suppose to be in objects and that which we experience in our sensation' (*Principles*, Part I, art. 70; emphasis supplied).

The Cartesian account of colour may thus be said to have three components. In the first place, in the realm of physics, there is a 'bleached out' scientific description which will reduce all colour-talk to descriptions of how external particles vary in respect of their shape, size and motion. Thus when we encounter the light we call 'blue', all that is strictly occurring, from the physical point of view, is that the speed of rotation of the relevant particles is lesser than their speed of approach; while in the light we call 'red' the reverse is the case (*Description of the Human Body*, AT XI 265: CSM I 323). In the second place, in the realm of physiology, the Cartesian account will proceed to describe, still in purely quantitative terms, the various changes in the nervous system that will occur when the eye is stimulated by various kinds of light (see *Treatise on Man*, AT XI 141ff: CSM I 101ff; *see* QUALITIES, SENSIBLE). And lastly (and it is only here that talk of 'red' or 'blue' as irreducibly qualitative notions becomes appropriate) there are the purely mental images or representations which will occur in the mind 'on the occasion' of the nervous system's being stimulated in various ways (cf. *Comments on a Certain Broadsheet*, AT VIIIB 359: CSM I 304). The explanation for the particular qualitative character of our colour sensations has, for Descartes, to be sought outside the realm of physical science: God has simply decreed that the soul should have sensations of various kinds corresponding to the various ways in which the brain can be stimulated via the nervous system (*Treatise on Man*, AT XI 143: CSM I 102); in so far as the explanation for these divinely decreed correlations is accessible to us, it relates to the benevolent purposes of God in wishing to help the soul monitor the condition of the body and the external world in a way which is conducive to personal health and survival (cf. Sixth Meditation: AT VII 82ff: CSM II 56ff).

Comments on a Certain Broadsheet   This short work was written in Latin and published under the title *Notae in Programma quoddam* early in 1648, by the house of Elzevir at Amsterdam. The work is sometimes known as the 'Notes against a Programme' (a crudely literal rendering of the Latin title). In the *Comments*, Descartes replies to the points made in a broadsheet published anonymously by Henri le Roy (Henricus Regius) towards the end of 1647. Regius, Professor of Medicine at the University of Utrecht, had strongly supported Descartes' ideas earlier in the 1640s, but Descartes was angered by the publication of Regius' *Foundations of Physics*, in 1646, which, he claimed, repeated many of his ideas (some gleaned from private correspondence), and distorted others, 'but all in such a confused manner, and with so few arguments, that the book can only make my views look ridiculous' (AT IV 510: CSMK 296). Descartes publicly dissociated himself from Regius in the Prefatory Letter to the French edition of the *Principles of Philosophy* in 1647, and Regius replied by publishing the *Broadsheet*, which set out a list of points on which they differered.

The main philosophical interest of the *Comments* lies in the remarks Descartes makes about INNATENESS. He argues that the class of innate ideas includes even sensory ideas: 'the ideas of pain, colours, sounds and the like must be . . . innate if, on the occasion of certain corporeal motions, our mind is to be capable of representing them to itself' (AT VIIIB 359: CSM I 304).

common notion   This term (Latin, *notio communis*) was originally a rendering of the Greek κοινή ἔννοια – the term used to refer to Euclid's axioms. Descartes frequently uses 'common notion' as a technical term for fundamental logical axioms such as 'things that are the same as a third thing are the same as each other' (AT X 420: CSM I 45; cf. AT VIIIA 9: CSM I 197, where one of the Euclidian axioms is explicitly quoted). In the *Principles of Philosophy* Descartes classifies 'common notions or axioms' as 'eternal truths which have no existence outside of our thought', and he gives as examples 'it is impossible for the same thing to be and not to be at the same time' and 'he who thinks cannot but exist while he thinks' (Part I, art. 49).

The Cartesian view that 'good sense or reason is equally distributed in all men' (AT VI 2: CSM I 111) suggests that everyone ought to have an equal grasp of the supposedly self-evident common notions. Descartes acknowledges, however, that not all of the common notions have an equal claim to be called 'common' among everyone, since they are not equally well perceived; his explanation is that PRECONCEIVED OPINIONS may obstruct the natural light of reason, so that not all of us perceive the common notions equally well. In principle, however, they are equally innate in all men. 'As regards the common principles and axioms, for example "it is impossible that one and the same thing should be and not be", men who are creatures of the senses, as we all are at a pre-philosophical level, do not think about these or pay attention to them. On the contrary, since they are present in us at birth with such clarity, and since we experience them within ourselves, we neglect them and think about them only in a confused manner, and never in the abstract, or apart from material things and particular instances' (*Conver-*

sation with Burman, AT V 146: CSMK 332; cf. *Principles of Philosophy*, Part I, art. 50 and Part II, art. 3).

'common' sense   Aristotle, in the *De Anima*, argues that, in addition to the five senses, there is an organ of 'common' sense (κοινή αἴσθησις) where the data from the five specialized senses are integrated. (cf. *De Anima*, Book III, ch. 1, 425a14). The notion of such a common sensorium was standard doctrine among the scholastics. One might have expected Descartes to have rejected this notion, both in the light of his resolute hostility to received scholastic doctrine, and also because of his conception of the mind as an incorporeal substance; in fact, however, he not only accepted it, but incorporated it into his own theory of mind–body interaction. The basis of this theory is that the mind receives information from the body, and initiates movements in it, at a single location: the conarion, or PINEAL GLAND. This gland receives data (via the nerves) from all parts of the body, and it is only after the data have been integrated in the gland into a unitary signal or impression that any conscious awareness can occur. 'The mind', Descartes wrote in the Sixth Meditation, 'is not immediately affected by all parts of the body, but only by the brain, or perhaps just by one small part of the brain, namely the part containing the "common sense"' (AT VII 86: CSM II 59). In his later work, the *Passions of the Soul*, Descartes takes the argument further in a way which explicitly trades on the traditional notion of a common sensorium: 'there must necessarily be some place where the two images coming through the two eyes, or the two impressions coming from a single object though the double organs of any other sense, can come together in a single image or impression before reaching the soul, so that they do not present to it two objects instead of one' (AT XI 353: CSM I 340). The argument is a curious one, since it is not at first sight apparent why a unitary image in the conscious mind requires a unitary signal or impression in the brain. Writing to Mersenne on 24 December 1640, Descartes reflected that 'the only alternative is to suppose that the soul is not joined immediately to any solid part of the body, but only to the animal spirits which are in its concavities, and which enter or leave it continually like the water of a river. That would certainly be thought too absurd' (AT III 264: CSMK 162). The suggestion seems far from absurd to the modern reader, accustomed to the notion that consciousness arises from just such a shifting and elusive interplay of electrical activity in the cerebral cortex. But it seems that Descartes is wedded to the idea of the soul as a kind of homunculus, whose operations *vis-à-vis* the brain consist of a series of simple one-to-one transactions (cf. AT XI 143: CSM I 102).

There are associated difficulties involved in the language Descartes uses to describe what is going on in the 'common' sensorium. Frequently he talks of 'images' or 'ideas' being imprinted there (see *Treatise on Man*, AT XI 202: CSM I 108); but since whatever happens in the organs of the brain must, for Descartes, be describable in strictly material terms, he is not entitled to mean by 'image' anything more than some kind of purely physiological or corporeal pattern. But why, we may then ask, is it necessary for the sensory data to be integrated by the 'common' sense into a *single* pattern, to enable us (for example) to see or hear? Again, a rather crude 'homunculus' model of the soul seems to be presupposed here, with a kind of naive reduplication, inside the brain, of the perceptual events which it is Descartes' purpose to explain in the first place. If we begin, for example, with an ordinary statement like 'René sees a cat', on the Cartesian account this is explained by reference to light striking René's eyes and setting up certain disturbances in each of the optic nerves. So far so good. But then the two 'images' formed on the retinas of the eyes are combined together in the 'common' sense, to form a little image of a cat, which René's soul then inspects. For one of the many passages which illustrate Descartes' tortuous manoeuvres on the psycho−physiology of vision, compare *Passions of the Soul*, art. 35: 'If we see some animal approaching us, the light reflected from its body forms two images, one in each of our eyes; and these images form two others, by means of the optic nerves, on the internal surface of the brain facing its cavities. Then, by means of the spirits that fill these cavities, the images radiate towards the little gland which the spirits surround. . . . In this way the two images in the brain form only one image on the gland, which acts directly upon the soul and makes it see the shape of the animal' (AT XI 355–6: CSM I 341–2). The all too evident problem here is that if the original item to be explained is a person's ability to see things, our understanding is hardly significantly advanced by being told that, at the end of the complex series of physiological events involved, what happens is that his soul 'sees' images of things. Descartes' use of the notion of a 'common sense' seems, in short, an awkward attempt to bridge the gulf between the purely physical events in the brain, and the conscious experiences of the perceiving mind or soul – a gulf which his own dualistic philosophy of mind is in large part responsible for creating.

See also MIND AND BODY; IMAGES.

Compendium Musicae The 'Compendium of Music' is the first work Descartes composed; it was completed on 31 December 1618, when he was twenty-two years of age. (It was not published, however, until 1650, just after his death.) The *Compendium* was dedicated to Isaac Beeckman (*see* INTRODUCTION), and attempts to explain the basis of harmony and dissonance in mathematical terms. The book contains a large number of diagrams and mathematical tables illustrating the proportional relationships involved in various musical intervals. We also find early signs of Descartes' interest in the relationship between psychological and physical phenomena: 'It seems that the human voice is agreeable to us because it is most in conformity with our spirits. Such affective sympathy or antipathy also perhaps explains why the voice of a close friend is more agreeable than that of an enemy, in the same way in which, they say, a drum made of sheepskin will suddenly go quiet and muffled if there is a drum of wolfskin being played in the vicinity' (AT X 90).

concurrence Following traditional terminology, Descartes employs this word to denote the continuous 'cooperative' power of God, whereby he preserves things in existence, once created, and without which they would simply collapse into nothingness. Thus although a created substance is, says Descartes, 'by nature incorruptible', it could still be 'reduced to nothingness' by God's 'denying his concurrence' to it (AT VII 14: CSM II 10). The 'ordinary concurrence' of God is invoked, in *Principles*, Part II, art. 36, to explain the CONSERVATION of motion in the universe. The term 'divine concurrence' might seem to have the connotation of God's merely *allowing* things to continue 'under their own steam' as it were, but Descartes makes it clear that he holds the much stronger thesis that the divine acts of creation and of preservation are in reality identical: 'It is quite clear . . . that the same power and action are needed to preserve anything at each individual moment of its duration as would be required to create that thing anew if it were not already in existence' (Third Meditation, AT VII 49: CSM II 33). Compare Thomas Aquinas: 'a thing could not abide if there were a cessation in the action of the agent that is the cause not merely of the effect's coming into being, but of its very being' (*Summa theologiae*, I, qu. 104, art. 1); cf. Descartes, Fifth Replies: God is the cause of created things in the same way that the sun is the cause of light – not just the cause of coming into being, but the cause of being itself (AT VII 369: CSM II 254–5).

See also TIME.

conservation, principle of In his early work on physics, *Le Monde*, Descartes lays it down that the total quantity of motion in the cosmos always remains the same; the principle is derived from, or associated with, the immutability of God (AT XI 43: CSM I 96). In the *Principles of Philosophy*, the principle is stated, more fully, as follows: 'it is most in agreement with reason to think that God moved the parts of matter in different ways when he first created them, and that he now conserves the whole of that matter in the same way and by the same principle [*eadem ratione*] by which he originally created it; and this also makes it most reasonable to think that God likewise always preserves the same quantity of motion in matter' (Part II, art. 36). This notion of the conservation of motion was highly influential for the subsequent development of physics. In later Newtonian physics, however, what is conserved is mass times velocity, and neither of these notions are to be found in Descartes: as the working out of Descartes' 'rules of impact' make clear, what is conserved is what Descartes calls 'quantity of motion', measured simply as the product of size (volume) and speed (the latter factor, unlike the more modern notion of velocity, is not held to be affected by a change in direction of motion; see *Principles*, Part II, arts 45–52).

cosmology   It was a major part of Descartes' ambition as a philosopher-scientist to provide a comprehensive account of the origins and structure of the universe. In chapter 6 of his *Le Monde*, written in the early 1630s, Descartes launched this project, by unfolding the general physical character-istics of what (perhaps to avoid open conflict with the theologians) he calls an 'imaginary new world'. The most striking feature of this universe is its simplicity: the nature of the matter of which it is composed contains 'nothing that everyone cannot know as perfectly as possible'. In keeping with its simplicity, Descartes' universe is perfectly homogeneous: somewhat in the manner of the 'perfect cosmological principle' proposed by some present-day astronomers, Descartes suggests that the application of the basic laws of physics yields a universe which is always and everywhere perfectly regular and uniform. Thus, even if one were to suppose an initially chaotic configura-tion of matter, 'the laws of nature are sufficient to cause the parts of the chaos to disentangle themselves and arrange themselves in such good order that they will have the form of a quite perfect world' (AT XI 34: CSM I 91).

The effect of Descartes' approach is to subsume cosmology under physics. No special creative acts, no divine purposes are invoked (*see* CAUSE, FINAL); rather, the universe is like a machine whose operations unfold automatically in accordance with the laws of matter in motion. This does not displace God: Descartes frequently stresses, both in his *Le Monde* and even more emphati-cally in his later *Principles of Philosophy*, that the uniform laws of motion operate in virtue of the power and constancy of the deity (see *Principles*, Part II, art. 36). But Cartesian cosmology is none the less austere and impersonal in character as compared with the special creation described in Genesis, of which man is the centrepiece and crowning purpose. In a letter to Chanut of 6 June 1647, Descartes observes that 'we are not obliged to believe that man is the end of creation', and argues that if Genesis suggests the reverse, this may simply be because 'Genesis was written for man'. Descartes' perpetual fear of becoming embroiled in theological disputes made him use highly oblique language here as elsewhere, but earlier in the same letter he comes close to asserting, in defiance of Scripture, that the universe may be not only infinite in spatial extent, but infinite in time: 'If we consider the [indefinite and unbounded] extension of the universe, and compare it with its duration, it seems to be that there is no imaginable time before the creation of the world in which God could not have created it if he had so willed' (AT V 52: CSMK 320).

A closely connected feature of Descartes' cosmology is its implicit denial of the traditional geocentric conception of the universe. The condemnation of Galileo by the Inquisition in 1633, for advocating the heliocentric hypothesis, led Descartes to withdraw his own *Le Monde* from publication, and in the later *Principles of Philosophy*, designed to be accepted as a university textbook, he goes through various laborious manoeuvres designed to distance him from Galileo's *eppur se muove* (see *Principles*, Part III, arts 17–19). None the less he manages in spite of the smokescreen to make it clear that he is committed to regarding the solar system as a great vortex with 'all the planets including the earth' turning about a central sun (Part III, art. 30). Descartes' insistence on dethroning the earth from its central position is all of a piece with his general programme for an autonomous physics, freed from the constraints of theological dogma, and based purely on mathematical principles. He was well aware that the loss of special status for the earth, and therefore the human race, might be seen as diminishing our value; but that this result necessarily followed from the acceptance of the new cosmology was something he firmly denied. The new science made it probable that the earth was only one of many other worlds which might support intelligent life, but 'the goods which belong to all the intelligent creatures in an indefinite world do not diminish those which we humans possess; they are not in any way lessened through being found in many others' (AT V 55–6: CSMK 322). In these and similar passages Descartes anticipates in part the line taken by Spinoza later in the century: the dignity and ethical worth of mankind does not depend on a cosily anthropocentric cosmology.

Conversation with Burman   This document is the result of a meeting held on 16 April 1648 between Descartes and the young Dutchman Frans Burman. Burman came to interview Descartes (who was living at the time at Egmond Binnen, near Alkmaar), and questioned him closely about a large number of passages in the *Meditations*, *Principles of Philosophy* and *Discourse*. He took full notes of Descartes' replies, and the result is what purports to be a verbatim report of the interview. Through the efforts of Burman's friend, the young philosopher John Clauberg (later to publish several works on Descartes), a copy of the manuscript was preserved; it was not, however, until the end of the nineteenth century that the work was first published. The text is in Latin, and is to be found in AT V 146ff; an English translation by J. Cottingham, with introduction and notes, was published in 1976, and substantial extracts of this version are printed in CSMK 332ff. The *Conversation* is a valuable source for the views of the mature Descartes on several important issues, including the Cartesian CIRCLE, INNATENESS, the COGITO and FREE WILL. Since, however, the work gives us Descartes' remarks only at second hand, it does not have the authority of his published work or his correspondence.

creation   Although Descartes felt obliged, as a good Catholic, to accept the revealed truths of Holy Scripture, there seems little doubt that he believed that the way in which the universe in fact evolved was inconsistent with the biblical account of creation given in Genesis. In the *Principles of Philosophy*, he makes an awkward attempt at compromise by saying that even though 'Adam and Eve were created fully grown', 'we may be able to think up certain very simple and easily known principles which can serve, as it were, as the seeds from which we can demonstrate that the stars, the earth, and indeed everything we observe in this visible world could have sprung; for although we know for sure that they never did arise in this way, we shall be able to provide a much better explanation of their nature by this method' (Part III, art. 45). The prudent, if somewhat tortuous, allegiance to the official creation story is retracted in a private interview, where (if he is reported correctly) Descartes implies that the Genesis story can only be accepted if it is construed metaphorically, not as the literal truth (*Conversation with Burman*, AT V 169: CSMK 349). *See* COSMOLOGY.

Despite these sources of conflict in Descartes' thinking, he certainly followed religious orthodoxy in so far as he regarded God as the cause of the existence of the universe – the reason why it was there at all. As far as the physical universe was concerned, this meant that God created *res extensa* – the all-pervasive extended substance of which the visible world is composed (cf. *Principles*, Part I, arts 51–4). Descartes further attributed to God's creative power the fact that the universe is in motion; for although, in the official Cartesian classification of matter, motion appears as a mere mode of *res extensa*, the purely geometrical notion of extension in three dimensions evidently does not of itself yield a dynamic universe of moving particles. Hence we find Descartes asserting in *Principles*, Part II, art. 36, that 'God is the universal and primary cause of all the motions in the world'. In creating matter, he imparted a determinate quantity of motion to it, and 'now merely by his regular concurrence, he preserves the same amount of motion and rest in the material universe as he put there in the beginning' (AT VIIIA 61: CSM I 240).

The notion of God's immutability is important here. God's perfect and unchanging nature does not permit any variations in his creative power. Indeed, God, as Descartes asserts elsewhere, does not strictly act through time, but rather accomplishes all things by means of a single timeless act (AT VIIIA 14: CSM I 201). The cash value for physics of these metaphysical reflections on the immutability of God is the Cartesian law of the conservation of motion. Divine creation and divine conservation (which Descartes elsewhere asserts to be only conceptually distinct – AT VII 49: CSM II 33) fuse together to form a kind of metaphysical underpinning for the principle that the net quantity of motion in the universe is never increased or diminished (*Principles*, Part II, art. 37).

See also MOTION; CONSERVATION, PRINCIPLE OF.

D

deceiving God dilemma In the First Meditation Descartes presents, as part of his systematic exploration of the limits of doubt, the following dilemma. I have been taught to believe in the existence of an omnipotent deity. Either there is such a being or there is not. If there is, it seems possible that he might have given me the kind of nature that allows me to go wrong 'every time I add two and three or count the sides of a square, or in some even simpler matter if that is imaginable'. If, on the other hand, there is no God, then I owe my existence not to a divine creator, but to some imperfect chain of chance events; but in this case it is even more likely that I am 'so imperfect as to be deceived all the time' (AT VII 21: CSM II 14). The possibility of my being wrong even with respect to the simplest truths of mathematics pushes doubt to its furthest limits (*see* CIRCLE, CARTESIAN). In the recapitulation of the argument at the end of the First Meditation, the deceiving God reappears in the guise of 'a malicious demon of the utmost power and cunning'.

See DEMON, MALICIOUS.

deduction In Descartes' theory of knowledge, all primary truths are directly perceived by means of the direct mental vision which Descartes terms INTUITION. But in addition to intuition, there is another mode of knowing, namely deduction, 'by which we mean the inference of something as following necessarily from some other propositions which are known with certainty' (*Regulae*, Rule III). Descartes goes on to explain that 'many facts which are not self-evident are known with certainty, provided they are inferred from true and known principles through a continuous and uninterrupted movement of thought' (AT X 369: CSM I 15).

The metaphor which Descartes employs both in the *Regulae* and in the *Discourse* to illustrate his notion of deduction is that of a chain composed of many links. Geometers manage to prove complex theorems by a long series of simple inferences, with each step in the argument tightly connected to its predecessor, so that the whole process of reasoning forms an unbroken chain (*Discourse*, Part II, AT VI 19: CSM I 120). Such deductive demonstrations succeed, as it were, in passing on to the conclusions the self-evidence enjoyed by the premises. 'This is similar to the way in which we know that the last link in a long chain is connected to the first: even if we cannot take in at one glance all the intermediate links on which the connection depends, we can have knowledge of the connection provided we survey the links one after the other, and keep in mind that each link from first to last is attached to its neighbour' (*Regulae*, Rule III, AT X 370: CSM I 15).

It is often said that Descartes, like other so-called 'rationalist' philosophers, attaches great importance to deductive knowledge, and there is some truth in this. Yet for all his enthusiasm for the 'long chains of reasoning' of the geometers, Descartes consistently regarded deduction as a second-best form of cognition. Intuition alone carries the self-evident certainty that arises when the mind's eye is directed towards a proposition whose content is entirely clear and manifest. But because of the finite scope of the human mind, our ability to attend to a plurality of propositions at any one time is severely limited (AT V 148: CSMK 335); hence the need for deduction, which involves temporarily leaving behind one proposition and moving on to the next, so that 'in a certain sense deduction gets its certainty from memory' (AT X 370: CSM I 15). In his quest for an absolutely certain and reliable system of knowledge, Descartes was well aware of the potential faultiness of memory, and in the *Regulae* he goes as far as to recommend that deduction should be dispensed with altogether, or at least assimilated as closely as possible to intuition: 'deduction sometimes requires such a long chain of inferences that when we arrive at a result it is not easy to recall the entire route which led us to it . . . Hence . . . to make good the weakness of memory . . . I shall run through [a chain of reasoning] several times in a continuous movement . . . simultaneously intuiting one relation and passing on the next, until I have learnt to pass from the first to the last so swiftly that memory is left with practically no role to play' (AT X 387–8: CSM I 25). There seems, however, to be some doubt about the practical feasibility of grasping complex scientific results via this kind of 'continuous and wholly uninterrupted sweep of thought' (ibid.); although the notion of a wholly indubitable system of knowledge remained an ideal for Descartes, he was often in practice content with less rigorous standards.

See also CERTAINTY; ASSUMPTION.

demon, malicious   In the introduction to his metaphysics in Part IV of the *Discourse*, Descartes deploys various reasons for subjecting his previous beliefs to systematic doubt. Three types of reflection generating doubt are presented: (1) reflections about reliability of the senses; (2) reflections on the possibility of going wrong even in the simplest reasonings of mathematics; and (3) reflections on the possibility that we might be dreaming, and hence that the judgements we make while (supposedly) awake might not in fact be true (AT VI 32: CSM I 127). In the *Meditations*, published four years later, a further device for shaking our previous beliefs is introduced, the scenario of the malicious demon (*malignus genius*) bent on systematic deception: 'I will suppose that . . . some malicious demon of the utmost power and cunning has employed all his energies in order to deceive me. I shall think that the sky, the air, the earth, colours, shapes, sounds and all external things are merely the delusions of dreams which he has devised in order to ensnare my judgement' (AT VII 22–3: CSM II 15).

What does the malicious demon add to the doubt-generating considerations previously outlined in the *Discourse* (and redeployed in the First Meditation)? Commentators have argued at length about the precise role of the demon, but it seems clear from the structure of the First Meditation that the supposition of such a supremely powerful deceiver is not supposed to be an additional *argument* for doubt (alongside the arguments about the senses, dreaming and possible error in mathematical reasoning). Rather the demon scenario is introduced as a deliberate act of will ('I will suppose therefore . . .') designed to counteract the force of preconceived opinion which 'occupies my belief' as a result of long habituation (AT VII 22, lines 3ff: CSM II 15). The demon, in other words, is an artificial device introduced to help the meditator to persevere in the suspension of his ordinary, comfortable beliefs. In terms of its scope, the demon scenario does not impugn any beliefs that had not already been called into question by previous arguments; rather, it reinforces my determination to keep focusing on already established doubts. Thus, the dreaming argument had raised the possibility that the objects around me which I believe to exist might be no more than mental figments; the demon reiterates this in more vivid form – 'all external things' might be no more than 'the delusions of dreams which he has devised to ensnare my judgement' (AT VII 22, line 28).

The malicious demon represents extreme or 'hyperbolical' doubt pushed to its farthest limit; his appearance thus paves the way for the attainment of Descartes' 'Archimedian point' – the meditator's certainty of his own existence which survives all the efforts of the demon to deceive in every conceivable way (*see* COGITO ERGO SUM).

One thing left unclear, however, by the conjuring up, and subsequent defeat, of the demon, is what relation it bears to the DECEIVING GOD DILEMMA introduced earlier in the First Meditation. That there is a close connection is suggested by the way in which Descartes introduces the demon: 'I will suppose that *not God who is supremely good and the source of truth* but rather some malicious demon . . .' (AT VII 22, emphasis supplied). In the remainder of the *Meditations* Descartes frequently asserts that it is contradictory to attribute deception to a supremely perfect being, and this premise plays an important role in the Cartesian project of constructing a reliable edifice of human knowledge (see Fourth Meditation, AT VII 53: CSM II 37; and Sixth Meditation, AT VII 79–80: CSM II 55). Descartes' eventual position, then, will be that the existence of a perfect being can be established, divine deception ruled out as an absurdity, and the reliability of the human mind (created by God) established. From the perspective of the First Meditation, however, nothing is yet certain: there may be an omnipotent deity, but then for all I know (as yet), he may deceive me. Against this background, the defeat of the demon, and the proof of the existence of an all-perfect God, becomes the vital prerequisite for any further progress towards a reliable system of knowledge. Descartes' most fully worked out discussion of the complex interrelations between doubt, divine deception, the Cogito argument, and the goal of certain knowledge, occurs in the fourth paragraph of the Third Meditation (AT VII 36: CSM II 25).

Description of the Human Body This unfinished treatise (written in French) dates from the winter of 1647–8, and was published posthumously in 1664 under the title *La Description du Corps Humain*. It provides evidence of Descartes' continued interest in physiology (especially the circulation of the blood), and it also attempts to put forward a purely mechanistic explanation of the formation and growth of the foetus (albeit of a highly speculative and schematic kind). The tone throughout is strongly reductionistic: 'It is true that we may find it hard to believe that the mere disposition of the bodily organs is sufficient to produce in us all the movements which are in no way determined by our thought. So I will now try to prove the point, and to give such a full account of the entire bodily machine that we will have no more reason to think that it is our soul which produces in it the movements which we know by experience are not controlled by our will than we have reason to think that there is a soul in a clock which makes it tell the time' (AT XI 226: CSM I 315).

Discourse on the Method Descartes' first published work appeared anonymously at Leiden in 1637. Its full title is *Discours de la Méthode pour bien conduire sa raison, et chercher la vérité dans les sciences* ('Discourse on the Method of rightly conducting one's reason and seeking the truth in the sciences'). The volume included three other works described as 'Essays in this method', namely the *Optics, Meteorology* and *Geometry*. In 1644 a Latin translation of the *Discourse* and *Essays* (omitting the *Geometry*) was published at Amsterdam.

The *Discourse*, which is written in the first person, and addressed directly to the plain man of 'good sense', that 'best distributed thing in the world (AT VI 1: CSM I 111), takes the form of a kind of intellectual autobiography. Part I describes the schooling which the young Descartes received, and his dissatisfaction with the way in which many of the standard curriculum subjects were taught. Part II describes his vision, as a young man, of a new philosophical METHOD. Part III sets out the rudiments of a provisional moral code 'consisting of just three or four maxims' (*see* MORALITY). Part IV, the metaphysical core of the work, describes his search for the foundations of a reliable system of knowledge, and contains the famous pronouncement *je pense donc je suis* ('I am thinking, therefore I exist'; *see* COGITO ERGO SUM). Part V outlines Descartes' views on physics and cosmology, discusses the particular scientific issue of the circulation of the BLOOD, and presents an argument based on LANGUAGE for the radical distinction between humans and ANIMALS. Finally, Part VI makes important general points about the role of observation and experiment in science (*see* EXPERIENCE), and outlines Descartes' future plans for research.

The *Discourse* is a fluent and stylish work, but the argumentation is often quite loose and informal; the metaphysical arguments in Part IV, for example, are presented with far less detail and rigour than we find in the *Meditations* (published four years later). Descartes himself wrote that the title *Discourse* was meant to convey the sense of a 'Preface or Notice on the Method', to show that the Method was not to be fully expounded, but only 'discussed'. 'As can be seen from what I say, it is concerned more with practice than with theory. I call the treatises that follow "Essays in this Method" because I claim that they could never have been discovered without it, so that they show how much it is worth. I have also inserted a certain amount of metaphysics, physics and medicine in the opening *Discourse*, in order to show that my method extends to topics of all kinds' (letter to Mersenne of 27 February 1637, AT I 349: CSMK 53).

distinction, real   The subtitle of the Sixth Meditation refers to the 'real distinction' between mind and body. By a 'real' (Latin *realis*) distinction between X and Y, Descartes means that X and Y are distinct things (Latin *res*); thus a thinking thing (*res cogitans*) is really distinct from a bodily or extended thing (*res extensa*) and 'can exist without it' (AT VII 78: CSM II 54). In the *Principles of Philosophy*, Descartes explains that 'strictly speaking a real distinction obtains only between two or more substances' – a substance being that which is capable of independent existence (AT VIIIA 28: CSM I 213; cf. AT VIIIA 24: CSM I 210). Descartes contrasts a 'real distinction' (such as that between corporeal and thinking substance) with a 'modal distinction' (such as that between a mode of extension, say shape, and the substance in which it inheres). The reason for calling the latter distinction modal rather than real is that the shape could not exist apart from the relevant substance (for a fuller explanation, see *Principles*, Part I, art. 62). Finally, following traditional terminology, Descartes distinguishes both the real and the modal distinction from the purely conceptual distinction or 'distinction of reason' (*distinctio rationis*): an example of this last would be the way in which, when considering corporeal or extended substance, one might distinguish the substance in question from the attribute of extension: the separation involved is a purely mental abstraction, since the substance cannot intelligibly be grasped without its defining attribute, nor vice versa (*Principles*, Part I, art. 63; *see* SUBSTANCE). The classification of distinctions which Descartes made is, like much of his metaphysical terminology, derived from his scholastic predecessors – in this case Francisco Suárez and Eustachius a Sancto Paulo (cf. Gilson, *Index Scolastico-Cartésien*, 86–90).

divisibility   Body or extended substance is, Descartes frequently asserts, by its very nature always divisible: 'there is no corporeal or extended thing which in my thought I cannot easily divide into parts; and this very fact makes me understand that it is divisible' (Sixth Meditation, AT VII 86: CSM II 59). The reasoning is not at first sight wholly perspicuous: the fact that one can mentally divide an extended body into parts does not seem to entail that it is therefore actually divisible. Descartes however has defined extended substance as 'the whole of that corporeal nature which is the subject matter of pure mathematics' (AT VII 71: CSM II 49); and it is a necessary truth of mathematics that whatever has a quantifiable extension (for example a line) must be infinitely (or as Descartes preferred to say 'indefinitely') divisible. From this piece of mathematical reasoning Descartes deduced the impossibility of atoms: 'if there were any atoms, then no matter how small we imagined them to be, they would necessarily have to be extended, and hence we could in our thought divide each of them into two or more smaller parts, and hence recognize their divisibility'. The same principle would hold good even if God had created particles that we could not in fact split into smaller ones: 'by making a particle indivisible by any of his creatures, God certainly could not thereby take away his own power of dividing it, since it is quite impossible for him to diminish his own power, and hence strictly speaking the particle will remain divisible' (*Principles*, Part II, art. 20).

Although the validity of these arguments seems guaranteed by the way Descartes has defined his terms, problems none the less arise from the application of his mathematically defined notion of extended substance to the real physical universe. For is it conceivable to maintain that the particles of which matter is composed are divisible again and again, ad infinitum? In *Principles*, Part II, arts 33 and 34, Descartes maintains that this is indeed the case, although he admits that it is beyond our power to grasp (*comprehendere*) how this indefinite division comes about: although it 'follows most evidently from what we know of the nature of matter, we perceive that it belongs to the class of things which are beyond the grasp of our finite minds' (AT VIIIA 60:

CSM I 239). The problem with this is that it seems to involve a partial retreat from what was supposed to be the chief advantage of Cartesian physics over its scholastic predecessors: its claim to employ only utterly transparent notions. The problem of grasping the idea of indefinitely divisible extension became known in the decades following Descartes' death as the 'labyrinth of the continuum', and was to form a principal plank in Leibniz' critique of the Cartesian conception of physics (cf. Leibniz, *A Specimen of Discoveries* [*c.* 1686]. The label 'labyrinth of the continuum' comes from the title of a book by Libert Froidmont, *Labyrinthus, sive de compositione continui*, 1631).

doubt 'Descartes' method of doubt' is the label often applied to the procedure whereby Descartes attempts to clear away the rubble of prejudices or preconceived opinions, in order to lay down a reliable metaphysical base for his new science. 'I realized that it was necessary, once in the course of my life, to demolish everything and start again right from the foundations if I wanted to establish anything at all in the sciences that was stable and likely to last' (First Meditation, AT VII 17: CSM I 12). Although Descartes was sometimes maliciously accused of being a sceptic (cf. AT VII 574: CSM II 387), he made it clear, right from the first public presentation of his metaphysics, that his purpose in raising systematic doubts was to *eliminate* doubt and find something secure and indubitable: 'since I wished to devote myself solely to the search for truth, I thought it necessary to do the very opposite and reject as if absolutely false everything in which I could imagine the least doubt, in order to see if I was left believing anything that was entirely indubitable' (*Discourse*, Part IV, AT VI 31: CSM I 126–7). Doubt, in short, is a means to an end, not an end in itself. And at the end of the *Meditations*, it is striking that the meditator is able, with relief, to dismiss his earlier doubts as 'laughable' and 'exaggerated' (Latin, *hyperbolicae*, AT VII 89: CSM II 61).

These manoeuvres need to be understood partly against the background of the sceptical debates of the late sixteenth and early seventeenth centuries. In 1562, some thirty years before Descartes' birth, Henri Etienne (Stephanus) had published a Latin translation of one of the great classics of Greek philosophy, Sextus Empiricus' *Outlines of Pyrrhonism* (*c.* AD 190). This work, named after the founder of ancient scepticism, Pyrrho of Elis, presented a host of arguments designed to show that suspension of judgement was the only rational course in the face of the contradictory and shifting evidence available for our beliefs. Sextus in his *Outlines* had drawn up ten 'modes' of scepticism – argument patterns designed to induce suspension of belief by drawing attention to a variety of evidential conflicts showing that what appears to be the case from one point of view, or against the background of a particular set of circumstances, could well appear otherwise in different conditions, or from a different standpoint.

The subsequent development of the branch of philosophy now known as 'epistemology' has tended to see the theory of knowledge as a perpetual battleground between the sceptic and the anti-sceptic, with the latter attempting to establish such basic truths as the existence of the external world, in the face of extreme or 'hyperbolical' doubts of the kind raised in the *Meditations*. Descartes' own philosophical motivations were certainly not of this sort. He wrote in the Synopsis to the *Meditations* that the great benefit of the arguments he had provided was 'not that they prove what they establish – namely that there really is a world, and that human beings have bodies, and so forth – since no sane person has ever seriously doubted these things, but rather that in considering these arguments we come to realize that they are not as solid or as transparent as the arguments which lead us to knowledge of our own minds and of God, so that the latter are the most certain and evident of all possible objects of knowledge for the human intellect' (AT VII 16: CSM II 11). One of the objects of the exercise in suspension of previous beliefs was to 'lead the mind away from the senses' and towards the truths accessible to the light of reason which Descartes believed to be innate in each soul (cf. INNATENESS and INTUITION).

For details of the various phases of doubt which Descartes employs at the start of the Meditations, *see* ILLUSION; DREAMING; DEMON, MALICIOUS; DECEIVING GOD DILEMMA.

dreaming In his search for new and reliable foundations for knowledge, one of the principal arguments which Descartes uses for challenging the basis of his previously held beliefs is the so-called 'dreaming argument'. Presented in its fullest form in the First Meditation, the argument is based on the claim that 'there are no certain marks by means of which being awake can be distinguished from being asleep' (AT VII 19: CSM II 13). Because of this, any proposition which the meditator asserts about 'external' objects (including what he is doing with his own body) are seen to be suspect. The meditator believes himself to be 'sitting by the fire, wearing a winter dressing gown'; but if he might now be asleep and merely dreaming these events, the beliefs just cited could well be false. 'How often, asleep at night, am I convinced of just such familiar events – that I am here in my dressing gown, sitting by the fire – when in fact I am lying undressed in bed!' (ibid.).

Critics of Descartes' argument have insisted that, so far from there being 'no certain marks' to distinguish being awake from being asleep, there are indeed many significant differences between dreaming and waking experiences. Descartes does not deny that dreams are 'vastly different' from waking life (Sixth Meditation, AT VII 89: CSM II 61), but this does not affect the validity of his claim in the First Meditation that there is no test available to the meditator which will provide a logically watertight guarantee that the experience he is now having is real (as opposed to being a dream). Indeed, Descartes proceeds to develop the argument further, to reach the much more radical conclusion, not just that any particular proposition about what I now think I am experiencing might be false, but that there might not be any real external objects at all. This much more extreme level of doubt (the thought, as it were, that the whole of life might be a dream) leaves Descartes with the conclusion that any science (such as physics, astronomy or medicine) which claims to refer to actually existing objects is now subject to doubt, and that only mathematics, which 'deals only with the simplest and most general things, regardless of whether they exist in nature or not', may contain something reliable (AT VII 20: CSM II 14). The upshot of this second, more extreme, phase of the dreaming argument is that belief in the 'external world' (the existing material universe which we take to be the cause of our sensory perceptions) is entirely suspended, only to be reinstated at the very end of Descartes' quest for knowledge, in the Sixth Meditation (AT VII 79–80: CSM II 55).

For more on the character and philosophical motivation for this extreme level of doubt (which Descartes himself termed 'hyperbolical'), *see* DOUBT.

dualism　Standard label given to the Cartesian claim that there are two distinct kinds of substance, mind (or 'thinking substance') and body (or 'extended substance'), whose natures are radically opposed. 'Each substance', wrote Descartes in the *Principles*, 'has one principal property which constitutes its nature and essence, and to which all its other properties are referred. Thus extension in length, breadth and depth constitutes the nature of corporeal substance, and thought constitutes the nature of thinking substance' (AT VIIIA 25: CSM I 210). As is explained in the Sixth Meditation, the properties of extension and of thought are mutually incompatible: an extended thing is a non-thinking thing, and a thinking thing is a non-extended thing (cf. AT VII 78: CSM II 54).

But how many substances, exactly, does the Cartesian universe contain? From an ontological point of view, the term 'dualism' suggests a contrast, on the one hand with monism (the view, taken most famously by Spinoza, that there is but one substance), and, on the other hand, with pluralism (the view of, for example, Leibniz that the universe contains an indefinite plurality of substances). But the numbers ('one', 'two', 'many') can be highly misleading here. For as far as minds are concerned, Descartes is a pluralist: each individual human mind is a distinct and separate substance. 'From the mere fact that each of us understands himself to be a thinking thing, and is capable in thought of excluding from himself every other substance, whether thinking or extended, it is certain that each of us, regarded in this way, is distinct from every other thinking substance . . .' (*Principles*, Part I, art. 60). In the case of corporeal substance, by contrast, Descartes' view is monistic: individual bodies such as rocks and stones and planets are not substances, but merely modifications of a single all-pervasive extended stuff (*see* BODY). Despite this asymmetry of number, Descartes frequently speaks of mind and matter as two basic classificatory categories or notions, and it is this which has given rise to the label 'dualism': 'we can easily have two clear and distinct notions or ideas, one of created thinking substance and the other of corporeal substance' (*Principles*, Part I, art. 54). The classification is not complete, however, unless we add to these two notions the further notion of 'uncreated and independent thinking substance', i.e. God, who alone qualifies as a substance in the strict sense (cf. *Principles*, Part I, art. 51; *see* GOD; SUBSTANCE).

The term 'Cartesian dualism' is most frequently introduced in contemporary philosophy of mind to refer to Descartes' doctrine of the incorporeality of the mind, i.e. the view that, as Descartes put it, 'this "I" – that is the soul by which I am what I am – is entirely distinct from the body, and would not fail to be whatever it is even if the body did not exist' (AT VI 33: CSM I 127). For the many philosophical problems which arise from this doctrine, *see* MIND AND BODY.

E

Early Writings   During his travels in Europe in 1619–22, Descartes kept a notebook to record his philosophical reflections. This notebook was mentioned in an inventory of his papers made at Stockholm after his death, but is now lost. However, a copy, taken by Leibniz, was later discovered and published under the title *Cogitationes Privatae* ('Private Thoughts') in 1859. By a further twist to the story, the Leibniz copy, which was the basis of this publication, has since been lost.

According to Descartes' biographer, Adrien Baillet, who saw the original notebook, it was divided into various sections, including *Praeambula* ('Preliminaries'), *Experimenta* ('Observations') and *Olympica* ('Olympian matters'), and included a detailed account of Descartes' night of troubled dreams, in November 1619, when he became convinced of his mission to found a new scientific and philosophical system. Baillet relates three consecutive dreams: in the first, Descartes felt himself assailed by phantoms and a whirlwind, and felt a pain in his side which he feared had been caused by an evil demon; in the second he heard a terrible noise like a thunderclap; the third and most complex dream involved an anthology of poetry (containing the poem of Ausonius beginning *Quid vitae sectabor iter* – 'What road in life shall I follow?') and an encyclopedia or dictionary 'signifying all the sciences collected together'. A translation of Baillet's account of the dreams may be found in the Appendix to J. Cottingham, *Descartes*, pp. 161ff. The surviving extracts from Descartes' notebook are printed (in a mixture of French and Latin) in AT X, 213ff, and translated in CSM I 2ff.

error   The problem of error is one which bulks large in Cartesian metaphysics, assuming the same kind of importance as the problem of evil assumes for theologians. Indeed, Descartes, in the Fourth Meditation, wrestles with an exact epistemological analogue of the ancient theological puzzle about how a benevolent God can allow evil in his creation: if we are created by a perfect God, who is the source of all truth and incapable of deception, then how does it happen that we so often go wrong in our judgements? Descartes' answer is that the source of error lies in the will, which 'extends more widely than the intellect'. The intellect itself is a God-given instrument which is, so far as its scope extends, free from error: whatever we clearly and distinctly perceive is true. But because of our nature as finite beings, there are many things that our intellect does *not* perceive clearly. In such cases we ought to withhold judgement; but instead the wide-ranging will often jumps in and gives assent to a proposition even though the evidence is not clear: 'in this incorrect use of free will may be found the privation which is the essence of error' (AT VII 60: CSM II 41; cf. *Principles*, Part I, art. 38). From this analysis, Descartes deduces what he takes to be a reliable recipe for the avoidance of error: 'restrain the will so that it extends only to what the intellect clearly and distinctly reveals, and no further' (AT VII 62: CSM II 43).

The recipe does not provide an infallible or easy route to the truth, since as Descartes admits 'there are few people who correctly distinguish between what they in fact perceive clearly and distinctly and what they think they so perceive' (AT VII 511: CSM II 348. *See* CIRCLE, CARTESIAN and CLARITY AND DISTINCTNESS). A further problem arises, moreover, in respect of our ordinary sensory apprehension of the world around us, which turns out, on Descartes' account of the true nature of the physical world, to be seriously misleading. We fall into error if we attribute to objects sensible qualities such as being hard, or heavy or coloured, since their true nature consists solely in extension in length, breadth and depth (cf. *Principles*, Part II, art. 4). Descartes' general 'theodicy' – the project of vindicating the truthfulness and goodness of God and explaining away error as due to human misuse of the freedom of the will – thus seems threatened. For it appears to be the case that our strong natural propensities incline us to construct a picture of the world (yellow sun, green grass, sweet honey, heavy stone, and so on) which just does not correspond to the way things really are. This is the issue which Descartes attempts to confront in the Sixth Meditation, and his general conclusion is that although it is in a certain sense 'natural' to think of objects as possessing colours and other sensible qualities, we are none the less guilty of 'misusing' our God-given natural propensities if we jump to the conclusion that such qualities really inhere in the objects around us. 'The proper purpose of the sensory perceptions given me by nature is simply to inform the mind of what is beneficial or harmful to the composite [human being] of which the mind is a part; and to this extent they are sufficiently clear and distinct. But I misuse them by treating them as reliable touchstones for immediate judgements about the essential nature of the bodies located outside us, this being an area where they provide only very obscure information' (AT VII 83: CSM II 58). The upshot is that the senses are, for Descartes, a source of error only if we treat their deliverances as the basis for constructing our scientific under-standing of the structure of the physical world. We should instead accept them for what they are, as survival mechanisms whose primary purpose is to flag external events in a way which conduces to the self-protection and health of the body. The importance of this conclusion is underlined by Descartes in the final paragraph of the *Meditations* (AT VII 89: CSM II 61), and the opening of Part II of the *Principles* (see esp. art. 3).

See also SENSATION.

essence Descartes' scholastic predecessor, Eustachius a Sancto Paulo, defined 'essence' as the 'reason, nature, form, formal definition or formal concept of some thing' (*Summa Philosophica* [1609] IV, 33–4; cited in Gilson, *Index Scolastico-Cartésien*, 104). Thus we might say that the essence of a circle is that it is a plane figure described by a point equidistant from a given point, or such that all the points on its circumference are equidistant from the centre. The notion derives ultimately from Aristotle's 'formal cause', which specifies the essence of a thing, or 'what it is to be something' (cf. *Posterior Analytics*, Book II, ch. 11). Descartes makes use of this traditional terminology in order to explicate his own theory of ideas. An idea is a mental item, a modification of my thought; but it also has a representative aspect – ideas are said in the Third Meditation to be 'like images', or to be 'as it were of things' (*comme des images*, AT IXA 34; *tanquam rerum*. AT VII 44; cf. CSM II 30, n. 2). Now concerning the things represented by our ideas, we may ask two questions. The most obvious question is whether they actually exist (and this is the subject of Descartes' arguments about the external world in the Sixth Meditation). But before this question, there is a prior question about essences, which Descartes introduces as follows in the Fifth Meditation: 'I find within me countless ideas of things which, even though they may not exist anywhere outside me still cannot be called nothing; for although in a sense they can be thought of at will, they are not my invention, but have their own true and immutable essences. When, for example, I imagine a triangle, even if perhaps no such figure exists, or has ever existed, outside my thought, there is still a determinate nature or essence or form of the triangle which is immutable and eternal, and not invented by me or dependent on my mind' (AT VII 64: CSM II 44–5). The notion of an immutable nature or essence which Descartes invokes here is of vital importance for his version of the ONTOLOGICAL ARGUMENT, since it enables him to avoid the objection that the argument is question-begging; compare letter to Mersenne of 16 June 1641, AT III 383: CSMK 183–4. For the contrast between essence and existence, cf. *Principles*, Part I, art. 16, and *Conversation with Burman*, AT V 164: CSMK 346. See also Cottingham (ed.), *Descartes' Conversation with Burman*, pp. 24 and 94.

For the status of truths about the essences of things, *see* ETERNAL TRUTHS.

eternal truths The class of eternal truths includes, for Descartes, COMMON NOTIONS, such as the proposition 'it is impossible for the same thing to be and not be'; cf. *Principles*, Part I, art. 49; truths about ESSENCES, for example, the fact that the radii of a circle are equal, are also included. The crucial point about such truths, for Descartes, is that we can assert them without committing ourselves to the actual existence of any object; cf. *Principles*, Part I, art. 48.

One of Descartes' most striking doctrines is that the eternal truths depend wholly on the will of God. He is their 'efficient and total cause', Descartes wrote to Mersenne on 27 May 1630, and he established them by 'the same sort of causality as that involved in all his creation'. From this it follows that, from the perspective of God, they are in no sense necessary: 'he was just as free to make it not true that all the radii of a circle are equal as he was not to create the world' (AT I 152: CSMK 25). This directly contradicts the official doctrine, formulated by St. Thomas Aquinas, that the necessity of such truths is prior to and independent of the will of God: 'the principles of sciences like Logic, Geometry and Arithmetic are solely derived from the formal principles of those things on which their essence depends, from which it follows that to bring about the opposite of these principles is not within the power of God' (*Contra Gentiles*, Book II, ch. 25; cf. Gilson, *Index Scolastico-Cartésien*, 105).

Several results follow from the Cartesian insistence on the total omnipotence and sovereignty of God, even over the truths of logic and mathematics. To begin with, Descartes cannot, despite what is sometimes suggested, be in a position to claim that the human mind is a faithful 'mirror of nature', or microcosm of the divine intellect. On the contrary, there must be a radical difference between our human perception of the fundamental truths of logic and mathematics, and their true nature. For us, such truths appear necessary: it is impossible for us to conceive of the radii of a circle being unequal (cf. AT V 224: CSMK 358–9). But no such necessity can apply to these truths as perceived by God: 'they are not known as true by God in any way which would imply that they are true independently of him' (AT I 149: CSMK 24). Reflection on this last point suggests that the very idea of the propositions of logic and mathematics being 'true' for God, is misleading. They are, rather, the result of a divine creative fiat; but precisely because humans cannot fully grasp the idea of such truths being subject to the will in this way, the ultimate rationale for such truths remains, in an important sense, beyond our comprehension. Coupled with Descartes' insistence that we can never fully grasp the infinite nature of God (AT VII 46: CSM II 32, n. 2), this generates important results for Descartes' overall conception of knowledge. While human beings have (thanks to the God-given NATURAL LIGHT) access to the fundamental logical and mathematical principles in accordance with which the universe is structured, the light of nature does not enable us to discern their ultimate basis. In a certain sense we simply have to accept them as emanations from the inscrutable will of God. If 'rationalism' is defined as the view that the basis for all truths is, in principle, transparently accessible to human reason, then Descartes' doctrine of the divine creation of the eternal truths makes his philosophy, in this respect at least, diverge substantially from the rationalist paradigm.

existence Existence is described by Descartes as a 'common' simple nature, since it is ascribed indifferently both to corporeal things and to minds or spirits (AT X 419: CSM I 45. *See* SIMPLE NATURES). In order to reach the first truth of Cartesian metaphysics, 'I am thinking, therefore I exist', one must of course understand what existence is. Commenting on this, Descartes wrote: 'to know what existence is, all we have to do is to understand the meaning of the word, for it tells us at once what the thing is which the word stands for, in so far as we can know it. There is no need here for a definition, which would confuse rather than clarify the issue' (*The Search for Truth*, AT X 525: CSM II 418).

In Descartes' proof of God's existence in the Fifth Meditation, existence is treated as a property (a property which must be attributed to God, defined as the sum of all perfections). Most modern logics do not treat existence in this way, and indeed some of Descartes' contemporary critics objected to the listing of existence as one of the perfections of God, alongside, for example, his omnipotence. Descartes replied: 'I do not see why existence cannot be said to be a property, just like omnipotence, provided of course that you take the word "property" to stand for any attribute, or for whatever can be predicated of a thing' (AT VII 382: CSM II 263).

See also ONTOLOGICAL ARGUMENT.

experience 'Our experience', Descartes observes in the *Regulae*, 'consists of whatever we perceive by the senses, whatever we learn from others, and in general whatever reaches the intellect from external sources or from its own reflexive contemplation' (AT X 422: CSM I 46). With respect to data from external sources, Descartes frequently (e.g. in the First Meditation) warns against sensory experience as a potential source of error; but he also frequently underlines the importance of observational evidence in science. When judiciously used, he suggests in the *Regulae*, experience assists the intellect in reaching the truth. The Latin term used in the *Regulae* is *experimentum*, which to the modern ear is suggestive of the scientific experiment, and indeed something of this connotation is present in the Latin, the term being derived from the verb *experiri*, to test. The same root is present in the French *expérience*, which is the word Descartes most frequently employs when talking of scientific observations. 'The further we advance in our knowledge', he points out in the *Discourse*, 'the greater is the necessity for *expériences*'. This is because what can be deduced *a priori* are only very simple and general structural features of the material universe. When we descend to more particular things, we 'encounter such a variety that the human mind cannot possibly distinguish the forms or species of bodies that are on the earth from an infinity of others that God might have put there' ; the only way forward is to 'proceed to the causes by way of the effects, by making many special observations'. Descartes goes on to assert that future progress in science will depend in large part on the systematic search for such observational evidence (AT VI 63–5: CSM I 143–4. *See* ASSUMPTIONS).

Descartes' scientific writings and his correspondence are full of references to experiments and observations, and we know that he performed a considerable number of experiments himself, particularly in the area of animal physiology (cf. letter to Plempius of 15 February 1638, AT I 526ff: CSMK 81ff; *Description of the Human Body*, AT XI 241ff: CSM I 317). A keen interest in experiment is also shown in his early work on the refraction of light; compare the letter to Golius of 2 February 1632, AT I 236ff: CSMK 34ff. This last letter is instructive, however, since although Descartes here discusses in considerable detail the design for a possible experiment to confirm his theory of refraction, he goes on to admit that he has actually performed the experiment only once (AT I 240: CSMK 36). It would certainly be wrong to represent Descartes as a dedicated experimental scientist; he is aware of the general importance of observational results in testing theories, but his own practice often appears to display a certain perfunctoriness, and in not a few cases he seems content merely to suggest experiments for others to perform (cf. letter to Mersenne of 13 December 1647, AT V 98ff: CSMK 327f.). It is also worth noting that when Descartes talks of *expériences*, he sometimes means, not systematic attempts to verify or falsify his theories against the bar of experience, but rather more or less commonplace everyday observations which he invokes to support, in a fairly loose sense, his supposition that mechanisms of a similar kind are operating at the micro level. For examples of observations of this kind, cf. *Principles*, Part III, art. 30 (the behaviour of whirlpools in a river, invoked to explain planetary motions); *Principles*, Part IV, art. 26 (the behaviour of droplets of water in a tub, invoked to explain the gravity or heaviness of terrestrial particles). *See also* ANALOGIES.

extension   Extension in length, breadth and depth is, for Descartes, the defining characteristic of matter or 'corporeal substance', and in principle all the various properties of matter can be exhibited as 'modes' of extension, i.e. various ways in which something can be extended. Thus although the famous piece of wax discussed in the Second Meditation can take on an indefinite variety of shapes, these are all simply modes of extension (AT VII

31: CSM II 20). Compare the definition of 'body' (*corpus*) in the Second Replies, as 'the substance which is the immediate subject of local extension and of the accidents [i.e. modes] which presuppose extension, such as shape, position, local motion and so on' (AT VII 161: CSM II 114).

It may be doubted, however, whether all the things that Descartes wants to say about body or material substance can in fact be reduced to modes of extension. Motion is officially described as such a mode, yet it does not seem to be derivable from the definition of matter as something extended in three dimensions; it is significant that in Descartes' physics, God is invoked as the primary cause for the quantity of motion that is to be found in the physical universe, which suggests that the divine power is needed to impart motion to extended substance (cf. *Principles*, Part II, art. 36; *see* CREATION). The ideas of solidity and impenetrability also seem to presuppose something more than mere geometrical extension, despite Descartes' claim that 'the true extension of a body is such as to exclude any interpenetration of the parts (Sixth Replies, AT VII 422: CSM II 298). In correspondence with Henry More, Descartes was challenged on this issue, and argued in reply that 'it is impossible to conceive of one part of an extended thing penetrating another equal part without thereby understanding that half the total extension is taken away or annihilated; but what is annihilated does not penetrate anything else, and so in my opinion it is established that impenetrability belongs to the essence of extension' (AT V 342: CSMK 372). The main text where Descartes unfolds his account of matter or body as pure extension is Part II of the *Principles of Philosophy*; see especially arts 4, 8, 11 and 12. In these passages, extension is used as almost equivalent to 'quantity', or that which can be measured. Compare the resounding declaration in the concluding article of *Principles*, Part II: 'I recognize no matter in corporeal things apart from that which the geometers call *quantity* and take as the object of their demonstrations, i.e. that to which every kind of division, shape and motion is applicable. . . . My consideration of such matter involves absolutely nothing apart from these divisions, shapes and motions' (AT VIIIA 79: CSM I 247).

F

faith, religious Descartes, like many philosophers of the seventeenth century, was troubled by the potential conflict between the demands of reason on the one hand and of religious faith on the other. Sometimes he was able to present himself as the ally of the Church, as in the prefatory letter to the Theology Faculty of the Sorbonne, which was printed at the front of the first edition of the *Meditations*: in establishing the existence of God and the immortality of the soul, he was following the edict of Pope Leo X that Christian philosophers should use all the powers of reason to support the faith (AT VII 3: CSM II 4). Some of the results of Cartesian physics, however, appeared to conflict with the revealed truths of the Bible (*see* COSMOLOGY; CREATION); and the very definition of matter which Descartes put forward was taken by many to conflict with the Catholic doctrine of transubstantiation. This latter difficulty was pursued, among others, by Antoine Arnauld, who pointed out that an ontology which identified matter with extension, of which properties like shape and motion were merely modes, could not allow for 'what we believe on faith, namely that the substance of the bread is taken away from the bread of the Eucharist, and only the accidents remain' (Fourth Replies, AT VII 217: CSM II 153). For Descartes' somewhat contorted reply, see Fourth Replies, AT VII 249ff; CSM II 173ff; see also the letter to Mesland of 9 February 1645, AT IV 162ff: CSMK 241ff.

Descartes' natural caution, and his distaste for theological controversy (AT V 159: CSMK 342) led him to make a number of formal declarations of allegiance to religious authority and the demands of faith. The most striking is at the end of the *Principles of Philosophy*: 'Mindful of my own weakness, I make no firm pronouncements, but submit all these opinions to the authority of the Catholic Church, and the judgement of those wiser than myself. And I would not wish anyone to believe anything except what he is convinced of by evident and irrefutable reasoning' (AT VIIIA 329: CSM I 291). But however submissive the tone, there is, nevertheless, something of a sting in the tail here, since if Descartes' own philosophical system is indeed (as he clearly believes it to be) based on 'evident and irrefutable reasoning', then the unavoidable implication is that any religious doctrine that conflicts with it must be suspect. A few years later, when composing the Preface to the French translation of the *Principles*, Descartes distinguished four sources of wisdom (rational intuition, sensory experience, opinion of others and book learning), and then proceeded simply to set the revealed truths of faith on one side as an honoured, but politely ignored, category of their own: 'I am not including divine revelation in the list, because it does not lead us on by degrees, but raises us at a stroke to infallible faith' (AT IXB 5: CSM I 181). Descartes' private view seems to have been that the main conflict was not so much between his philosophy and the revealed truths of of the Bible, but rather between his philosophy and the scholastic orthodoxy which the theologians had, mistakenly, invested with the full authority of the Church. He wrote to Mersenne on 31 March 1641: 'I have decided to fight with their own weapons the people who confuse Aristotle with the Bible and abuse the authority of the Church – I mean the people who had Galileo condemned . . . I am confident that I can show that none of the tenets of their philosophy accords with the Faith so well as my doctrines' (AT III 349–50: CSMK 177). Compare also the more formal statement in the Letter to Dinet published with the second edition of the *Meditations*: 'As far as theology is concerned, since one truth can never be in conflict with another, it would be impious to fear that any truths discovered in philosophy could be in conflict with the truths of faith. Indeed, I insist that there is nothing relating to religion which cannot be equally well or even better explained by means of my principles than can be done by means of those which are commonly accepted' (AT VII 581: CSM II 392).

See also SCHOLASTIC PHILOSOPHY.

force Since Cartesian physics attempts to describe and explain all physical phenomena using only the austere geometrical notion of extension and its associated modes (*see* EXTENSION), there is no place for notions such as 'force' 'influence' and the like, if such notions are taken to imply that matter possesses intrinsic dynamic qualities or real causal powers. See especially *Principles*, Part IV, art. 187, where Descartes extols the superiority of his system to those of his predecessors, with their array of occult powers – 'mysterious powers in stones and plants, marvels attributed to sympathetic and antipathetic influences and the like' (AT VIIIA 314: CSM I 279). Despite Descartes' attempts to purge his own physics of all such notions, he none the less sometimes slips into language which appears to attribute to objects more than can be derived from the concept of extended matter in motion. One such notion is that of 'force' (Latin *vis*), which crops up from time to time in Descartes' scientific writings. Compare *Principles*, Part III, art. 55, where we are offered an explanation of 'the force whereby the globules of the second element . . . strive to move away from their centres of motion'. In the next article, however, Descartes notes: 'when I say that the globules of the second element "strive" (Latin *conari*) to move away from the centres around which they revolve, it should not be thought that they have some thought from which this striving proceeds. I mean merely that they are positioned and pushed into motion in such a way that they will in fact travel in that direction...' (AT VIIIA 108: CSM I 259). This manoeuvre is not entirely satisfactory, since although Descartes can correctly claim that he resists the temptation to anthropomorphize matter (by attributing to it any 'thought' or inclination to move in a certain way) the revised description he offers nevertheless makes use of the idea of push or impulse, which in turn might be thought to presuppose the concept of force. To this Descartes might reply that all the movements in question are straightforwardly derivable from the laws of motion, which presuppose only that God imparted a certain quantity of motion into matter when he created it (*see* CREATION; CONSERVA-TION, PRINCIPLE OF). If this line of thought, which is implicit in much of Cartesian physics, is developed to its logical conclusion, it leads to the Malebranchian thesis that matter is essentially inert and that force or causal power is, strictly speaking, to be attributed to God alone (cf. Malebranche, *Entretiens sur la métaphysique* [1688], Dialogue VII).

free will 'That there is freedom in our will, and that we have power in many cases to give or withhold our assent at will, is so evident that it must be counted among the first and most common notions that are innate in us' (*Principles*, Part I, art. 39). This resounding declaration accords with many other passages where Descartes refers to the inner awareness which each of us has of our freedom (cf. AT V 159: CSMK 342). The traditional problem of reconciling human freedom with causal determinism or divine preordination is one which Descartes prefers to leave on one side: 'we have a clear and distinct perception that the power of God [whereby he wills and preordains all things] is infinite, but we cannot get a sufficient grasp of it to see how it leaves the free actions of men undetermined' (*Principles*, Part I, art. 41).

Although the remark just quoted sidesteps the ancient philosophical puzzle concerning free will and determinism, it nevertheless at least appears to acknowledge that there is a logical tension between the two notions, since free action is, apparently, equated with undetermined action (compare the French version of the same passage: the power of God leaves human actions *entièrement libres et indéterminées*). In the *Meditations*, however, Descartes takes a very different line, when considering the relationship between the intellect and the will. The central doctrine affirmed in the Fourth Meditation is what may be called the 'doctrine of the irresistibility of the natural light': when the intellect is confronted with a clear and distinct perception, the will is immediately and spontaneously impelled to give its assent to the truth of the relevant proposition. But such determination of the will, Descartes insists, does not mean that the assent is not freely given: 'the more I incline in one direction, either because I clearly understand that reasons of truth and goodness point that way, or because of a divinely produced disposition of my inmost thought, the freer is my choice; neither divine grace nor natural knowledge ever diminishes freedom, but on the contrary they increase and strengthen it' (AT VII 57–8: CSM II 40). On this analysis, liberty does not require a 'two-way' or contra-causal power to select x or not-x; rather it involves the spontaneous but unavoidable selection of x as the self-evidently correct answer. The existence of such 'liberty of enlightenment' as it has been called, is very far from being in tension with determinism; on the contrary it seems to presuppose it. When the internal light of reason makes the truth plain, assent is determined, but still free (it is regarded as unfree only when it is constrained by some *external* force). This reconciliationist line of thought perhaps explains why Descartes explicitly revises his definition of freedom of the will in the Fourth Meditation. Having at first suggested that it is the power 'to do or not to do something (to affirm or deny, to pursue or avoid)', he shifts his ground: 'or rather it consists simply in the fact that when the intellect puts something forward, we are moved to affirm or deny or pursue or avoid it in such a way that we do not feel ourselves determined by any external force; for in order to be free there is no need for me to be capable of movement in each of two directions' (ibid.).

If true human freedom consists, for Descartes, not in some two-way power, but in the unavoidable submission of the will to the divinely implanted light of reason within each of us, this raises two problems. The first is why Descartes appears to favour a more robustly contra-causal account in the passage from the *Principles* quoted above. And the second is how the 'submissive' or reconciliationist account squares with what seems to be presented in the opening of the *Meditations* as the complete autonomy of the will to suspend judgement, withholding assent from all former beliefs (including apparently, such seemingly irresistible truths as that two and three make five; AT VII 21–2: CSM II 14–15). A possible solution to these problems may be found in the letter of Mesland of 9 February 1645, where Descartes apparently continues to maintain that the will is irresistibly determined while we are actually in process of contemplating an evident truth (AT IV 174, line 27: CSMK 246), but none the less suggests that 'it is always open to us to hold back from pursuing a clearly known good, or from admitting a clearly perceived truth, provided we consider it a good thing to demonstrate the freedom of our will by so doing' (AT IV 173: CSMK 245). What may be underlying Descartes' position here is the point that although the truth of any given self-evident proposition will command assent when presented to the intellect, we can always direct our attention elsewhere, and so avoid following the light of truth. And since attention itself is wholly within the power of the will, it follows that humans do, in a sense, have an autonomous power of self-determination with respect to the judgements they make. (For the notion that the will is constrained only so long as the truth is actively attended to, compare *Conversation with Burman*, AT V 148: CSMK 334: see also Cottingham (ed.), *Descartes' Conversation with Burman*, pp. 6 and xxixff.)

In cases where a proposition is *not* clearly and distinctly perceived, the situation is far more straightforward. Here Descartes indeed believes that we have a two-way power to assent or not to assent, and that the correct response is to withhold assent (*see* ERROR). But the state of 'indifference' in which we find ourselves in such cases, where the light of reason fails to discern sufficient information to establish the truth, is classified by Descartes as 'the lowest grade of freedom' (AT VII 58: CSM II 40; cf. INDIFFERENCE).

G

generosity In Descartes' conception of the good life, *la générosité* is the crowning virtue – the 'key to all the other virtues and a general remedy for every disorder of the passions' (*Passions of the Soul*, art. 161). The translation of the French term is a difficult matter. The English transliteration 'generosity' is almost unavoidable, and is not entirely misleading (it would have been perfectly natural, even in seventeenth-century France, to apply the term *générosité* to acts which we should nowadays call acts of generosity); but for Descartes the term had powerful resonances which are largely absent in our modern usage. As a fluent Latinist, Descartes would have been vividly aware of the connotations of the cognate Latin adjective *generosus*, of which the primary meaning is 'noble' or 'well born' (compare the Latin noun *genus*, whose basic meaning is 'race' or 'family'). By a simple shift, *generosus* then came to mean 'noble-minded' or 'magnanimous' (and was used by some Latin writers to indicate the possession of that overarching virtue which the Greeks had termed μεγαλοψυχία or 'great souledness'; cf. Aristotle, *Nicomachean Ethics*, Book IV, ch. 3). Descartes himself compares his own notion of generosity to the scholastic concept of magnanimity in *Passions*, art. 161.

One of the principal themes among the ethical philosophers of classical times had been the possibility of achieving the solid and lasting goods constitutive of a worthwhile life despite the vulnerability of the human condition to chance. Descartes' own ethics is highly sensitive to this problem; indeed the general aim of his entire philosophical system is to give human beings mastery over their own lives and over the environment (cf. *Discourse*, Part VI, AT VI 62: CSM I 142). In the *Passions of the Soul*, the cultivation of *générosité* is presented as the major remedy (apart from reflection on divine providence) against human vulnerability to fortune. The person of *générosité* will never passionately desire things which are outside of our power to achieve, and whose non-attainment may frustrate us and thus destroy our well-being (art. 145). The reason for this (as is explained at the start of Part III of the *Passions*) is that true *générosité* implies 'the knowledge that nothing truly belongs to us but the freedom to dispose our volitions, and that we ought to be praised or blamed for no other reason than using our freedom well or badly' (art. 153). When this knowledge is coupled with the other essential ingredient of *générosité*, namely the 'firm and constant resolution to undertake and carry out what we judge to be best' (ibid.), the result, according to Descartes, will be a life of perfect virtue, a life whose goodness depends not on external circumstance, but on what is wholly within our own power.

It is perhaps not entirely clear what the Cartesian virtue of *générosité*, characterized in this way, has to to with the traditional notion of nobility or 'great-souledness'. The connection which Descartes makes is that the virtue of noble-mindedness, as traditionally conceived, implied a certain dignity and legitimate self-esteem, and this will precisely be true of the person of *générosité*: it 'causes a person's self-esteem to be as high as it legitimately may be' (AT XI 445–6: CSM I 384). But such self-esteem, Descartes implies, will be unlike that of the person of 'nobility' in the genetic sense, since this latter quality depends on accidents of birth and natural endowment. 'It is easy to believe that the souls which God puts into our bodies are not equally noble and strong'; and while 'good upbringing is of great help in correcting defects of birth' (art. 161), this too, will presumably depend largely on factors outside the agent's control. By contrast, true *générosité*, self-esteem for the resolute and well-directed use of free will, is within the power of all. Those possessed of *générosité* 'will not consider themselves much inferior to those who have greater wealth or honour, or even to those who have more intelligence, knowledge or beauty, or generally to those who surpass them in some other perfections; but equally they will not have much more esteem for themselves than for those they surpass. For all these things seem to them to be very unimportant by contrast with the virtuous will for which they alone esteem themselves, and which they suppose also to be present, or at least capable of being present, in every other person' (*Passions*, art. 154, AT XI 446–7: CSM I 384).

The philosophical importance of Descartes' theory of *générosité* lies in the fact that his ideas here, as in so many other areas of his philosophy, form a kind of bridge between the ancient and modern worlds. The primacy which his account gives to the autonomous power of the will as the only true basis for moral appraisal clearly looks forward to Kant. But his thinking is also sufficiently rooted in the robust naturalism of traditional virtue-theory for him to acknowledge the importance of upbringing and above all training and habituation (*Passions*, art. 50) for the development of a worthwhile human life.

For more on the importance of the will on the one hand and of training on the other in Descartes' account of the good life, *see* PASSIONS.

geometry   The science of geometry is of central importance in the Cartesian system in at least two respects. First, it serves as a kind of model for all knowledge: 'those long chains composed of very simple and easy reasonings which geometers customarily use to arrive at their most difficult demonstrations gave me occasion to suppose that all the things which come within the scope of human knowledge are interconnected in the same way' (*Discourse*, Part II, AT VI 19: CSM I 120). Second, Descartes' programme for the 'mathematicization' of physics officially restricts the language of science to whatever can be expressed in geometrical terms: 'I freely acknowledge that I recognize no matter in corporeal things apart from what the geometers call quantity and take as the object of their demonstrations' (*Principles*, Part II, art. 64; *see* EXTENSION.)

Descartes was himself an accomplished geometrician, and he chose to include his treatise *La Géométrie* as one of the three essays illustrating his method, which he published with the *Discourse* in 1637. Apart from presenting a number of important specific results (notably the solution of the longstanding puzzle known as Pappus' problem), the *Geometry* had a lasting general effect on the development of mathematics, by laying down the foundations for what is now known as analytic or coordinate geometry. The essay opens with the assertion of a close interrelationship between arithmetic and geometry (the first section is entitled 'Comment le calcul d'Arithmétique se rapport aux opérations de Géométrie'), and argues that any geometrical problem of a certain type can be reduced to one which requires only the knowledge of the lengths of lines, and which can therefore be solved using arithmetical operations. More importantly, Descartes then proceeds to show how the use of abstract algebraic notation enables us to proceed beyond the consideration of numerically specified lengths in such a way as to generate results of much greater power and generality. The idea of exhibiting abstract relations in a way that was free from specific numerical interpretations constituted a substantial advance on earlier classical conceptions of geometry which largely relied on spatial intuitions. It also symbolizes Descartes' grand reductionist design for encompassing the whole of science within the framework of a series of abstract relationships which would be applicable irrespective of the particular kind of subject-matter involved.

See also KNOWLEDGE.

Geometry   The third of the three 'specimen essays' published with the *Discourse* in 1637, *La Géométrie* is made up of three books, the first dealing with 'problems that can be constructed using only circles and straight lines', the second dealing with 'the nature of curved lines', and the third dealing with 'solids and sursolids'. The essay was written during the mid 1630s, but incorporates discoveries made several years earlier. For its philosophical significance, *see preceding entry.*

God   God plays a central role in Descartes' philosophical system. In the Cartesian validation of knowledge, the existence of a perfect creator has to be established to enable the meditator to pass from the isolated subjective awareness of his own existence to knowledge of other things; the movement outwards from self (Second Meditation) to the external world (Sixth Meditation) could not be accomplished without the argumentation of the intermediate Meditations, so much of which is taken up with an investigation into the existence and nature of God. Compare the Fifth Meditation: 'I see plainly that the certainty and truth of all knowledge depends uniquely on my awareness of the true God, to such an extent that I was incapable of perfect knowledge about anything else until I became aware of him. But now it is possible for me to achieve full and certain knowledge of countless matters, both concerning God and other intellectual natures, and also concerning the whole of corporeal nature which is the subject of pure mathematics' (AT VII 71: CSM II 49). (For the proofs of God's existence which Descartes offers in order to make this transition, see ONTOLOGICAL ARGUMENT and TRADEMARK ARGUMENT.)

Descartes' system of knowledge depends, on the one hand, on the power of the intellect to discern the truth by means of its 'clear and distinct perceptions' and, on the other hand, on the resolution of the will to confine itself to such perceptions (Fourth Meditation; see ERROR). The whole procedure presupposes the 'truth rule' – 'I seem to be able to lay it down as a general rule that whatever I clearly and distinctly perceive is true' (Third Meditation, AT VII 35: CSM II 24). The vital role of the deity in underwriting the truth rule is something that Descartes frequently insists on: 'if we did not know that everything real and true within us comes from a perfect and infinite being, then however clear and distinct our perceptions were, we should have no reason to be sure that they had the perfection of being true' (Discourse, Part IV, AT VI 39: CSM I 130). The human intellect, in other words, is one of the creative works of God, and since God is supremely perfect, it cannot be an inherently unreliable instrument for discerning the truth. This does not, of course, mean that the human intellect is itself perfect; it is a self-evident truth that there are many things of which it is ignorant (many things, indeed, which are wholly beyond its grasp; cf. AT VII 47; CSM II 32). But (following a standard line of reasoning in Christian apologetics), Descartes observes that such deficiencies are merely absences or negations; what positive (though limited) powers the intellect does possess are derived from the perfect creator, and are therefore reliable. 'Every clear and distinct perception is undoubtedly something real and positive, and hence cannot come from nothing, but must necessarily have God for its author. Its author, I say, is God, who is supremely perfect, and who cannot be a deceiver on pain of contradiction; hence the perception is undoubtedly something true' (Fourth Meditation, AT VII 62: CSM II 43). The explicit invoking of God as a guarantor of our clear and distinct perceptions in turn raises the question of how the Cartesian meditator can be sure of the truth of those premises which are needed to prove God's existence in the first place (for this long-standing puzzle in Cartesian epistemology, *see* CIRCLE, CARTESIAN).

A fundamental paradox, which lies at the heart of Descartes' theocentric metaphysics, is that the very being who is invoked as the guarantor of truth and of the reliability of the perceptions of the intellect is also frequently declared by Descartes to be beyond our human grasp: 'We cannot comprehend [or 'grasp' – *comprendre*] the greatness of God, even though we know it [*connaissons*]' (to Mersenne, 15 April 1630: AT I 145: CSMK 23); 'since God is a cause whose power exceeds the bounds of human understanding, and since the necessity of these truths [the eternal truths of mathematics] does not exceed our knowledge, these truths are therefore something less than, and subject to, the incomprehensible power of God' (to Mersenne, 6 May 1630: AT I 150: CSMK 25; cf. ETERNAL TRUTHS); 'I say that I know it, not that I conceive or comprehend it, because it is possible to know that God is infinite and all-powerful even though our soul, being finite, cannot comprehend or conceive him' (to Mersenne, 27 May 1630: AT I 152: CSMK 25). Descartes' position in these and similar passages is, however, tolerably consistent, and relies on a crucial distinction between knowing something and fully grasping it: 'just as we can touch a mountain but not put our arms round it, so to grasp something is to embrace it in one's thought, while to know something it suffices to touch it with one's thought' (AT I 152: CSMK 25). The infinite perfections of God, then, cannot be fully encompassed or grasped by the human mind; indeed in a certain sense incomprehensibility is the very hallmark of the infinite (AT VII 368: CSM II 253). But nevertheless we can attain to sufficient knowledge of the divine attributes to enable us to be sure at least of those aspects of the divine nature which need to be established to validate knowledge: we can prove that God exists, and that he is no deceiver (AT VII 70: CSM II 48). Throughout Descartes' metaphysical writings we find a tension between what might be called the rationalist mode, where the project is that of making the structure of reality utterly transparent to the light of reason, and what might be called the devotional mode, where the meditator humbly reflects on the greatness of the deity and the weakness of the human mind before the incomparable majesty of the creator. For the devotional mode, see especially the 'wonder and adoration' expressed in the last paragraph of the Third Meditation; the refrain is taken up again in the First Replies, where it is said that we should try 'not so much to take hold of the perfections of God as to surrender to them' (*perfectiones . . . non tam capere quam ab ipsis capi*, AT VII 144: CSM II 82).

In Cartesian physics, the role of God is rather different. The divine creative power is invoked as the ultimate cause of the quantity of motion in the universe (*see* CONSERVATION), but once the laws of motion have been laid down, little further reference is made to God. In this sense, Cartesian science may be said to be relatively 'autonomous' in comparison with the systems of many of Descartes' predecessors, which had invoked the presumed purposes of the Deity to explain countless details concerning the structure and operation of natural phenomena. Descartes' approach to the natural world is firmly mechanistic: phenomena are explained solely by reference to the size, shape and movement of particles of matter, and any mention of divine purpose is ruled out as beyond the proper scope of science (*see* CAUSE, FINAL).

The only area of Cartesian science in which the purposes of God are invoked in a more direct manner is that of human psychology – an area which involves reference to mental as well as material phenomena, and which therefore may be said to fall outside the scope of physics proper. When the nervous system of a human being is in a particular state, a sensation of a particular kind will be produced in the mind; there is thus a kind of 'natural institution' directly ordained by God, whereby brain states give rise to sensory states. Descartes introduces this idea in his *Treatise on Man* (see AT XI 143: CSM I 102), and it is developed further in the Sixth Meditation: 'Any given movement occurring in the part of the brain that immediately affects the mind produces just one corresponding sensation; and hence the best system that could be devised is that it should produce the one sensation which of all possible sensations is the most especially and most frequently conducive to the preservation of the healthy man. And experience shows that the sensations which nature has given us are all of this kind and so there is absolutely nothing to be found in them that does not bear witness to the power and goodness of God' (AT VII 87: CSM II 60). Appeal to divine goodness thus enables us, in a certain sense, to understand how psychological phenomena fit into the scheme of things, even though the qualitative nature of such phenomena puts them beyond the reach of Descartes' mathematical physics.

See also MIND AND BODY.

gravity There is no conception in Descartes' writings of gravity in the modern (post-Newtonian) sense of a universal attractive force operating between any two bodies, and measured as the product of their masses divided by the square of the distance between them. Indeed, the concept of mass is itself absent from Cartesian physics: Descartes refuses to admit that there can be variations in the density of bodies, and his determination of the 'quantity of matter' in any given vessel depends on its extension (volume) alone (see *Principles*, Part II, art. 19; cf. EXTENSION). Descartes uses the Latin term *gravitas* merely to refer to the ordinary perceived 'heaviness' of terrestrial particles, and in accordance with his general programme for physics, he attempts to explain this without reference to any inherent 'real qualities' in matter, but instead purely in terms of the mechanical interactions of micro-particles. The theory which he offers is that the fast-moving particles of 'celestial matter' which surround the earth displace the slower-moving terrestrial particles which they encounter, and that the net effect of all the collisions and displacements involved is that the particles of terrestrial matter are driven downwards (see *Principles*, Part IV, arts 20–7). The point which Descartes underlines is that terrestrial particles are not heavy 'in themselves'; indeed, were it not for the complicated action of the celestial matter above them, they would 'fly away from the earth in all directions' by centrifugal force (Part IV, art. 21).

H

---

human being   The status of a human being (Latin *homo*; French *homme*) is highly problematic in Descartes' philosophy. His official dualistic ontology allows for only two kinds of substance, mind (*res cogitans*) and matter (*res extensa*), and the effect of this is to make a human being not an organic whole, but an uneasy amalgam of two incompatible elements – on the one hand, a pure incorporeal spirit and, on the other hand, the mechanical structure of the body, which is merely 'a certain configuration of limbs and other accidents of this sort' (AT VII 14: CSM II 10). This result puts Descartes completely at odds with the traditional Aristotelian account of man as a 'rational animal'. For Descartes, the true self – 'this "I" by which I am what I am' – is entirely distinct from the body (AT VI 33: CSM I 127), and our biological nature as a certain species of animal is, if not denied, at least made extraneous to our essence as conscious beings.

The disintegration of our organic unity as human beings was a result that some of Descartes' disciples were prepared to embrace; Henricus Regius, for example, advanced on Descartes' behalf the thesis that a human being (*homo*) is not an essential unity (*see* ANGEL). Descartes himself, however, was reluctant to present his views in this way, partly no doubt, for fear of provoking the followers of Aristotle (see AT III 460: CSMK 200), but also because, despite his official dualistic doctrine, he was always prepared to acknowledge, and try to find room for, the facts of our ordinary experience that testify to our embodied nature as humans. 'Nature teaches me', he wrote in a famous passage in the Sixth Meditation, 'that I am not merely present in my body as a sailor is present in a ship, but that I am very closely joined and, as it were, intermingled with it, so that I and the body form a unit' (AT VII 81: CSM II 56). The assertion of such a unity, despite the previous insistence on the stark opposition between mind and matter, is remarkable; the evidence for it, as the context of the passage makes clear, is the nature of our sensory experience. Hunger, thirst, pleasure and pain are, says Descartes, 'confused modes of thinking which arise from the union and, as it were, intermingling of mind and body' (ibid.). This suggests that sensory experience is not an essential part of my nature as a *res cogitans*, but belongs to me, rather, in so far as I am an embodied creature – a human being. This is confirmed by Descartes' treatment of sensation (along with IMAGINATION) as a 'special' mode of consciousness, and 'not a necessary constituent of my own essence, that is, of the essence of my mind' (cf. AT VII 73: CSM II 51). A pure *res cogitans*, then, would be endowed only with intellect and volition, the two 'modes of thinking' (*Principles*, Part I, art. 32). A purely material creature, on the other hand, would not have any experiences at all, but would operate purely as a mechanical automaton (*see* ANIMALS). But when a thinking thing is 'united' with a body, then we have a distinct type of phenomenon, sensory experience, which cannot be attributed to mind *simpliciter*, or to body, but which must be ascribed to the hybrid entity which is a human being.

Modern interpreters of the Cartesian system have often tended to ignore Descartes' introduction of this third category of sensation, alongside thought and extension. Indeed, the term 'Cartesian dualism' as used nowadays lumps together all forms of 'consciousness' (not a term normally used by Descartes) under the single category of the mental. But Descartes himself is at pains to draw a threefold distinction, which he explicitly refuses to reduce to a simple duality. In his correspondence with Elizabeth on the mind/body issue, he advances not two but three 'primitive notions', which are, he says, 'the patterns on the basis of which we form all our other conceptions': 'As regards body, we have only the notion of extension, which entails the notions of shape and motion; as regards the soul on its own, we have only the notion of thought, which includes the perceptions of the intellect and the inclinations of the will; lastly, as regards the soul and the body together, we have only the notion of their union, on which depends our notions of the soul's power to move the body, and the body's power to act on the soul and cause its sensations and passions' (letter of 21 May 1643, AT III 665: CSMK 218).

The union, or 'substantial union' as Descartes elsewhere calls it, represents a distinct and irreducible category of its own (irreducible, because the phenomenon of sensation neither belongs to body, nor falls within the essential concept of a mind or thinking thing in the strict sense). Hence, argues Descartes: 'human beings are made up of body and soul, not by the mere presence or proximity of one to another, but by a true substantial union. . . . If a human being is considered in itself, as a whole, it is an essential unity, because the union which joins a human body and soul to each other is not accidental to a human being, but essential, since a human being without it is not a human being' (to Regius, 31 January 1642, AT III 508: CSMK 209). Although these manoeuvres go some way towards reintegrating the concept of the human being which had apparently been torn asunder by the doctrine of the 'real distinction between mind and body', it is by no means clear that they solve the central problems which that distinction creates. In particular, it is not clear whether any convincing, or even intelligible, account can be given of what a 'union' of distinct and incompatible substances might amount to. In so far as Descartes answers this question, it is by an appeal to everyday experience, which, he seems to suggest, must take over and convince us of what the intellect fails to grasp: 'it is the ordinary course of life and conversation, and abstention from meditation . . . that teaches us how to conceive of the union of the soul and the body' (to Elizabeth, 28 June 1643, AT III 692: CSMK 227).

I

idea The term 'idea' is one of the most slippery and ambiguous of all philosophical concepts. The word is a transliteration of the Greek ἰδέα, which was generally rendered as *forma* ('form') in the philosophical Latin of the Middle Ages. ('By ἰδέα in Greek or *forma* in Latin is meant that by means of which the form of some thing is understood over and above the existing thing itself'; Aquinas, *Summa theologiae* I, 15, 1.) For Plato and his followers 'ideas' or 'Forms' are the eternal unchanging objects of understanding which exist over and above the everyday objects which we perceive by the senses (cf. *Republic* 479). Although the Platonic philosopher aims to direct his mind towards the Forms, ideas or Forms as conceived by Plato are not psychological items which depend for their existence on the human mind, but rather objects which possess independent reality (cf. *Parmenides* 132b). Plato often describes the Forms as paradigms or archetypes which we aspire to grasp in their full perfection, and which are the originals of which ordinary everyday objects are mere shadows or copies. Christian writers who were influenced by this Platonic conception spoke of Forms as eternally existing archetypes in the mind of God (cf. Augustine, *De diversis quaestionibus*, LXXXIII, 46), and this notion reappears later in the writings of Thomas Aquinas: 'the ideas which are the exemplars, of which the things created in the world are imitations, must be located nowhere else but in the mind of God (*Sententiae*, I, 36, 2, 1). As far as human cognition is concerned, however, the status of 'ideas' is something which Aquinas leaves somewhat unclear. Influenced by the anti-Platonic arguments of Aristotle, he tends to resist the temptation to make ideas into independent entities; the intellect has the power to abstract a universal concept from its particular manifestations, but the idea is the 'means of cognition' (*id quo intelligitur*) not a separate object of cognition (*id quod intelligitur*) (*Summa theologiae* I, 5, 2).

Descartes is sometimes said to have 'psychologized' the concept of an idea, and turned it from a formal notion into some kind of modification of consciousness – thus prefiguring the notion later developed by Locke: 'Every Man being conscious to himself That he thinks, and that which his mind is employ'd about whilst thinking, being the *Ideas*, that are there, 'tis past doubt that Men have in their Minds several *Ideas*, such as those expressed by the words, *Whiteness, Hardness, Sweetness, Thinking, Motion, Man, Elephant, Army, Drunkenness* and others' (*Essay concerning Human Understanding* [1689], II, ch. i, §1). In fact, however, Descartes' use of the terminology of ideas is not as revolutionary as is often supposed. Frequently, he harks back in his usage to the classical and medieval traditions: 'I used the word "idea" because it was the standard philosophical term used to refer to the forms of perception belonging to the divine mind' (AT VII 181: CSM II 127). Compare the Third Meditation: 'although one idea may perhaps originate from another, there cannot be an infinite regress here, but eventually one must reach a primary idea, the cause of which will be like an archetype [Latin *archetypum*; the French version says 'model/pattern or original' – *un patron ou un original*], which contains in itself formally and in fact all the reality which is present representatively in the idea' (AT VII 42 and IXA 33: CSM II 29). When I think of God, in other words, my thought has a certain representational content, or form; and this fact is expressed by saying that I have an 'idea' of God, which ultimately derives from God himself.

The table of definitions which Descartes provides in the Second Replies distinguishes a *thought* ('that which is within us in such a way that we are immediately aware of it') from an *idea*, which is 'the *form* of any given thought' (AT VII 160: CSM II 113, emphasis supplied). There is thus a tolerably clear distinction in Descartes between what we should nowadays call the psychological and the logical realms. Considered from a psychological point of view, 'the nature of an idea is such that of itself it requires no reality except what it derives from my thought of which it is a mode, i.e. a manner or way of thinking' (AT VII 41: CSM II 28). But considered from a logical point of view, it has a certain representational content. 'Considered simply as modes of thought, there is no inequality among my ideas – they all appear to come from within me. But in so far as ideas are considered as representing different things, they differ widely [in that some contain more 'objective reality' or representational content, than others]' (AT VII 40: CSM II 28). It may be seen from passages like this that Cartesian ideas are in some respects more like publicly accessible concepts than private psychological items: two people could not be said to have the same *thought*, since a thought is a (private) mental item or mode of consciousness; but they could be said to have the same *idea* in so far as their thoughts have a common representational content. It is significant that Descartes links the possession of an idea to the ability to use a linguistic term correctly: 'whenever I express something in words, and understand what I am saying, this very fact makes it certain that I have an idea of what is signified by the words in question' (AT VII 160: CSM II 113). He is thus careful to distinguish an idea, in his sense, from the scholastic notion of a phantasm or impression received via the senses: 'it is not only the images depicted in the imagination which I call "ideas"; indeed, in so far as these images are in the corporeal imagination, that is are depicted in some part of the brain, I do not call them "ideas" at all; I call them "ideas" only in so far as they give *form* to the mind itself' (AT VII 160: CSM II 113, emphasis supplied). Descartes sometimes laid himself open to misinterpretation on this point by saying that ideas were 'like images of a certain sort' (*veluti quasdam imagines* – AT VII 42, line 12: CSM II 29); but when questioned by critics he made it perfectly clear that the availability of a quasi-pictorial image or impression was quite irrelevant to the criteria for the possession of an idea. Thus anyone who has a conception corresponding to the expressions 'God' and 'soul' must *eo ipso* know what is meant by the 'ideas' of God and the soul, 'namely nothing other than the conception he has' (letter to Mersenne of July 1641, AT III 392: CSMK 185; cf. the misunderstanding of Hobbes, and Descartes' brusque rejoinder, in the Third Objections and Replies, AT VII 180–1: CSM II 126–7).

In classifying ideas, Descartes makes a celebrated distinction between those that are innate, those that are acquired or 'adventitious' and those that are invented or constructed by the mind (AT VII 38: CSM II 26). Firmly breaking with the traditional maxim of the scholastics 'nothing in the mind which was not previously in the senses', he insists that many of our most important ideas (including the concepts of thought, and of God, and of mathematical objects like triangles) are present at birth, having been directly implanted in the soul by God (*see* INNATENESS). It is crucial to Descartes' account of knowledge that if we rely on the clear and distinct perceptions of the intellect with respect to its innate ideas, error can be avoided (*see* CLARITY AND DISTINCTNESS; ERROR; JUDGEMENT). A complication here is that Descartes suggests that some of our ideas are what he calls 'materially false' – that is, while they may appear to have some representational content, they do not succeed in representing anything, or, as Descartes puts it, they 'represent non-things as things'. Thus the idea of cold is 'materially false', since it represents as a real and positive quality something which is in fact merely negative – an absence of heat (AT VII 43: CSM II 30). Descartes' notion of 'material falsity' is presented in a way which is not easy to follow: if such ideas lack genuine representative content, how can they be said to 'represent non-things as things' (compare the criticisms of Antoine Arnauld in the Fourth Objections, AT VII 206: CSM II 145, and the somewhat obscure reply at AT VII 233: CSM II 163). Descartes' general point, however, seems to be that in the case of sensory impressions, whether 'internal' such as those of pain and hunger, or 'external' such as those of coldness, there is so little clarity of content that those who go on to make judgements about existing objects corresponding to those sensations cannot really know what they mean. 'If someone says he sees colour in a body or feels pain in a limb, this amounts to saying that he sees or feels something there of which he is wholly ignorant, or, in other words, that he does not know what he is seeing or feeling. . . . If he examines the nature of what is represented by the sensation of colour or pain – what is represented as existing in the coloured body or the painful part – he will realize that he is wholly ignorant of it' (*Principles*, Part I, art. 68). What this appears to come down to is that the 'ideas' of sensible qualities should hardly be counted as ideas in the strict sense, since they lack intelligible content – a notion that anticipates the views of Descartes' successor Nicolas Malebranche, who refuses to classify sensations as ideas (*Recherche de la Vérité* [1674–5], III, 2, 6). In the case of Descartes, however, a certain tension remains: in order to rebut those of his critics who denied that we have a genuine idea of God, Descartes insists that the mere ability to understand the use of the word implies the possession of the relevant idea (see preceding paragraph); but it now appears that there are many words (like 'cold') with whose employment we are perfectly familiar, but where there is something suspect about the corresponding idea. Descartes' reply to this difficulty would probably be to insist on the distinction between merely using a word in conformity with prevailing linguistic conventions, and fully understanding what we mean. Our use of words, he points out in the *Principles of Philosophy*, is often the result of blind habit and preconceived opinion, rather than clear analysis of the content of what we are saying: 'the thoughts of almost all people are more concerned with words than with things, and as a result people very often give their assent to words they do not understand, thinking they once understood them, or that they got them from others who did understand them correctly.' The task of the philosopher will be to subject our ideas to systematic scrutiny, in order to distinguish 'those concepts which are clear and distinct from those which are obscure and confused' (Part I, art. 74; *see* SENSATION).

illusion, argument from   At the start of the *Meditations*, embarking on his programme for 'leading the mind away from the senses', Descartes reflects on the unreliability of sensory perception: 'I have found from time to time that the senses deceive, and it is prudent never to trust completely those who have deceived us even once' (AT VII 18: CSM II 12). No examples of such sensory deception are provided in the First Meditation, but later on Descartes cites cases which are supposed to 'undermine our faith in the senses': 'sometimes towers which had looked round from a distance appeared square from close up; and enormous statues standing on pediments did not seem large when observed from the ground'; even 'internal' senses like that of pain may mislead (Descartes instances the case of the PHANTOM LIMB – the patient who on waking from an operation feels pain 'in the arm' even though the limb has in fact been amputated: AT VII 77: CSM II 53). Defenders of the trustworthiness of the senses have not been too impressed with Descartes' use of the 'argument from illusion', as it has come to be known today; and even in his own day, Descartes' critics were unpersuaded by the conclusion that the reliability of the intellect is greater than that of the senses: 'how can the intellect enjoy any certainty unless it has previously derived it from the senses when they are working as they should . . . Owing to refraction, a stick which is in fact straight appears bent in water. What corrects the error? The intellect? Not at all; it is the sense of touch' (Sixth Objections, AT VII 418: CSM II 282).

On this last point, Descartes replied to his critics that 'the sense of touch alone does not suffice to correct a visual error: in addition we need to have some degree of reason which tells us that in this case we should believe the judgement based on touch rather than that elicited by reason' (Sixth Replies, AT VII 439: CSM II 296). In general, however, Descartes' disparaging comments on the senses are not, in fact, designed to show that they are always deceptive; on the contrary, the argument of the *Meditations* concludes with the resounding declaration that 'I should not have any further fears about the falsity of what my senses tell me every day; indeed, the exaggerated doubts of the last few days should be dismissed as laughable' (AT VII 89: CSM II 61). The senses are, for Descartes, instruments which are, for the most part, reliable indicators of the conditions which conduce to the health and survival of the body (Sixth Meditation, AT VII 83: CSM II 57). In the light of these conclusions, it is important not to take Descartes' use of the 'argument from illusion' out of context. The initial stress on sensory illusions is designed to play its part in testing the assumptions of the 'pre-philosophical man' (AT V 146: CSMK 332) by means of a deliberately willed demolition of our previously held beliefs: 'because our senses some-times deceive, I decided to suppose (*j'ai voulu supposer*) that nothing was such as they led us to imagine' (*Discourse*, Part IV, AT VI 32: CSM I 127). After the Cartesian reconstruction of knowledge has been completed, much of our confidence in the senses can be reinstated – but always with the proviso that they 'cannot be used as reliable touchstones for judgements about the essential nature of external bodies' (AT VII 83: CSM II 58). This last caveat makes it appropriate to say that, although Descartes certainly does not dispense with sensory observation in his eventual programme for science (*see* ASSUMPTION), his account of knowledge does belong firmly in the rationalist tradition which proposes to set up the foundations of science from premises derived not from the senses, but from the deliverances of the pure intellect.

images Descartes' account of the physiology of sense perception aims to provide a detailed account of the mechanisms which operate in the brain when the sense organs are stimulated by external objects. In his early work the *Treatise on Man*, written during the period 1629–33, he describes how the stimulation of the optic nerves sets up movements of the ANIMAL SPIRITS, which in turn lead to certain 'figures' or 'images' being traced out 'on the internal surface of the brain', or, more specifically, 'on the surface of the gland where the seat of the imagination and the common sense is located' (AT XI 176–7: CSM I 106; cf. PINEAL GLAND; 'COMMON' SENSE). At first sight, this notion seems to owe a good deal to traditional scholastic theories of sense-perception, according to which we perceive physical objects by means of the imprinting, first on the particular sensory organs and then on the so-called 'common sense', of 'phantasms' or simulacra resembling those objects. But in the essay on *Optics*, which he published with the *Discourse* in 1637, Descartes takes care to distance his views from those of his scholastic predecessors: 'We must take care not to assume – as our philosophers commonly do – that in order to have sensory awareness the soul must contemplate certain images transmitted by objects to the brain; or at any rate we must conceive the nature of these images in an entirely different manner from that of the philosophers' (AT VI 112: CSM I 165). He goes on to explain that such traditional accounts make a crucially false assumption – that the only way the mind can be stimulated to conceive of objects must be by images in the strict and literal sense of 'little pictures formed in the head' (ibid.). Descartes allows that the process of sense-perception must involve the presence to the mind, via brain activity, of representations of some kind; but he makes the vital point that representation does not require resem-blance: 'our minds can be stimulated by many things other than images – by signs and words, for example – which in no way resemble the things they signify' (ibid.). So exactly what sort of 'images' (for Descartes continues to use this term) are formed in the brain when we perceive objects? The analogy which Descartes draws with signs (another analogy he uses is that of an engraving which depicts the layout of a town) suggests that what is involved is some kind of coded representation whereby certain features of an object are 'mapped' onto the interior surface of the brain; the resultant pattern will correspond, albeit often in an indirect and 'coded' way, with the structure of the original object. Finally, when the mind or soul 'contemplates' the pattern, it will as a result have sensory awareness of the object. (For the notion of the mind residing in the brain and 'contemplating' (Latin *inspicere*) the patterns that are traced out on the pineal gland, compare the *Conversation with Burman*, AT V 162: CSMK 344–5, and the Sixth Meditation, AT VII 73: CSM II 51.)

It is clear that there are certain instabilities in Descartes' account of the 'images' involved in sensory perception. On the one hand, as just noted, he is keen to get away from the scholastic notion of the transmission from object to observer of some kind of pictorial copy of the object: we need to deliver ourselves from 'all those little images flitting though the air called "intentional forms" which so exercise the minds of philosophers' (*Optics*, AT VI 85: CSM I 153–4). He aspires, in other words, to a wholly reductionistic physiology of sense-perception which will replace pictorial language with purely mechanical descriptions of micro-events in the sense-organs and brain: 'when I see a stick, it should not be supposed that certain "intentional forms" fly off the stick towards the eye, but simply that rays of light are reflected off the stick and set up certain movements in the optic nerve and, via the optic nerve, in the brain, as explained in the *Optics*' (Sixth Replies, AT VII 437: CSM II 295). But if the Cartesian account of a non-physical 'mind' or 'soul' is wedded to this mechanistic conception, it is not clear why there should be any direct or intrinsic relationship at all between the brain events and the mind's resulting sensory awareness of an object; one might say instead (as Descartes in fact sometimes does) that God simply *ordains* that the mind should have sensory awareness of a certain sort whenever the micro-structure of the brain is configured in a certain way. This 'occasional-ist' solution is hinted at in several Cartesian texts, and it evidently does not require the brain happenings to be 'images' even in the most attenuated sense; all that seems necessary is that there be certain regular (divinely decreed) correlations between brain happenings (neural events) and mental states. For passages where Descartes seems to want to move towards this kind of occasionalist and non-imagistic account of sensory perception, com-pare *Treatise on Man*, AT XI 143: CSM I 102, and *Optics*, AT VI 114: CSM I 166.

Notwithstanding these passages, however, the way in which Descartes seems to have conceived of the mind as a kind of homunculus, located in the pineal gland and 'contemplating' the images presented there (*see* 'COMMON' SENSE), made him reluctant to abandon the notion that the end-product of the stimulation of the sense organs was, in some sense of the word, an actual, physically delineated, picture or image: 'when external objects act on my senses, they print on them an idea or rather a figure of themselves; and when the mind attends to the images imprinted on the gland in this way it is said to have sensory perception' (AT V 162: CSMK 344). This last comment is an indirect report of Descartes' words rather than a quotation from one of his published works, but it is of a piece with those passages where he seems to have felt it necessary to give some account of the precise way in which 'the images formed in the brain can enable the soul to have sensory awareness' (AT VI 113: CSM I 166); and in attempting to construct such an account, he could not quite free himself of the bizarre conception of the soul dwelling in the pineal gland and contemplating the images served up to it there. In Discourses Five and Six of the *Optics* we find Descartes wrestling with these issues, and ending up with an account which is predominantly occasionalist (in the sense explained above), but which is still partly committed to the notion of pictorial images generated deep within the brain: 'the objects we look at do imprint quite perfect images of themselves on the back of the eye. . . . These pass beyond the eye to the inside of the brain, where they still bear some resemblance to the objects from which they proceed. But we must not think that it is by means of this resemblance that the picture causes our sensory awareness of these objects – as if there were yet other eyes within our brain by which we could perceive it – but rather that the movements composing the picture act directly upon our soul, being ordained by nature to make it have such and such sensations' (AT VI 114 and 130: CSM I 166–7). What is interesting about this passage is the way in which Descartes is alive to the dangers of conceiving the soul as a miniature self viewing little pictures inside the head; but by locating the soul inside the pineal gland, and introducing a psycho-physical transaction at the end of a physiological chain of events culminating in the formation of an image inside the brain, he showed that he could not, after all, completely escape the homunculus conception and its attendant conceptual confusions. But if Descartes' account is flawed, it has to be said that the problem which he tackled – that of giving a satisfying account of the relationship between the physiological and the psychological aspects of sense-perception – is one to which, more than three centuries later, there is still no readily agreed solution.

imagination   Despite the tendency of modern writers to foist on Descartes the view that all psychological processes are to be ascribed to an incorporeal mind or spirit, Descartes himself makes it clear that imagination (and the same goes for SENSATION) is a faculty which belongs to me not *qua* pure mental substance but only in so far as I am an embodied creature – a HUMAN BEING. In the Sixth Meditation he writes that 'the power of imagining which is in me, differing as it does from the power of understanding, is not a necessary constituent of my own essence, that is of the essence of the mind' (AT VII 73: CSM II 51). Understanding, or intellection is, for Descartes, a purely cognitive faculty which could operate in the absence of any physical substrate; imagination, by contrast, is 'the application of the cognitive faculty to a body which is intimately present to it, and which therefore exists' (AT VII 72: CSM II 50). Corresponding to this difference in the ontological status of the two faculties is a phenomenological difference: when we imagine some object, it is presented to consciousness in terms of an actually visualized image: 'when I imagine a triangle, I do not merely understand that it is a figure bounded by three sides, but at the same time I also see the three lines with my mind's eye as if they were present before me' (ibid.). This in turn connects with what Descartes calls the 'peculiar effort of mind' (ibid.) which is necessary for imagination: in order actually to visualize something, I need to make the relevant image 'come' before the mind, and this (since it involves the occurrence of brain events over which I have only indirect control; cf.

IMAGE) may require training and habit; thus most people can easily imagine a triangle, but will find it quite hard to imagine a ten-sided figure. Understanding, by contrast, which is a 'purely mental' process, is not attended by such physiological constraints, and hence we can quite well understand what is meant by a chiliagon (thousand-sided figure), even though we cannot imagine (visualize) such a figure, 'since the mind cannot trace out and form a thousand lines in the brain except in a very confused manner' (AT V 162: CSMK 345). Descartes aptly sums up the distinction between the two faculties in a letter to Mersenne of July 1641: 'Whatever we conceive of without an image is an idea of the pure mind (*une idée du pur esprit*), and whatever we conceive of with an image is an idea of the imagination' (AT III 395: CSMK 186).

The role of the imagination in the development of knowledge is one which Descartes often downplays. In the letter to Mersenne just referred to, he describes its scope as very restricted: 'As our imagination is tightly and narrowly limited ... there are very few things, even corporeal things, which we can imagine, even though we are capable of conceiving them. One might perhaps think that the entire science which considers only sizes, shapes and movements would be most under the sway of our imagination, but those who have studied it know that it rests not at all on the phantasms of our imagination, but only on the clear and distinct notions of our mind' (ibid.). In general, the fact that the faculty of imagination, like sensation, involves bodily as well as mental operations led Descartes to regard it as in a certain sense a contaminated source of knowledge, particularly with respect to metaphysical inquiries. For the aim of metaphysics is to lead the mind away from the senses in order to allow the pure perceptions of the intellect to flourish; hence when planning the writing of the *Meditations*, Descartes wrote to Mersenne that although he had found imagination helpful in his mathematical work, he found it 'more of a hindrance than a help in metaphysical speculation' (AT II 622: CSMK 141). An example of this occurs in the Second Meditation, where Descartes canvasses various (as it later emerges incorrect) views of the soul that are associated with corporeal images. 'As to the nature of the soul [speaking as a pre-philosophical 'man of the senses'], I either did not think about it, or else imagined it to be something tenuous, like a wind or fire or ether, which permeated my more solid parts' (AT VII 26: CSM II 17); but later reasoning reveals that 'I am not some thin vapour which permeates the limbs – a wind, fire, air, breath, or whatever I depict in my imagination. ... None of the things which the imagination enables me to grasp is at all relevant to the [true] knowledge of myself which I possess, and hence the mind must be most carefully diverted from this way of conceiving things if it is to perceive its own nature as distinctly as possible' (AT VII 27–8: CSM II 18–19).

A rather more positive view of the imagination emerges in Descartes' earlier writings, notably in the *Rules for the Direction of our Native Intelligence*. In Rule XII, anticipating the *Meditations*, Descartes stresses the need to curb the senses and the imagination when dealing with matters 'in which there is nothing corporeal or similar to the corporeal' (AT X 416: CSM I 43). But he goes on to describe in considerable detail how the imagination, properly controlled, can be a considerable aid to the intellect in its perception of the corporeal natures which are the subject of pure mathematics (see esp. Rule XIV, *passim*, and cf. letter to Elizabeth of 28 June 1643, AT II 692: CSMK 227). However, although Descartes waxes very enthusiastic about the gains to be derived from exercising the imagination in mathematics (at one point noting that 'we shall undertake nothing without the aid of the imagination', AT X 443: CSM I 59), it is important to note that its role is essentially an auxiliary one – it is simply a 'help' (*adjumentum*; Rule XIV, opening sentence). It remains the prerogative of the INTUITION of the pure intellect to apprehend the true nature of things, whether corporeal or intellectual; cf. Rule III, AT X 368: CSM I 14). This strongly intellectualistic, or Platonic, strand in Descartes' philosophy is one which can be found right through his thinking, from the early reflections in the *Regulae*, to his later writing on ethics in the *Passions of the Soul*, where the remedy advanced for the unruly influence of the passions which may disturb our tranquillity consists in learning how to control the imagination, which presents things 'in a way which tends to mislead the soul and makes the reasons for pursuing the object of its passion appear much stronger than they are' (AT XI 487: CSM I 403).

See also PASSIONS.

indifference   The term 'indifference' was generally used in medieval philosophy to refer to a contra-causal or two-way power of the will – the power to choose x or not-x 'indifferently' (i.e. without any causal necessitation). Thus, for example, we find William of Ockham, in the fourteenth century, defining freedom as 'the power by which I can indifferently and contingently produce an effect in such a way that I can cause or not cause that effect' (*Quodlibet* I, 16). This usage survived well into Descartes' time and beyond; thus Leibniz writes that 'the will is in a state of indifference in so far as this is the opposite of necessity, and it has the power to act otherwise, or to suspend its action entirely, since both alternatives are and remain possible' (*Discourse on Metaphysics* [1686] §30). In his account of human freedom in the Fourth Meditation, Descartes seems, on the face of it, to question the importance and value of such liberty of indifference: 'The indifference I feel when there is no reason pushing me in one direction rather than another is the lowest grade of freedom; it is evidence not of any perfection of freedom, but rather of a defect in knowledge, or a kind of imperfection. For if I always saw clearly what was true and good, I should never have to deliberate about the right choice, and ... it would be impossible for me ever to be in a state of indifference' (AT VII 58: CSM II 40). The conception of freedom which Descartes favours, as the next paragraph makes clear, is one in which the will spontaneously (but none the less freely) assents to the irresistible deliverances of the NATURAL LIGHT: 'the spontaneity and freedom of my belief was all the greater in proportion to my lack of indifference' (AT VII 59: CSM II 41).

The upshot of these passages appears to be, first, that true human freedom consists not in liberty of indifference (as traditionally understood) but in liberty of spontaneity or 'freedom of enlightenment'; and, second, that indifference, so far from being a condition which we ought to aspire to if we wish to be free, is in fact a low-grade state, or defect, which arises only when the evidence for a given proposition is cloudy or inadequate. When, however, he was later questioned about his views as presented in the Fourth Meditation, he made an important distinction between two senses of the term 'indifference': 'indifference' [in the context of the Fourth Meditation] means that state of the will when it is not impelled one way rather than another by any perception of truth or goodness; this is the sense in which I took it [when I spoke of] "the lowest grade of freedom". But perhaps others mean by "indifference" a positive faculty of determining oneself to one or other of two contraries, and I do not deny that the will has this positive faculty' (letter to Mesland of 9 February 1645, AT IV 173: CSMK 245). The distinction is clear enough, but the concluding point is puzzling. Given the position set out in the Fourth Meditation, one might have expected Descartes to maintain that indifference in the sense of an undetermined two-way power was, firstly, not so much an impressive 'positive power' as a low grade, and rather suspect, faculty of 'plumping' for one of two alternatives when the truth was not properly clear; and, second, that such a power was available only in cases of inadequate evidence, and was not available (or desirable) when the truth was clearly perceived. In fact, however, Descartes affirms in the letter to Mesland both that he accepts that such undetermined power of the will is a 'positive' faculty, and, more remarkable still, that he believes it is available 'not only with respect to actions where the will is not pushed by any evident reasons on one side rather than on the other, but also with respect to all other actions' (ibid.). The resolution of this apparent inconsistency appears to be as follows: indifference considered as a *state* or *condition*, which we find ourselves in when the evidence is not clear, is not something admirable, but low-grade – a mere defect. But indifference in the sense of a *faculty of choice* is a genuine autonomous power of the will which is unrestricted in its scope. This accords with the comment in the Fourth Meditation that 'I know by experience that the will or freedom of choice which I received from God is not restricted in any way ... indeed, there is nothing else in me which is so perfect and so great that the possibility of a further increase in its perfection or greatness is beyond my understanding' (AT VII 56: CSM II 39. Cf. *Principles*, Part I, art. 41, where Descartes asserts that the 'free actions of humans are undetermined' and that we have a close inner awareness of the 'freedom and indifference' which makes this possible). This still leaves one question unanswered: how such positive power could be available in cases where the truth of a given proposition is irresistibly clear; for Descartes' attempts to deal with this question in the letter to Mesland already referred to, *see* FREE WILL.

induction   The 'problem of induction' as we understand it today (namely the problem, famously examined by Hume, of how in science we are entitled to generalize from particular instances, or to infer the operation of universal laws from limited data) finds little place in Descartes' writings. In his physics, Descartes takes it for granted that the human mind has the innate power to formulate the mathematical principles in terms of which the material universe operates; experiential data come in only at a later stage, when the scientist is confronted with several possible explanatory ASSUMP-TIONS, each consistent with the basic laws, and wishes to establish which of these assumptions accords best with observation.

In the *Regulae*, Descartes uses the term 'induction' in a sense that is rather different from the modern usage of the term. He distinguishes two types of cognitive process which lead to scientific knowledge. The first involves a linear series of inferences beginning with a SIMPLE NATURE that is accessible to us, where each link in the chain is readily intuited; the second arises when no complete reduction to a series of intuitions is possible. 'If we infer a proposition from many disconnected propositions, our intellectual capacity is often insufficient to enable us to encompass them all in a single intuition, in which case we must be content with a level of certainty which the operation of induction or enumeration allows' (AT X 389: CSM I 26). Descartes goes on to observe that, while the ideal situation is one where this inductive or enumerative operation is 'distinct and complete', there are other occasions where all we can expect is that it should be 'sufficient' (AT X 390). The fact that 'induction' involves lesser standards of certainty than INTUITION arises from the finite scope of the human intellect. Enumeration or induction is defined as 'the well-ordered scrutiny of all the relevant points relating to a given problem'; but there are many areas of inquiry where 'if every single thing relevant to the question in hand were to be separately scrutinized, one lifetime would generally be insufficient for the task'. The limitations of the human condition can be overcome in a way which is sufficient for all practical purposes, provided that 'we arrange all of the relevant items in the best order, so that for the most part they fall under definite classes; it will then be sufficient if we look closely at one class, or at a member of each particular class' (AT X 391: CSM I 27). It may be seen from this passage that Cartesian 'induction' is not so very far removed from the type of scientific inference from particular to general which Hume was later to subject to radical criticism; in the light of this, Descartes' confident assertion of the 'sufficiency' of enumerative or inductive reasoning appears somewhat over-optimistic, not to say glib. It may be that his confidence is partly due to the fact that he has mathematical examples predominantly in mind: 'if I wish to show by enumeration that the area of a circle is greater than the area of any other geometrical figure whose perimeter is the same length as the circle, I need not review every geometrical figure, since if I can demonstrate that this fact holds for some particular figures, I shall be entitled to conclude by induction that the same holds true in all other cases' (AT X 390: CSM I 27). We may accept the validity of the reasoning in this type of case, since it operates within a closed and strictly defined system where the possibility of counter-examples is foreclosed; but it is far from clear that the same procedure could be readily transferred to the other example Descartes gives – an enumeration of categories of body which licences the conclusion that 'the rational soul is not corporeal' (ibid.). For Descartes' attempts to use the 'inductive' method in metaphysics, namely in order to construct a reliable conception of the attributes of God, compare the letter to Silhon of March or April 1648 (AT V 138: CSMK 332).

inertia   In the *Principles of Philosophy*, Descartes states as his 'first law of nature', the principle that 'each and every thing, in so far as it can, always continues in the same state, and thus what is once in motion always continues to move' (Part II, art. 37). In the same article, he pointedly distances himself from the Aristotelian preconception that 'it is in the very nature of motion to come to an end, or to tend towards a state of rest'. This, he argues, is a prejudice derived from the senses: 'we live on the earth, where all motions near it are soon halted, often from causes undetectable by the senses, and hence from our earliest years we have often judged that such motions, which are in fact stopped by causes unknown to us, come to an end of their own accord' (ibid.).

The term 'inertia' was often used by the scholastics to refer to the supposed inherent tendency of terrestrial matter to be 'inert' or sluggish, so that it would always 'naturally' come to rest. Descartes is to be credited with promoting the transition from this traditional Aristotelian conception to the modern conception of inertia as the persistence of motion – a conception later enshrined in Newton's First Law (*Mathematical Principles of Natural Philosophy*, 1687). In a remarkably modern-sounding passage in the *Principles*, Descartes points out that 'no more action is needed for motion than for rest; for example, the action needed to move a boat which is at rest in still water is no greater than that needed to stop it suddenly when it is moving' (Part II, art. 26). It should be noted, however, that Descartes was by no means the only seventeenth-century figure responsible for the transition from the traditional to the modern conception of inertia. The principle of the persistence of motion may well have been suggested to Descartes by his early mentor Isaac Beeckman (cf. AT X 58, and AT I 72: CSMK 8), and it had also been put forward by Galileo in his *Dialogue concerning the Two Chief World Systems* [1632]: in fact, the example found in Descartes of the ship continuing in motion was employed much earlier by Galileo in a letter of 1612 (cf. Galileo, *Opere*, V, 227). It is notable, however, that while Galileo formulates his principle in terms of circular motion, Descartes anticipates the Newtonian version, maintaining that 'all motion is in itself rectilinear' (*Principles*, Part II, art. 39), although he argues that the result of the interactions between bodies will always be a complex series of circular movements (Part II, art. 33).

infinite   The principal task in Descartes' reconstruction of knowledge is to move outwards from the awareness of the thinking self, to the objective world of science. This transition is effected, in the *Meditations*, by reflecting on the idea of the infinite which I find within myself, but which, in virtue of its representational content, I recognize as coming from something outside of myself. 'I clearly understand that there is more reality in an infinite substance than in a finite one, and hence that my perception of the infinite, that is, God, is in some way prior to my perception of the finite, that is myself' (AT VII 46: CSM II 31). The notion of the infinite thus plays a crucial role in Cartesian epistemology, and this gives rise to a central difficulty: Descartes needs to be able to say, on the one hand, that I am capable of forming a perfectly clear and distinct idea of the infinite (indeed, that it is the 'truest and most clear and distinct of all my ideas', AT VII 46: CSM II 32), but on the other hand, that the content of this idea is so great as to exceed the capacity of my mind to construct it. Descartes is aware of this problem, and attempts to resolve it by making a distinction between understanding (*intelligere*) and fully grasping or comprehending (*comprehendere*): 'it does not matter that I do not grasp the infinite, or that there are countless additional attributes of God which I cannot in any way grasp, and perhaps cannot even reach in my thought; it is enough that I understand the infinite' (ibid.; cf. *Conversation with Burman*, AT V 154: CSMK 339. *See* GOD).

The distinction is not entirely adequate to rescue Descartes from trouble. For although he may plausibly claim that the human mind can understand the meaning of the term 'infinite' without being able fully to grasp or encompass it, an objector might point out that such understanding could be derived purely from our own resources, simply from a process of extrapolation or negation: we might reflect on our own restricted knowledge and power, and thus construct for ourselves the notion of a being who is immune to such restrictions (cf. Gassendi's criticisms in the Fifth Objections, AT VII 304: CSM II 212). To this type of objection, Descartes replies with the somewhat obscure claim that our idea of God represents him as a being who is 'infinite in the positive sense', and that this 'positive' notion of infinity could not be generated by a finite mind alone: 'In the case of God alone, not only do we fail to recognize any limits in any respect, but our understanding positively tells us there are none; in the case of other things, by contrast, our understanding does not in the same way positively tell us that they lack limits in some respect, but we merely acknowledge in a negative way that any limits that they may have cannot be discovered by us' (*Principles of Philosophy*, Part I, art. 27). In order to mark this (not entirely happy) distinction, Descartes tends to reserve the term 'infinite' for God alone; for other items, such as the infinite extension of the physical universe, he prefers the term 'indefinite'. For this usage, compare *Principles*, Part I, art. 26, and the correspondence with More: 'In my view it is not a matter of affected modesty, but of necessary caution to say that some things are indefinite rather than infinite. God is the only thing I positively understand to be infinite, whereas in the case of other things, like the extension of the world, and the number of parts into which matter is divisible, I confess I do not know whether they are absolutely infinite; I merely know that I know no end to them, and so looking at them from my own point of view, I call them indefinite' (letter of 5 February 1649, AT V 274: CSMK 364). The reason why this manoeuvre is not fully satisfactory is that it fudges Descartes' own theses about the infinite extension and infinite divisibility of matter: elsewhere he provides what amount to strict deductive arguments that there can be no boundaries to the extended universe, and no limits to the repeated divisibility of matter (cf., for the former, letter to Chanut of 6 June 1647, AT V 52: CSMK 320, and, for the latter, *Principles*, Part II, art. 20). The upshot is that, in those cases where Descartes fastidiously prefers to use the less honorific label 'indefinite', just as clear, and arguably even clearer, reasoning seems to be available than anything which the human mind can come up with in the case of God; and this must leave a doubt about the supposedly privileged 'positive' notion of infinity which he claims to be available in respect of our understanding of the divine nature.

innateness It is basic to Descartes' account of science that clear and distinct knowledge of the nature of the universe can be constructed on the basis of the innate resources of the human mind. 'I noticed', he writes in Part V of the *Discourse*, 'certain laws which God has so established in nature, and of which he has implanted such notions in our minds, that after adequate reflection we cannot doubt that they are exactly observed in everything which exists or occurs in the world' (AT VI 41: CSM I 131). The claim is not merely that the human mind is capable of developing knowledge of these laws, but that the relevant concepts and propositions are literally present in the soul at birth: 'the mind of the infant has in itself the ideas of God, of itself, and of all the truths which are called self-evident, in the same way as adult human beings have these ideas when they are not attending them; it does not acquire these ideas later on, as it grows older. I have no doubt that if it were released from the prison of the body, it would find them within itself' (letter to 'Hyperaspistes' of August 1641, AT III 424: CSMK 190).

The celebrated attack on innate ideas mounted by John Locke later in the century raises the problem that if the imprinting of ideas on the mind means anything, it must surely entail (what is false) that the infant mind actually perceives them; 'for to imprint anything on the Mind without the Mind's perceiving seems to me hardly intelligible' (*Essay concerning Human Understanding* [1689], Book I, ch. ii, §5). The Cartesian reply to this type of objection is that the ideas which are present from birth tend, in infancy, and often even in adult life, to be swamped by bodily stimuli (AT III 425: CSMK 190; cf. *Principles*, Part I, art. 47); it requires undistracted effort and attention to allow the deliverances of the inborn natural light to become manifest (*Conversation with Burman*, AT V 150: CSMK 336). This is the purpose of the programme of metaphysical reflection which 'leads the mind away from the senses' (AT VII 12: CSM II 9) so that it can draw the innate ideas forth from the 'treasure house of the mind' (AT VII 67: CSM II 46; cf. AT VII 189: CSM II 132).

Descartes contrasts the IDEAS that are innate in this sense, with those that are 'adventitious' (acquired later via the senses), and those that are invented or made up (AT VII 38: CSM II 26). The third category includes mythological creations like the 'sirens, hippogriphs and the like' (ibid.), and Descartes carefully distinguishes such artificial constructs from innate ideas like that of a triangle, which 'are not my own inventions', but which represent 'true and immutable essences' (AT VII 64: CSM II 44; *see* ESSENCE). In the second category, that of the adventitious, Descartes puts observational ideas like the idea of the sun which is based on sensory observation (that of a smallish bright yellow disc in the sky), and he is at pains to point out that this kind of sense-based idea may mislead us, unless it is corrected by the 'idea of the sun based on astronomical reasoning, that is, derived from certain notions which are innate in me' (AT VII 39: CSM II 27). The contrast between the 'adventitious' ideas of sense, and the innate ideas of pure reason is, however, not entirely unproblematic, since Descartes recognizes that there is an innate element in all sensory perception. When we perceive objects, 'neither the motions themselves, nor the figures arising from them are conceived exactly as they occur in the sense organs, and hence it follows that the very ideas of the motions themselves and of the figures are innate in us' (*Comments on a Certain Broadsheet*, AT VIIIB 359: CSM I 304). The Cartesian account of sense-perception rejects the scholastic theory that sensory representations are impressions or copies of external objects (*see* IMAGES); hence, although corporeal motions in the brain act as a stimulus, the way in which the mind conceives of objects (the way in which it processes the data, as we might say nowadays) is in terms of its own innate conceptual apparatus. It is interesting to see Descartes applying this model not only to the kind of processing which involves the clear and distinct concepts of size, shape and motion, but also to 'confused' ideas like those of colour: 'since nothing reaches our mind from external objects through the sense organs except certain corporeal motions ... the ideas of pain, colours, sounds and the like must be all the more innate, if, on the occasion of certain corporeal motions, our mind is to be capable of representing them to itself; for there is no similarity between these ideas and the corporeal motions' (ibid.; *see* COLOUR). It may be seen from this just how far the Cartesian account of the mind differs from the empiricist notion that it is sensory experience, and this alone, which furnishes the mind with the 'vast store of materials' out of which our knowledge is constructed (cf. Locke, *Essay*, II, i, 1).

intellect A persistent theme running through Descartes' philosophy is that the unencumbered operations of the pure intellect will enable us to arrive at truths which are obscured to those who rely on preconceived opinion and the confused deliverances of the senses. The theme is summed up in the opening of the *Search for Truth*: 'Man came into the world in ignorance, and since the knowledge which he had as a child was based solely on the weak foundation of the senses and the authority of his teachers, it was virtually inevitable that his imagination should be filled with false thoughts before reason could guide his conduct. . . . But I shall bring to light the true riches of our souls, opening up to each of us the means whereby we can find within ourselves, without any help from anyone else, all the knowledge which we may need for the conduct of life, and the means of using it in order to acquire all the most abstruse items of knowledge which the human mind is capable of possessing' (AT X 496: CSM II 400; compare also the opening of the *Meditations*, and of the *Principles of Philosophy*).

For more on the powers of the intellect, *see* INNATENESS and INTUITION. For the relation between the pure incorporeal intellect and the faculties which are contaminated by union with the body, *see* IMAGINATION and SENSATION. For the involvement of the intellect in the search for truth and the development of knowledge, *see* ERROR; JUDGEMENT and FREE WILL.

For Descartes' distinction between intellection (or understanding) and comprehension (or grasping), *see* GOD.

intentional forms   The intentional form or species (Latin *species intentionalis*) was a key notion in the standard scholastic account of sense-perception. Eustachius a Sancto Paulo, whose works Descartes had studied as a young man, provided the following definition: 'an intentional form is a formal sign of the thing which is presented to the senses, or a quality which is transmitted from the object and which when received by the senses has the power of representing the object . . . . For example, when the eye perceives a distant colour, the eye receives a simulacrum of the colour, that is a quality which is transmitted through the air from the colour itself, and when received in the sense of sight has the power of representing the colour' (*Summa philosophica quadripartita* [1609], III, 330). Originally, the notion was apparently supposed to explain how the senses could receive information about an object, without the object actually entering the sense organs (hence the talk of transmission of 'form' rather than matter); but the obscurities of the account had come under considerable pressure in the early seventeenth century; thus Pierre Gassendi developed instead a neo-Epicurean account according to which there was an actual material transmission of atoms from object to observer (*Exercitationes Paradoxicae Adversus Aristotelicos*, 1624). Descartes himself was utterly dismissive of the scholastic notion of 'all those little images flitting though the air called "intentional forms" which so exercise the minds of philosophers' (*Optics*, AT VI 85: CSM I 154), and seems to have been more favourable to the neo-Epicurean account (although he rejected the concept of ATOMS). Writing to Gassendi he observed that, while no corporeal image is required for the 'pure understanding' to operate, in the case of imagination and sensation 'we do indeed require a semblance which is a real body, which the mind applies itself to, though without receiving it' (AT VII 387: CSM II 265).

For further details of Descartes' own account of the mechanisms of sensory perception, *see* IMAGES.

intuition   Descartes' account of human knowledge is indebted to a long philosophical tradition which draws a comparison between mental cognition and ordinary ocular vision. The notion goes back as far as Plato (*Republic* [*c.* 380 BC], 514–8), and plays a prominent role in the writings of Plotinus (*Enneads* [*c.* AD 250], III, viii, 11 and V, iii, 17) and Augustine (*De Trinitate* [AD 400–16], XII, xv, 24). Augustine puts the matter as follows: 'The mind, when directed towards intelligible things in the natural order, according to the disposition of the creator, sees them in a certain incorporeal light which is *sui generis*, just as the physical eye sees nearby objects in corporeal light' (loc.

cit.). This is the background which informs Descartes' use of the term 'intuition' (Latin *intuitus*) – the word being derived from the verb *intueri*, which in classical Latin means simply to look at or inspect. His claim is that the mind, when freed from interference from sensory stimuli, has the innate power to 'see', or directly apprehend, the truths which God has implanted within it. 'By intuition, I do not mean the fluctuating testimony of the senses, or the deceptive judgement of the imagination as it botches things together, but the conception of a clear and attentive mind which is so easy and distinct that there can be no room for doubt about what we are understanding. Alternatively, and this comes to the same thing, intuition is the conception of a clear and attentive mind which proceeds solely from the light of reason. . . . Thus everyone can mentally intuit that he exists, that he is thinking, that a triangle is bounded by just three sides and a sphere by a single surface, and the like' (AT X 368: CSM I 14). In the *Regulae* (*Rules for the Direction of our Native Intelligence*), from which this last quotation comes, intuition is put forward as the fundamental basis of all reliable knowledge; and although a finite mind will often be unable to 'see' a whole series of interconnected truths at a single glance, the ideal remains that it should attempt to survey the series 'in a single and uninterrupted sweep of thought', so that the process of DEDUCTION is reduced, as far as possible, to direct intuition.

Inseparable from Descartes' account of intuition is the Platonic–Augustinian notion that the mind is illuminated by the 'light of reason' or *lux rationis* (*Regulae*, loc. cit.). 'Everyone knows', Descartes wrote to Hobbes, who had questioned the metaphor, 'that a "light" in the intellect means transparent clarity of cognition' (AT VII 192: CSM II 135). In the *Meditations*, Descartes' preferred term is the 'natural light' (*lumen naturale*), and he invokes this notion whenever he wishes to introduce into the argument premises which are supposed to be self-evidently manifest to the intellect (for example, the principle that 'there must be as much reality in the cause as in the effect', AT VII 40: CSM II 28). The notion is not without its problems. Transparency of cognition suggests that there are certain truths which, when presented to the intellect, allow no room for denial ('from a great light in the intellect there follows a great propensity in the will [to give the assent]', AT VII 59: CSM II 41; cf. JUDGEMENT). But while this may be acceptable enough in the case of propositions which it is logically impossible to deny (since their negation manifestly implies a contradiction), principles like the causal axiom in the Third Meditation seem to contain too many complex and debatable implications to fit obviously into this category. It is hard to avoid the impression that Descartes sometimes uses the light metaphor to claim a spurious authority for the arguments which he deploys in his metaphysics. Sometimes, indeed, he verges on ranking the natural light equally with the light of faith, thus claiming for the 'natural' authority of reason the same kind of respect traditionally accorded to the teachings of the Church (see AT VII 598: CSM II 394; for a more typically cautious and diplomatic approach, contrast AT III 426: CSMK 191; *see* FAITH). The prevailing tenor of Descartes' philosophy is, however, firmly anti-authoritarian: he wishes others to be convinced only of what they themselves have seen as indubitable when they have internalized the arguments for themselves, and 'meditated along with the author' (AT VII 9: CSM II 8). Descartes was, nevertheless, not very sanguine about the ability and willingness of his readers to follow the path of reason: 'those who have long been in the habit of yielding to authority rather than lending their ears to the dictates of their own reason will find it difficult to submit themselves exclusively to the natural light' (AT X 522–3: CSM II 416). It may be seen from this last remark that Descartes' views on the natural light do not entail the implausible claim that any rational reader of his arguments will automatically and immediately assent to their truth: 'From the fact that all men have the same natural light, it might seem that they should all have the same notions, but there is a great difference between the criterion of universal assent and the criterion of the natural light, since hardly anyone makes good use of that light' (AT II 598: CSMK 139).

For more on the relation between the intuitions of the natural light and the Cartesian validation of knowledge, *see* CLARITY AND DISTINCTNESS.

J

judgement Scholastic philosophy made a distinction between merely perceiving the content of a proposition and judging it to be true or false. 'First the intellect intuits the things presented to it with a kind of simple vision, without any assent or denial; next, it collates the material and passes judgement on it, either assenting to it, by affirmation, or dissenting, by negation' (Eustachius, *Summa philosophica quadripartita* [1604], I, 20–1). Thomas Aquinas had classified judgement as 'an act of the cognitive faculty' (*Summa theologiae* [*c.* 1270], I, 84, 3), but Descartes stresses the crucial role of the will in the giving or withholding of assent: 'In order to make a judgement, the intellect is of course required, since in the case of something which we do not in any way perceive, there is no judgement we can make; but the will is also required, so that once something is perceived in some manner, our assent may then be given' (*Principles of Philosophy*, Part I, art. 34). This is important for Descartes' recipe for the avoidance of falsehood. When the intellect simply contemplates the ideas within it, and no judgement about truth or falsity is made, then it is not possible to fall into error. Error arises, according to Descartes, 'only when, as often happens, we make a judgement about something even though we do not have an accurate perception of it' (*Principles*, Part I, art. 33; *see* ERROR).

Descartes' theory of judgement is developed fully in the Fourth Meditation, where he attributes the human tendency to fall into error not to the intellect, which is in itself error-free, although limited in its scope, but to the 'misuse of our freedom of the will in making judgements about matters which we do not fully understand' (AT VII 61: CSM II 42). Compare also the letter to 'Hyperaspistes' of August 1641: 'In many matters, people's judgements disagree with their perceptions; but if we never make any judgement except about things we clearly and distinctly perceive – a rule which I always keep as well as I can – then we shall be incapable of making different judgements at different times about the same thing' (AT III 431: CSMK 194–5). The Cartesian distinction between judgement, *qua* active power of the will, and understanding, *qua* passive faculty of the intellect (see *Principles*, Part I, art. 32, and *Passions of the Soul*, art. 17), is not without its problems, however. In the first place, Descartes allows that a certain kind of falsity, called 'material falsity', can arise in the intellect even though no judgement is made (for this notion, *see* IDEAS). Secondly, and more importantly, the separation of the two faculties of intellect and will is in some respects artificial, since (as Spinoza was later to point out), the clear and distinct perception of, for example, a mathematical object like a triangle, is inseparable from the judgement that certain properties are true of it (Spinoza, *Ethics* [*c.* 1665], Part II, scholium to proposition 49). Hence, for Spinoza, 'the intellect and the will are one and the same', and the much-vaunted Cartesian programme for the avoidance of error through the suspension of judgement turns out to rest on a confusion, for 'when we say that someone suspends judgement, we are merely saying that he sees that he does not perceive the thing adequately' (ibid.). To this criticism Descartes would no doubt have replied that through the influence of bad habits and preconceived opinions, many people mistakenly suppose that their perceptions are clear, when in fact they are obscure and confused (cf. First and Sixth Meditation, and *Principles*, Part I, art. 1); and the power of the will to suspend assent in such cases is therefore crucial for the avoidance of error (cf. *Principles*, Part I, art. 35). However, in cases where our intellectual perceptions are completely clear and distinct, the assent of the will does indeed follow automatically and unavoidably (AT VII 58–9: CSM II 41); but in such cases, we can still make a conceptual distinction between intellect and will, since the operation of the judgement is determined by the perception of the intellect ('it is clear by the natural light that the perception of the intellect should always precede the determination of the will'; AT VII 60: CSM II 41).

For more on the relation between the intellect and the will in judgement, *see* FREE WILL.

K

knowledge Throughout his writings, Descartes advances an elevated and demanding conception of knowledge. In his early work the *Regulae*, or *Rules for the Direction of Our Native Intelligence*, he introduces what was to become almost a technical term in his philosophy, namely *scientia*. The word is derived from the ordinary Latin verb for to know, *scire*, but it also has connotations that look forward to the Cartesian programme for achieving a unified *science* which will encompass all the objects of human cognition – the programme (as he later put it in the *Discourse*) for 'rightly conducting one's reason and seeking the truth in the sciences' (AT VI 1: CSM I 111). Rule II of the *Regulae* defines *scientia* as 'certain and evident cognition', and tells us that we should reject all belief that is merely probable, and 'resolve to believe only what is perfectly known and incapable of being doubted' (AT X 362: CSM I 10).

In order to achieve the kind of indubitability he sought, Descartes proposed to make a fresh start, seeking new and utterly reliable foundations for his system of knowledge. 'Ancient cities which have gradually grown up from mere villages into large towns are usually ill-proportioned compared with the orderly towns which planners lay out . . . on level ground' (*Discourse*, Part II, AT VI 11: CSM I 116). Hence the insistence in the opening of the *Meditations* on total demolition of what has gone before (AT VII 17: CSM II 12). The buildings to be demolished are the entrenched, often uncritically accepted, 'preconceived opinions' of past ages, while the new foundations required are what Descartes elsewhere calls *principles* – clear and self-evident starting points for inquiry. As Descartes develops his idea of a rebuilt system of knowledge, two specific components of the Cartesian vision emerge. The first is a radical individualism: traditional science, 'compounded and amassed from the opinions of many different persons' can never come as near the truth as the 'simple reasonings performed by an individual of good sense' (AT VI 12: CSM I 117). The second component is an emphasis on unity and system: 'All the things which come within the scope of human knowledge are interconnected' (AT VI 19: CSM I 120).

Both these claims represent a declaration of war by Descartes against orthodox scholasticism. In the first place, he pits the individual's innate powers of reasoning (*see* INNATENESS) against the accumulated wisdom of the authorities: custom and example, so far from deserving to be accepted courts of appeal, are specifically opposed to certain knowledge (*la connaissance certaine*, AT VI 16: CSM I 119). In the learned academic disputations of the early seventeenth century, a standard method of establishing a thesis was to build up a barrage of textual authorities to support it. Descartes, by contrast, states quite uncompromisingly that in the search for truth a majority of voices is worthless (ibid.). In the second place, Descartes attacks the established dogma, going back to Aristotle, that each branch of knowledge has separate methods of inquiry and standard of precision. Thomas Aquinas, the founding father of scholasticism, had enshrined this view in his dictum that 'the intellectual virtues are not connected; one may have one science without having another' (*In Boethium de Trinitate*, qu. 1, art. 1, cited in Gilson E. (ed.), *Descartes, Discours de la méthode*, p. 138). Descartes' bold aim is to overturn this dogma by showing that there are abstract structures which can be shown to underlie a whole range of seemingly diverse subjects. Thus astronomy, music and optics all have a common base, in so far as 'they consider nothing but the various proportions or relations between their objects' (AT VI 20: CSM I 120).

Although the inspiration behind this unified conception of knowledge is a mathematical one (cf. GEOMETRY), the scientific reasoning which Descartes envisages is of a very general and abstract kind. 'I came to see', he wrote in the *Regulae*, 'that the exclusive concern of mathematics is with questions of order and measure, and that it is irrelevant whether the measure in question involves numbers, shapes, stars, sounds, or any other object whatsoever. This made me realize that there must be a general science (*generalis scientia*) which explains all the points that can be raised concerning order and measure, irrespective of subject matter (AT X 377–8: CSM I 19). Descartes observes in the *Discourse* that if we are tied to a particular subject-matter – for example the nature of particular geometrical figures – the power of the intellect is restricted by the need to visualize the particular objects in question (AT VI 17; cf. IMAGINATION). But by devising a very simple general notation, that would designate only abstract proportions and relations, one should be able to develop a kind of universal algebra which would reveal the underlying structures common to all objects of enquiry. Descartes took the first step along this road in the *Geometry*, where he aimed to unify the apparently diverse studies of arithmetic and geometry by expressing arithmetical quantities in the form of geometrical lines. Next, as he explains in the *Discourse*, he took the lines themselves, and designated them by algebraic symbols: 'in order to keep them in mind, I thought it necessary to designate them by the briefest possible symbols (*quelques chiffres les plus courtes qu'il serait possible*); in this way I would take over all that is best in geometrical analysis and in algebra, using the one to correct all the defects of the other' (AT VI 20: CSM I 121). Finally, the scope of the method would be extended still further: 'As I practised the method, I felt my mind gradually become accustomed to conceiving its objects more clearly and distinctly, and since I did not restrict the method to any particular subject matter, I hoped to apply it as usefully to the problems of other sciences as I had to those of algebra' (AT VI 121). The Cartesian vision, in short, is nothing less than that of a *mathesis universalis* which would comprise all the objects of human knowledge (AT X 378: CSM I 19). Inspired as he was by the clarity and indubitability of sciences like arithmetic and geometry, Descartes clearly chose the term 'mathesis' in part because of its associations with mathematics; but the term (from the Greek μάθησις, literally 'learning') was one which, as he explains, was intended to have the wider sense of a universal science or 'discipline' (the Latin term *disciplina*, from *discere*, 'to learn', being the equivalent of the Greek μάθησις: AT X 377, line 17: CSM I 19, ns. 1–3).

The conception Descartes offers of a unified system of reliable knowledge presents several difficulties. First, by his own admission, there is a radical disparity between the nature of physical objects and the nature of thinking beings (*see* DUALISM); and notwithstanding Descartes' efforts to show that the truths of metaphysics can be as clearly or more clearly perceived than those of physical science, it is not easy how a model of knowledge based on simple and transparently clear relationships, of the kind found in geometry, can be applied to complex issues like the nature of the mind or the existence of God (compare *Regulae*, XII, AT X 421–2: CSM I 46). Second, the requirement of complete indubitability, which Descartes builds into his conception of *scientia*, seems to set the standards for scientific knowledge at an impossibly high level. To this objection, Descartes would probably reply that only the general framework of Cartesian science is supposed to be derivable from indubitable first principles; at a lower level, there is scope for more probabilistic reasoning backed up by observation (cf. ASSUMPTION; DEDUCTION; EXPERIENCE). Lastly, critics have attacked even the more restricted claim that at least the foundations of our knowledge ought to be indubitable. Compare Hume: 'much inculcated by Des Cartes ... as a sovereign preservative against error [is a method proceeding] by a chain of reasoning, deduced from some original principle which cannot possibly be fallacious. ... But neither is there any such original principle, which has a prerogative above all others ... [n]or if there were, could we advance a step beyond it, but by the use of those very faculties of which we are already supposed to be diffident' (*Enquiry concerning Human Understanding* [1748], Sect. XII, Part 1). In so far as Descartes anticipated this type of objection, his position appears to have been that in reasoning about the metaphysical foundations of knowledge we arrive at a state of conviction (Latin *persuasio*) which is 'so firm that it is impossible for us to have any reason for doubting what we are convinced of'; and in such cases, though we may be unable to assume the standpoint of 'God or an angel', or provide an 'absolute' vindication of our conclusions, none the less, 'we have all that we could reasonably want . . . for a conviction so firm that it cannot in any way be removed is plainly the same as the most perfect certainty' (Second Replies, AT VII 144–5: CSM II 103).

L

language In Part V of the *Discourse on Method,* Descartes lays great stress on the uniquely human ability to arrange words together and form speech (*d'arranger ensemble diverses paroles et d'en composer un discours,* AT VI 57; CSM I 140). Authentic linguistic output is, for Descartes, wholly different from anything that could be produced by a machine, or by a (non-human) animal. You may be able to train a magpie to utter 'words', he later wrote to the Marquess of Newcastle, but each word will be a fixed response to an external stimulus causing a given change in the nervous system (AT IV 574: CSMK 303). The point hinges on what counts as a genuine use of language: 'We can certainly conceive of a machine so constructed that it utters words (*paroles*) . . . corresponding to . . . a change in its organs (e.g. if you touch it in one spot it asks what you want of it, and if you touch it in another spot it cries out that you are hurting it). But it is not conceivable that such a machine should produce arrangements of words so as to give an appropriately meaningful answer (*pour répondre au sens*) to whatever is said in its presence, as even the dullest of men can do' (AT VI 56: CSM I 140). In short, the human language-user has the capacity to respond appropriately to an indefinite range of situations, and this capacity seems utterly different from anything that could be produced by a finite mechanism generating a fixed range of outputs from determinate inputs. The conclusion Descartes draws is that genuine language is a 'sure sign' of the presence within us of a wholly non-physical entity – the rational soul (ibid.; cf. letter to More of 5 February 1649, AT V 278: CSMK 366).

Descartes' views on the impossibility of a mechanical explanation of language contrast interestingly with his general belief in the *power* of mechanical explanations. The passage on language in Part V of the *Discourse* follows directly on a discussion of how the purely mechanized operations of the brain and nervous system can, provided that they are sufficiently complex, explain a whole range of actions which might, to the unprejudiced eye, seem entirely beyond the scope of a mere machine. The purely physical processes of the animal spirits, and the mechanical processing of the *fantasie* or 'corporeal imagination', can produce a rich array of behaviour which is entirely 'appropriate to the objects of its senses and internal passions' (*à propos des objets qui se presentent à ses sens et des passions qui sont en lui*). The sceptic is invited to consider just how complex the responses of ingeniously constructed man-made automata can be: if a physical artefact can exhibit such complexity of response, then why not accept that a purely physical body 'made by the hand of God' can do even more? 'This will not seem at all strange to those who . . . are prepared to regard the body as a machine (*consideront le corps comme une machine*) which, having been made by the hand of God (*ayant été faite des mains de Dieu*), is incomparably better ordered, and contains in itself far more remarkable movements than any machine that could be invented by man (*est incomparablement mieux ordonnée, et a en soi des mouvements plus admirables, qu'aucune de celles qui peuvent être inventées par les hommes*)' (AT VI 56: CSM I 139). At this point, however, a critic might object that if God has at his disposal minute physical mechanisms of such incomparable complexity, then surely we cannot know *a priori* that he could not construct, out of purely material structures, a thinking, talking machine – a human being. Descartes' perhaps surprising answer is that we cannot absolutely rule this out. The appeal to the flexibility and scope of human linguistic capacity generates an argument whose conclusion has the status only of an overwhelming probability, not of an absolute certainty: 'Since reason is a universal instrument (*instrument universel*) which can be used in all kinds of situations, whereas [physical] organs need some particular disposition for each particular action, it is *morally impossible* (*moralement impossible*) for a machine to have enough different organs to make it act in all the contingencies of life in the way in which our reason makes us act (AT VI 57: CSM I 140, emphasis supplied). 'Moral certainty', as Descartes later explained in the 1647 (French) edition of the *Principles of Philosophy*, is 'certainty which is sufficient to regulate our behaviour, or which measures up to the certainty we have on matters relating to the conduct of life which we never normally doubt, though we know it is possible absolutely speaking that they may be false' (Part IV, art. 205: AT IXB 323: CSM I 290). Descartes' reflections on our uniquely human ability to respond to 'all the contingencies of life' led him to believe that the 'universal instrument' of reason could not feasibly be realized in a purely physical set of structures; but the possibility of such a physical realization is one that he is not prepared absolutely to rule out.

The upshot of all this is that Descartes' appeal to linguistic capacities in support of his belief in the incorporeality of the mind has a rather different status from the metaphysical arguments for dualism which he presents elsewhere. What makes a physical realization of the 'instrument of reason' hard for him to envisage is, at least partly, a matter of *number and size* – of how many structures of the appropriate kind could be packed into a given part of the body. Descartes made no secret of his enthusiasm for anatomical dissection as the key to understanding the minute structures of the nervous system and other bodily organs. But what such investigations established, so he believed, was the essential underlying *simplicity* of those structures. Everything that went on in heart and brain, nerves, muscles and 'animal spirits' manifested, at the level of observation that was available to him, nothing more than elementary 'push and pull' operations – operations not in principle any different from the simple workings of cogs and levers and pumps and whirlpools that could be readily inspected in the ordinary macro-world of 'medium-sized hardware'. Everything happened 'in accordance with the rules of mechanics which are identical with the laws of nature' (AT VI 54: CSM I 139). The argument from language in the *Discourse* thus hinges ultimately on the practical impossibility of a physical mechanism possessing a sufficiently large number of different parts (*assez de divers organes*) to facilitate the indefinite range of human responses to 'all the contingencies of life' (AT VI 57: CSM I 140). Descartes thus poses, in effect, the following empirical challenge which remains applicable even today to those who advocate a materialist, or reductionist, account of linguistic capacity: can such reductionists show how the mechanisms of the brain or nervous system can generate enough responses of the complexity needed to constitute genuine thought or linguistic behaviour?

laws of nature   Two fundamental presuppositions of Cartesian science are that, first, the universe operates in accordance with certain immutable laws, established by God, and, second, that the human mind has the innate, God-given, capacity to discover the structure of those laws. Both these premises are explicitly asserted in the opening of Part V of the *Discourse*, where Descartes describes how, having established the metaphysical starting points of his philosophy, he will proceed to deduce a 'whole chain of truths' about the physical world (AT VI 40–1: CSM I 131). The immutability and constancy of the divine nature entails, for Descartes, that the operation of the universe is entirely uniform, and hence that, in order to explain the present arrangement of the cosmos as we observe it, only very minimal assumptions are required about its initial configuration: 'For God has established these laws in such a marvellous way that even if we suppose that he creates nothing beyond what I have described [an indefinitely extended universe of moving and infinitely divisible parts], and sets up no order or proportion within it, but composes from it a chaos as confused and muddled as any of the poets could describe, the laws of nature are sufficient to cause the parts of this chaos to disentangle themselves and arrange themselves in such good order that they will have the form of a quite perfect world – a world in which we will be able to see not only light but also all the other things, general as well as particular, which appear in the real world' (*Le Monde*, ch. 6, AT XI 34–5: CSM I 91).

In Part II of the *Principles of Philosophy*, Descartes sets out three fundamental 'laws of nature', which govern the operation of the physical universe. The first is that 'each thing, so far as it can, always continues in the same state, and thus what is once in motion always continues to move' (art. 37); the second is that 'all motion is in itself rectilinear' (art. 39); and the third is that 'if a body collides with another body that is stronger than itself, it loses none of its motion, but if it collides with a weaker body it loses a quantity of motion which is equal to that which it imparts to the other body' (art. 40). (For the first two laws, *see* INERTIA; for the third, *see* CONSERVATION.)

Although Descartes' 'laws of motion' are of a fairly general and abstract nature, his approach does exemplify the transition which occurred in the seventeenth century from a qualitative physics based on definitions of 'natural kinds' to a quantitative system of mathematically-based covering laws. Following the statement of his general laws in Part II of the *Principles*, he supplies a series of seven 'Rules of Impact', which specify, in quantitative terms, how the speed and direction of bodies after impact may be calculated. The seven ideal cases which he covers are (1) that in which two bodies of equal size and speed collide head on; (2) as in (1) but where one body is larger; (3) as in (1) but where one body is travelling faster; (4) where one body is at rest but larger; (5) where one body is at rest and smaller; (6) where one body is at rest, and the bodies are equal in size; and (7) where two bodies collide when travelling in the same direction (arts 45–52). The Cartesian rules, however, can hardly be considered to be a significant contribution to the development of physics, since they are based on the primitive notion that what is conserved is 'quantity of motion', measured simply as the product of size (extension) and speed; Descartes does not provide any serious attempt to test these rules by deriving precise concrete predictions from them, and his system thus falls far short of the rigour and predictive power of the laws formulated by Newton later in the century (which invoke the much richer and more sophisticated notion of the conservation of mass times velocity). Descartes himself admitted that 'experience often appears to conflict with the rules of impact', but insisted that 'the rules do not need proof, since they are self-evident, and the demonstrations are so certain that even if our experience seemed to show the opposite, we should still be obliged to have more faith in our reason than our senses' (*Principles*, Part II, arts 52 and 53). In short, Descartes' promise of an exact, mathematically based, science of matter in motion remained more of a programmatic vision than an achieved body of rigorous predictive principles. In his more modest moments, indeed, he acknowledged that the complexities of the physical phenomena were such that to hope for watertight demonstrative explanations was unrealistic: 'to require me to give demonstrations on a topic that depends on physics is to ask the impossible' (AT II 142: CSMK 103).

Letter to Dinet   Open letter, written in Latin (*Epistola ad P. Dinet*) and printed at the end of the Seventh Set of Objections and Replies in the 1642 edition of the *Meditations* with *Objections and Replies*. In the letter Descartes defends his philosophy against the venomous attacks to which it had been subjected both in France, by the Jesuit Pierre Bourdin (author of the Seventh Objections), and, in Holland, by Gisbertus Voetius (*see* LETTER TO VOETIUS). Dinet was the head of the Jesuit order in France, and had taught Descartes at the College of La Flèche. The letter is an important source for Descartes' attitude to scholasticism; it is also a good example of his tact and diplomacy in attempting to win the support of the Church for his own philosophy.

Letter to Voetius   Long open letter which Descartes had published by the Elzevirs of Amsterdam in May 1643. The original Latin text is entitled *Epistola Renati Descartes ad Celeberrimum Virum D. Gisbertum Voetium* ('Letter of René Descartes to that most distinguished man, Mr. Gisbertus Voetius'). The letter was designed as a reply to two essays Voetius had published which viciously attacked Descartes and his views; Voetius was also the instigator of the successful move to have the Cartesian philosophy formally condemned at the University of Utrecht, of which he was Rector. The *Letter to Voetius* is of interest in illustrating the furious opposition which Descartes' ideas aroused, and the success which his opponents had in branding him as a sceptic and an atheist, despite all his attempts to show that this was malicious slander. The text of the Letter is found in AT VIIIB 1–194, and extracts are translated in CSMK 220ff.

Letters   Descartes was a prolific letter writer, and his love of solitude and self-imposed exile from France meant that he depended greatly on correspondents for philosophical stimulus. He preserved copies of many of the letters he wrote, and when he died a very large number of these was found among his papers in Stockholm. Three volumes of letters were published by Claude Clerselier between 1657 and 1667, and the collection has since been augmented by the discovery of a considerable number of additional letters.

Descartes' correspondence, addressed to some forty different recipients, ranges over a vast number of topics, mathematical, scientific, metaphysical and ethical. It also provides a wealth of information about the planning and reception of his published works. Descartes' chief correspondent was his friend and literary editor Marin Mersenne, who frequently advised him about his planned publications, and was also an acute philosophical critic of his ideas. By common consent, however, the richest portion of the correspondence from a philosophical point of view consists of the letters exchanged between Descartes and Princess Elizabeth of Bohemia, where searching questions are raised regarding Descartes' views on MIND AND BODY. The original texts of Descartes' letters take up the first five volumes of the standard Franco-Latin edition of Descartes' works (AT); English translations of the great bulk of those letters which are of philosophical interes̈ may be found in CSMK.

light The investigation of the nature and properties of light was one of the most important projects that occupied Descartes' attention in the 1630s. In a letter of 22 August 1634, addressed to Beeckman, he describes certain experiments which he claims will confirm his view that light is transmitted instantaneously: 'if someone holds a torch in his hand after dark and moves it about, and looks at a mirror placed a quarter of mile in front of him, he will be able to tell whether he feels the movement in his hands before he sees it in the mirror. . . . If a time lag were to be detected in such an experiment, I admit that my philosophy would be completely overturned' (AT I 308: CSMK 46). The reason for the concluding admission (which will seem so embarrassingly rash to the modern reader armed with hindsight) is that Descartes maintains that 'the light in the bodies we call luminous is nothing other than a certain movement, or very rapid and lively action, which passes to our eyes through the medium of the air and other transparent bodies, just as the movement or resistance of the bodies encountered by a blind man passes to his hand by means of his stick. . . . Hence, light can extend its rays instantaneously from the sun to us, just as the action by which we move one end of a stick must pass instantaneously to the other end . . . even though the distance from the sun to us is far greater than that between the ends of the stick' (AT VI 84: CSM I 153).

In his treatise the *Optics* (*La Dioptrique*), which was one of the specimen essays published with the *Discourse* in 1637 and designed to illustrate his new scientific method, Descartes set out to 'deal with refraction and the manufacture of lenses, and also to give detailed descriptions of the eye, of light, and of vision, and of everything belonging to catoptrics and optics' (letter to Mersenne of March 1636, AT I 339–40: CSMK 51). It may be seen from this remark that the essay in question aims to be a general treatise on optics, that is, the science of light and the laws of vision, encompassing both 'Dioptrics' (the traditional name given to the subdivision of optics which deals with refracted light) and 'Catoptrics' (the study of reflected light). In the course of the essay, Descartes puts forward a version of what is now known as Snell's law, according to which $sin\ i = n\ sin\ r$, where i is the angle of incidence, r the angle of refraction and n a constant specific to the refractive medium (see letter to Mersenne of June 1632, AT I 255: CSMK 39). Descartes' achievements in this field are considerable, and it is probably fair to say that he achieved in this area the kind of mathematical precision which he hoped,

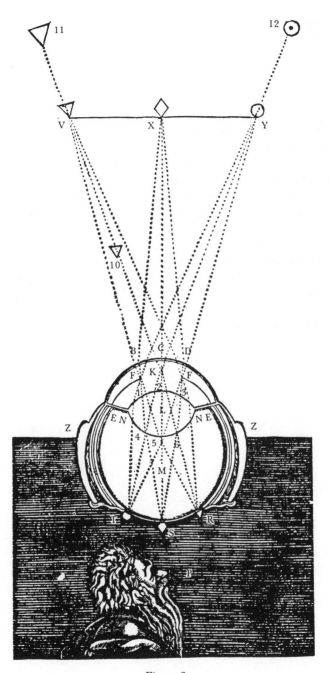

Figure 2

though without quite succeeding, to provide throughout his physics (cf. LAWS OF NATURE).

With respect to the way in which light is perceived, Descartes aimed to provide a 'geometry of vision' which would show how the distance and position of objects, together with their size and shape, is perceived by means of a complicated inferential process which depends on the configuration of 'the images imprinted on the back of the eye' (*Optics*, Discourse VI, AT VI 133–1: CSM I 170–2). But although the physiology of light perception was to be accounted for by reference to the magnitudes of the angles subtended by the rays of light passing from external objects via the lens of the eye through to the retina, Descartes makes it clear that the full explanation of our perception of light will involve more than physiology: 'it is the soul which sees, not the eye, and it does not see directly, but only by means of the brain' (AT VI 141: CSM I 172).

For more on the complexities of Descartes' account, *see* COLOUR and IMAGES. For Descartes' detailed discussions of the nature and properties of light, see his early account in *Le Monde*, ch. 2 (AT XI 7ff: CSM I 83f), and the more extended treatment in the *Principles of Philosophy*, Part II, arts 55ff.

light, natural   *see* INTUITION.

M

machine A pervasive feature of Descartes' approach to scientific explanation is the use of mechanistic models; indeed, the 'mechanistic' outlook is one of the hallmarks of the seventeenth-century scientific revolution of which he was among the principal inaugurators. The central idea behind this outlook is presented with remarkable clarity and explicitness in Part IV of the *Principles of Philosophy*: 'I do not recognize any difference between artefacts and natural bodies except that the operations of artefacts are for the most part brought about by mechanisms which are large enough to be easily perceivable by the senses – as indeed must be the case if they are to be capable of being manufactured by human beings. The effects produced in nature, by contrast, almost always depend on structures which are so minute that they completely elude our senses. Moreover, mechanics is a division or special case of physics, and all the explanations belonging to the former also belong to the latter; so it is no less natural for a clock constructed with this or that set of wheels to tell the time than it is for a tree which grew from this or that seed to produce the appropriate fruit. Men who are experienced in dealing with machinery can take a particular machine whose function they know, and by looking at some of its parts easily form a conjecture about the design of the other parts which they cannot see. In the same way, I have attempted to consider the observable effects and parts of natural bodies, and track down the imperceptible causes and particles which produce them' (art. 103, AT VIIIA 326: CSM I 288–9).

Four aspects of Descartes' use of machines or mechanisms in science are especially noteworthy. The first is that it is inspired by a radical reductionism: the operation of macro-phenomena is explained, without remainder, solely by reference to the interactions of micro-particles. A second feature, closely connected with the first, is the resolute rejection of any need to posit occult powers and forces: 'all the effects usually attributed to occult properties', such as the mysterious 'powers in stones or plants', and the 'marvels of sympathetic and antipathetic influences' can be explained purely on the basis of the shape and motion of the constituent parts of matter (*Principles*, Part IV, art. 187). Third, the Cartesian approach is what may be called 'simplicist': 'nature employs only means which are very simple' (AT III 797:

CSMK 215), and whatever complexities may appear to obtain on the surface, the underlying mechanisms are of the same perfectly straightforward and unproblematic type as those which ordinary craftsmen are familiar with in the macro-world. And fourth, the mechanisms of nature all exhibit a complete homogeneity: the distinctions between 'animate' and 'inanimate' nature, and between natural and man-made phenomena, are in fact quite arbitrary, since the same kinds of operations are at work in all cases. This last point is especially important in Cartesian physiology. The human body is frequently described as a machine: no 'vegetative or sensitive soul' needs to be introduced, since the full range of biological processes, including 'growth, digestion, respiration, the reception of sensory data, the internal movements of the appetites and the external movement of the limbs' can all be explained as 'following from the mere arrangement of the machine's organs as naturally as the movement of a clock or other automaton follows from the arrangement of its counter-weights and wheels' (*Treatise on Man*, AT XI 202: CSM I 108; compare also *Description of the Human Body*, AT XI 226: CSM I 315). It is only in the case of human beings that any kind of soul needs to be introduced, namely to explain the phenomena of THOUGHT and LANGUAGE, which Descartes regards as recalcitrant to mechanistic explanation. In the case of non-human animals or the 'beasts' (French, *bêtes*) or 'brutes' (Latin, *bruta*), as Descartes frequently calls them, there is nothing that cannot be explained mechanistically, and this gives rise to the notorious Cartesian doctrine of the *bête machine* – the view that non-human animals are simply mechanical automata.

See also ANIMALS.

mathematics Throughout his life, Descartes consistently regarded the study of mathematics as a paradigm of that 'right use of reason' which would lead to discovery of the truth: 'mathematics accustoms the mind to recognizing the truth, because it is in mathematics that examples of correct reasoning, which you will find nowhere else, are to be found. Accordingly, the man who has once accustomed his mind to mathematical reasoning will have a mind that is well equipped for the investigation of other truths, since reasoning is exactly the same in every subject' (AT V 177: CSMK 351–2). Mathematics appealed to Descartes both because of its deductive certainty, and also because it provided a kind of template for the investigation of those formal and abstract relationships which, he believed, underpinned a whole range of physical phenomena. Hence the student of mathematics would be able to extend the range of his inquiries 'beyond arithmetic and geometry, to sciences such as astronomy, music, optics and mechanics', all of which could be subsumed under *mathesis universalis* – the 'universal discipline' which encompassed the whole of human knowledge, irrespective of the particular nature of the subject-matter in any given case (for this notion, *see* KNOW-LEDGE).

Mathematics was a major preoccupation of the young Descartes. Many of the results later incorporated in his *Geometry* (1637) were worked out during the 1620s, and we know from his letters that a great inspiration during his early years was the Dutch mathematician Isaac Beeckman, whom he met in Holland in 1618. Beeckman seems to have played for Descartes something of the role which Hume was later to play for Kant – waking him from his dogmatic slumbers: 'you alone roused me from my state of indolence', wrote Descartes to Beeckman on 23 April 1619, 'and reawakened the learning that by then had almost disappeared from my mind' (AT X 163: CSMK 4). One of the chief points to strike Descartes was that mathematics could attain complete clarity and precision in its arguments, and that the demonstrations it employed were completely certain: no room was allowed for merely probabilistic reasoning. (Compare his later comment to Burman: 'mathematics accustoms the mind to distinguishing arguments which are true and valid from those which are probable and false. For in mathematics, anyone who relies solely on probable arguments will be misled and driven to absurd conclusions' (AT V 177: CSMK 352).) The mathematical model continued to influence Descartes' scientific work throughout the following decade, leading up to the composition of his treatise on physics and cosmology, *Le Monde* (written in the early 1630s), which announced, at any rate in outline, a comprehensive programme for the elimination of qualitative descriptions from science in favour of exact quantitative analysis. The arguments of his *Optics* (1637) also contained a great deal of mathematical reasoning, geometrical analysis playing the central role (*see* LIGHT); by the time of his major scientific treatise, the *Principles of Philosophy* (1644), he ventured to make the bold claim that his entire account of material things invoked 'nothing apart from what the geometers call quantity, and take as the object of their demonstrations, i.e. that to which every kind of division, shape and motion is applicable', and that with regard to such divisions, shapes and motions, nothing was to be admitted as true 'except for what has been deduced from indubitable common notions so evidently that it is fit to be considered as a mathematical demonstration' (Part II, art. 64).

Some of Descartes' critics objected that Cartesian science made the mistake of confusing the artificial objects of pure geometry with the concrete realities of the physical world: 'material things are not the subject matter of pure mathematics, since the latter include the point, the line, the surface, which cannot exist in reality' (Pierre Gassendi, Fifth Objections, AT VII 329: CSM II 228). Descartes himself described some of his scientific writings as 'a mixture of mathematics and philosophy [i.e. physics]' (AT I 370: CSMK 58), but he certainly maintained in the *Meditations* that the clear and distinct perceptions of the enlightened intellect were the key to understanding 'the whole of that corporeal nature that is the subject matter of pure mathematics' (AT VII 71: CSM II 49). This seems to promise a pure mathematical physics whose structure is determined largely *a priori*; but in reality the Cartesian system depends, at any rate for its detailed explanation of specific phenomena, on a good deal of empirical observation (*see* ASSUMPTIONS). Difficulties none the less remain for the Cartesian project of characterizing the general nature of matter in purely geometrical terms (*see* EXTENSION).

For more on the use of mathematics in Cartesian science, *see* CAUSE; GEOMETRY; IMAGINATION; KNOWLEDGE and LAWS OF NATURE. For the epistemic status of mathematical truths in the Cartesian system, *see* DECEIVING GOD DILEMMA and ETERNAL TRUTHS.

mathesis universalis   For this expression, which Descartes employs to convey his ideal of a universal science, modelled on and including mathematics, but wider and more abstract in its scope, *see* KNOWLEDGE.

matter   In his account of the physical universe, Descartes introduces three 'elements' out of which all material items are composed. The first element (of which the sun and stars are made) consists of very small fast-moving particles – 'so violently agitated that when they meet other bodies they are divided into particles of indefinite smallness'; the second is composed of slightly larger, but still minute and imperceptible, spherical particles, and goes to make up the 'heavens' (i.e. the matter which fills all the space between the stars and planets – Descartes firmly denying the existence of any VACUUM); and the third element, consisting of 'bulkier particles with shapes less suited for motion', makes up the matter of which the earth and other planets are composed (*Principles*, Part III, art. 52). Superficially, this classification seems partly to mirror the traditional scholastic division of matter into natural kinds, based on the ancient Aristotelian elements of fire, air, earth and water, except that the last two elements are reduced in Descartes to a single category. But Descartes makes it clear that his talk of 'elements' refers to nothing more than convenient classifications in respect of size, shape and motion; he firmly denies that there are any intrinsic generic differences involved. 'The nature of matter, or body considered in general, consists not in its being something which is hard, or heavy, or coloured, or which affects the senses in any way, but simply in its being something which is extended in length, breadth and depth' (*Principles*, Part II, art. 4; cf. art. 11; *see* BODY and EXTENSION). The doctrine of the homogeneity of all matter appealed to Descartes for two principal reasons, namely, because it enabled all physics to be unfolded in quantitative rather than qualitative terms, by means of laws describing the behaviour of particles by reference to their size, shape and motion (*see* LAWS OF NATURE and MATHEMATICS), and, in the second place, because the doctrine represented a spectacular reduction in the number of special entities or properties that needed to be invoked. Descartes makes his reductionist aspirations quite explicit in his essay on *Meteorology*, published with the *Discourse* in 1637: 'To make you accept all these suppositions more easily, bear in mind that . . . I regard these particles as all being composed of one single kind of matter, and believe that each of them could be divided repeatedly in infinitely many ways, and that there is no more difference between them than there is between stones of various different shapes cut from the same rock. Bear in mind too, that to avoid a breach with the philosophers [i.e. the scholastics], I have no wish to deny any further items which they may imagine in bodies over and above what I have described, such as "substantial forms" or their "real qualities" and so on. It simply seems to me that my arguments must be all the more acceptable in so far as I can make them depend on fewer things' (AT VI 239: CSM II 173, n. 2). The apparent concession to the scholastics in this passage is evidently heavy with irony; while Descartes does not aim to disprove the existence of the forms and qualities posited by the scholastics, his aim is clearly to show that appeal to such notions will simply die a natural death, once it has been shown that they are, for explanatory purposes, completely redundant (compare his elimination of the need to posit entities like 'the vegetative or sensitive soul' in physiology, AT XI 202: CSM I 108).

See also SCHOLASTIC PHILOSOPHY.

medicine   It is clear from many of Descartes' letters and published works that he was a keen student of anatomy and physiology, and he evidently hoped that these studies would eventually yield practical benefits in the field of medicine. Medicine is mentioned, along with mechanics and morals, as one of the principal branches of the tree of knowledge, of which metaphysics are the roots and physics the trunk. The metaphor implies that the eventual development of reliable and practically useful medical knowledge will be one of the crowning achievements of the Cartesian science, once the more fundamental principles of that science have been established: 'just as it is not the roots or the trunk of a tree from which one gathers the fruit, but only the ends of the branches, so the chief benefit of philosophy depends on those of its parts which can only be learnt last of all' (Preface to the French edition of the *Principles of Philosophy* [1647], AT IXB 14–15: CSM I 86). Ten years before this passage was written, Descartes had described in correspondence how he was working on a 'Compendium of Medicine based partly on my reading and partly on my own reasoning', and he declares his hope that such research would lead to a 'stay of execution' – a way of prolonging his life to 'a hundred years or more' (letter to Plempius of 20 December 1637, AT I 649: CSMK 76). The theme is developed at length in Part VI of the *Discourse on the Method*, where Descartes outlines his programme for a comprehensive practical philosophy which will make us 'lords and masters of nature' (*maîtres et possesseurs de la nature*): 'The maintenance of health is undoubtedly the chief good and the foundation of all the other goods in life. For even the mind depends so much on the temperament and disposition of the bodily organs that if it is possible to find some means of making men in general wiser and more skilful than they are now, I believe that we must look for it in medicine. It is true that the medicine which is currently practised does not contain much that is of practical use … but we might free ourselves from innumerable diseases both of the body and of the mind, and perhaps even from the infirmity of old age, if we had sufficient knowledge of their causes, and of all the remedies that nature has provided' (AT VI 62: CSM I 143). The promised 'Compendium of Medicine' was, however, never completed, although Descartes did, in the late 1640s, start work on a treatise entitled *The Description of the Human Body*, which was published posthumously, in its unfinished state, in 1664. The main theme of the *Description* is that progress can be made only by treating the body in purely mechanistic terms, 'so that we will have no more reason to think that it is our soul which produces in it the movements which we know by experience are not controlled by our will than we have reason to think that there is a soul in a clock which makes it tell the time' (AT XI 226: CSM I 315). But although the work opens with a repetition of Descartes' grand aim of 'curing illness and preventing it, and even slowing down the ageing process' (AT XI 223: CSM I 314), the extant portions of the *Description* comprise merely a recapitulation of Descartes' early work on the circulation of the BLOOD, together with a highly speculative and schematic account of the formation of the foetus. It seems likely that by the middle to late 1640s Descartes had accepted that there was no immediate prospect that his scientific principles could be made to yield significant practical advances in medicine; the best advice he could give to correspondents was to ignore the advice of professional doctors and consult their own common sense: anyone who had reached the age of thirty should know by their own experience what regime suited them best, and so be able to 'be their own doctor' (see letter to Newcastle of October 1645, AT IV 329–30: CSMK 275–6, and *Conversation with Burman* [1648], AT V 179: CSMK 354).

meditation There is considerable significance in Descartes' choice of the title 'Meditations' for the definitive presentation of his metaphysical system. In the first place, the way in which the work was conceived shows the influence of the large corpus of devotional writings of the sixteenth and early seventeenth centuries, such as those of Ignatius of Loyola (1491–1556), founder of the Jesuit Order. In his *Spiritual Exercises*, Ignatius defines a 'spiritual exercise' as 'a way of examining one's conscience by meditating, contemplating or praying, either silently or out loud', and notes that 'the needs of the soul are not usually satisfied by lots of facts, but by an inner sense and appetite for things' (*Exercitia Spiritualia* [1548], trans. Longridge, pp. 4 and 7). Descartes (who was educated by the Jesuits at their newly founded college of La Flèche) clearly designed his own *Meditations* not as a static set of 'facts', but as a dynamic series of exercises whose impact could be felt only by those who were willing to follow the author and internalize the reflections they contained; 'I would not urge anyone to read this book except those who are able and willing to meditate seriously with me' (Preface to the *Meditations*, AT VII 11: CSM II 8). This 'inner' or subjective orientation is evident from the start. The train of thought follows the reflections of the solitary thinker in retreat, isolated from the world: 'today I have expressly rid my mind of all worries and arranged for myself a clear stretch of free time . . . I am here quite alone' (AT VII 17–8: CSM II 12). Each Meditation is designed to occupy one day, and each concludes with a summary that recapitulates the insights gained to date, before the next stage of discovery is attempted (cf. especially the end of the Second Meditation, AT VII 34: CSM II 23, and the end of the Fourth, AT VII 62: CSM II 43). Although he was later, in the *Principles*, to expound his metaphysical views in textbook fashion, as a quasi-formal chain of propositions mapped out in seventy-six compact 'articles', there is no doubt that Descartes thought that the informal, reflective style of the *Meditations* was better suited to conveying the soul's solitary quest for truth. 'I do not attempt', Descartes wrote to Mersenne, 'to say in a single place everything relevant to a given subject, because it would be impossible for me to provide proper proofs, since my supporting reasons would have to be drawn in some cases from considerably more distant sources than others. Instead, I reason in a orderly way, from what is easy to what is harder . . . which is the right way in my opinion to find and explain the truth. The order of the subject-matter is good only for those whose reasoning is disjointed, and who can say as much about one difficulty as about another' (24 December 1640, AT III 266: CSMK 163; compare also the distinction between the 'order of exposition' and the 'order of discovery' in the *Conversation with Burman*, AT V 153: CSMK 337–8).

The motivation for this reflective, first-person approach to metaphysics arises partly from Descartes' programme for 'demolishing everything and starting again right from the foundations' (AT VII 17: CSM II 12). By retreating from the world of the senses, and divesting himself from the influences of 'preconceived opinion', the meditator aims to discover, within himself, the indubitable first principles on which a new system of knowledge can be built. But Descartes' conception of metaphysics as 'meditation' reaches beyond epistemology, and, at times, takes him into a 'devotional' style of reflection, where the prevailing mode ceases to be that of the autonomous seeker after truth and becomes instead a kind of spiritual submission to the divine will. Thus at the end of the Third Meditation, after establishing what appears to be a purely rational proof of the impossibility of divine deception, the meditator breaks off and exclaims: 'But before examining this point more carefully . . . I should like to pause here and spend some time in the contemplation of God; to reflect on his attributes, and to gaze with wonder and adoration at the beauty of this immense light, so far as the eye of my darkened intellect can bear it. For just as we believe through faith that the supreme happiness of the next life consists solely in the contemplation of the divine majesty, so experience tells us that this same contemplation, albeit much less perfect, enables us to know the greatest joy of which we are capable in this life' (AT VII 52: CSM II 35–6).

For more on the contrast between the 'rational' and the 'devotional' modes in Descartes, *see* GOD.

Meditations on First Philosophy   Descartes' philosophical masterpiece was written in Latin and first published in Paris in 1641 under the title *Meditationes de Prima Philosophia*. The subtitle adds 'in which the existence of God and the immortality of the soul are demonstrated'; but Descartes, commenting on the phrase 'first philosophy', explained to Mersenne that 'the discussion is not confined to God and the soul, but treats of all the first things to be discovered by philosophizing' (letter of 11 November 1640, AT III 235: CSMK 157). A (slightly revised) edition of the *Meditations* appeared in 1642, published this time by the Elzevirs of Amsterdam; the subtitle of this new edition omits the reference to the immortality of the soul, and substitutes 'the distinction between the human soul and the body'. A French translation of the *Meditations*, by the Duc de Luynes, was published with Descartes' approval in 1647.

The *Meditations* describes, in dramatic detail, the voyage of discovery of an isolated thinker, attempting to find secure foundations for science (*see* MEDITATION). Systematic DOUBT is used to question all preconceived opinions (First Meditation), but at last a point of certainty is reached with the meditator's indubitable awareness of his own existence (Second Meditation; *see* COGITO ERGO SUM). The Second Meditation goes on to examine the nature of the 'thinking thing' whose existence has been established and argues that the mind is better known than the body. In the Third Meditation, the meditator lays down the rule that 'whatever we very clearly and distinctly perceive is true' (AT VII 35: CSM II 24; *see* CIRCLE, CARTESIAN); but residual doubts about the reliability of the mind remain, only to be dispelled when the meditator reflects on the idea of God which he finds within him, and reasons that such an idea can only have come from an actually existing God, who is the source of all truth (*see* TRADEMARK ARGUMENT). The Fourth Meditation proceeds to examine the relationship between the intellect and the will (*see* JUDGEMENT) and uncovers a recipe for the avoidance of ERROR. In the Fifth Meditation, the nature of matter as EXTENSION is established, and there is a second argument for the existence of God, based on the claim that existence cannot be separated from the essence of a supremely perfect being (*see* ONTOLOGICAL ARGUMENT). Finally, in the Sixth Meditation, the existence of the external world is re-established, and Descartes goes on to argue that the nature of the mind is wholly different from that of the body, so that MIND AND BODY are entirely distinct substances; notwithstanding this conclusion, he also points out that the mind is closely 'intermingled' or 'united' with the body (*see* HUMAN BEING). The Meditation concludes with an explanation of how, notwithstanding the benevolence of God, 'the nature of man as a combination of mind and body is such that it is bound to mislead him from time to time' (AT VII 88: CSM II 61). Descartes himself provided a Synopsis to the *Meditations*, together with a Preface to the Reader, noting some difficulties in the argument (AT VII 7ff: CSM II 6ff). At the start of the volume is a Dedicatory Letter to the Theology Faculty at the Sorbonne, in which Descartes presents his arguments as designed to support the Church in its fight against atheism. Also included in the same volume as the *Meditations* was a series of OBJECTIONS AND REPLIES, containing Descartes' answers to difficulties raised by various critics.

memory   Descartes, in his physiological writings, describes the faculty of memory in purely corporeal terms. A completely mechanical android, if its internal parts were suitably organized, could not just perform all the functions associated with digestion, heartbeat, nutrition and growth, but also could have a nervous system facilitating the 'reception of light, sounds, smells, tastes, heat and other such sensible qualities, the imprinting of the ideas of these qualities in the organ of the "common" sense and imagination, *the retention or stamping of these ideas in the memory*, the internal movements of the appetites and the passions, and finally the external movement of all the limbs – movements which are *so appropriate* not only to the actions of objects presented to the senses but also *to the passions and impressions found in the memory*, that they imitate perfectly the movements of a real man' (*Treatise on Man*, AT XI 202: CSM I 108, emphasis supplied. For the details of this account, *see* IMAGES). In allowing for a non-cognitive type of memory shared by humans and animals, Descartes is partly following scholastic tradition: Aquinas had ascribed the ability to store sensory impressions to the *memoria sensitiva*, a faculty of the 'sensitive soul' present in both men and beasts (*Summa contra Gentiles*, II, 74). But the crucial difference in Descartes is that such a faculty is explained in resolutely reductionist terms: 'in order to explain these functions, it is not necessary to conceive of the [bodily] machine as having any vegetative or sensitive soul, or other principle of movement and life, apart from its blood and its spirits, which are agitated by the heat of the fire burning continuously in its heart – a fire which has the same nature as all the fires that occur in inanimate bodies' (*Treatise on Man,* ibid. The 'spirits' referred to in this passage are purely corporeal in nature; *see* ANIMAL SPIRITS).

In addition to the corporeal memory, Descartes posits, in the case of humans, a conceptual or 'intellectual' memory whereby concepts and meanings are stored, and this he insists is attributable to an entirely non-physical soul. 'When, for example, on hearing that the word "rex" [king] signifies supreme power, I commit this to my memory and then subsequently recall the meaning, it must be the intellectual memory which makes this possible. For there is certainly no affinity between the letters R-E-X and their meaning, which would enable me to derive the meaning from the letters. It is the intellectual memory that enables me to recall what the letters stand for' (AT V 150: CSMK 336–7). What this argument suggests is that concept storage and recognition could not possibly be explained by reference to any mechanical process, since the gap between sign and significatum is not of the kind which could be bridged by the causal laws of physics; compare *Principles,* Part IV, art. 198: 'we understand very well how the different size, shape and motion of the particles of one body can produce various local motions in another body, but there is no way of understanding how they can produce something else whose nature is quite different from their own.' Descartes' position is perhaps not entirely consistent here, since he allows that animals can be trained to react in various ways by stimuli which have no direct 'affinity' to the passions subsequently aroused: 'I reckon that if you whipped a dog five or six times to the sound of a violin, it would begin to howl and run away as soon as it heard that music again' (AT I 134: CSMK 20). His views on LANGUAGE, however, make it clear that there is a radical difference between stimulus response mechanisms of this kind and the sort of understanding necessary for the genuine grasp of concepts.

The role of memory in Cartesian epistemology is problematic in several respects. As just noted, the use of what might be called 'conceptual' memory seems necessary if any cognition at all is to be possible. But Descartes makes a distinction between the kind of cognition, called INTUITION, where the content of a proposition is directly present to the mind, and, on the other hand, DEDUCTION, where a 'long chain of inferences' is involved. To minimize the possibility of slips of memory contaminating the latter process, Descartes advocated the habit of 'running through a chain of inferences several times, simultaneously intuiting one relation and passing on to the next, until I have learnt to pass from the first to last so swiftly that memory is left with practically no role to play' (*Regulae*, Rule VII, AT X 388: CSM I 25). In connection with his validation of knowledge, Descartes was challenged to explain how we can prove the existence of God before the (divinely guaranteed) reliability of our clear and distinct perceptions has been established. His reply suggests that, while the existence of God needs to be established if we are to have confidence in developing systematic knowledge requiring a long series of inferences, in cases where truths are directly intuited, and no use of memory is involved, no such divine guarantee is required: 'when I said that we can know nothing for certain until we are aware that God exists, I expressly declared that I was speaking only of knowledge of those propositions which can be recalled when we are no longer attending to the arguments by means of which we deduced them' (Second Replies, AT VII 140: CSM II 100). It is probably a mistake to interpret this and other similar passages as making the ambitious claim that memory is, for Descartes, a process whose accuracy is guaranteed once God's existence is proved; for Descartes is in fact only too clearly aware of the weakness and fallibility of human memory (cf. *Regulae*, loc. cit.; and *Conversation with Burman*, AT V 148: CSMK 334). The point is, rather, that belief in a benevolent God allows us to embark with reasonable confidence, albeit slowly and cautiously, on the process of trying to construct a systematic body of knowledge; without such a well-grounded belief, we should not be in a position to extend our knowledge beyond the scope of actually intuited truths.

See also CIRCLE, CARTESIAN.

Meteorology Written in French, *Les Météores* is the second of the three specimen essays published with the *Discourse on the Method* in 1637. The essay is designed to illustrate Descartes' unificatory and reductionist approach to physical phenomena, and opens by suggesting that, although we have a natural tendency to wonder at things above us more than at those beneath our feet, there is in reality no obstacle to providing perfectly simple causal explanations for all the relevant phenomena (AT VI 231). Water, earth, air and all the other bodies in the environment are composed of particles of matter of various shapes and sizes (AT VI 233), and these differences in size and shape are sufficient to explain all the variety we observe, without the need to posit any qualitative differences between different kinds of matter (AT VI 239). The *Meteorology* is divided into ten chapters or 'Discourses': the first gives a general account of the nature of terrestrial bodies, and there then follow chapters on a variety of 'meteorological' phenomena, including vapours and exhalations, salt, winds, clouds, snow, rain and hail, storms and lightning, and the RAINBOW.

method   Descartes made much of his claim to have discovered a new method for 'rightly conducting reason and seeking the truth in the sciences' (AT VI 1: CSM I 111). Such claims were in fact relatively commonplace in the sixteenth and early seventeenth centuries; what is more, the approach which Descartes takes in his supposedly 'fresh start' for philosophy is by no means as original as is often supposed. For example, the radical tone which characterizes the opening of the *Meditations* is anticipated in remarkable detail in the work of Francisco Sanches, the Portuguese philosopher and medical writer, whose *Quod nihil scitur* was published in Lyons in 1581. Sanches begins his inquiry into the possibility of knowledge by 'withdrawing into himself' (*ad memetipsum retuli*) and 'calling all into doubt' (*omnia in dubium revocans*); this is the 'true way of knowing' (*verum sciendi modus*; ed. Thomson, 1988, p. 92). Sanches, like Descartes, sweeps away traditional appeals to authority: Aristotle, for all his wisdom, was just wrong on many points; at the end of the day '*homo ut nos*' – he was a man like us. To say 'thus spake the Master' is unworthy of a philosopher; better, in our reasonings, 'to trust nature alone' (ibid., p. 93). Sanches' motto 'I follow nature alone' sounds so Cartesian to the modern ear that we almost expect to find him appealing to the light of nature; but had he done so, this would not have been an anticipation, but a recapitulation, for the ancient metaphor had been revived earlier in the sixteenth century by the Spanish humanist Joannes Vives in his *De Disciplinis* (1531) – a work with which Sanches himself was almost certainly familiar, *see* INTUITION.

Even though his approach was not wholly original, there is no doubt that Descartes did devote a great deal of systematic and careful attention to the problem of specifying the correct method of philosophizing. In his early work, the *Regulae*, he offers the reader a barrage of methodological recommendations, some relating to mathematical problems in the narrow sense, others of much more general scope, describing the cognitive operations whereby the mind can achieve systematic KNOWLEDGE. The first twelve rules of the *Regulae* introduce such general maxims, and contain much discussion of the nature of INTUITION and DEDUCTION, and the relation between them, as well as such matters as how the pure apprehension of the INTELLECT can be assisted by the correct use of the IMAGINATION (cf. Rule XII). But there are signs that, even as he composed the *Regulae*, Descartes became impatient with the length of time it was taking him to set out his recommendations. The method, he often comes near to saying, is in essence a very elementary one, and should be capable of being stated in the simplest and briefest terms. Sometimes, indeed, his individual rules look more like encapsulated summaries of the whole procedure, as in Rule V: 'the whole method consists entirely in the ordering and arranging of objects on which we must concentrate our mind's eye if we are to discover the truth' (AT X 379: CSM I 20).

By the time he came to write the *Discourse*, Descartes had succeeded in boiling down his methodological rules to just four: 'The first, never to accept anything as true if I did not have evident knowledge of its truth. ... The second, to divide each of the difficulties I examined into as many parts as possible and as may be required in order to solve them better. The third, to direct my thoughts in an orderly manner, beginning with the simplest and most easily known objects in order to ascend, little by little, to knowledge of the most complex. ... The last, to make enumerations so complete ... that I could be sure of leaving nothing out' (AT VI 18–19: CSM I 120).

The much-vaunted rules are, it must be said, disappointingly bland, and it is hard to see them as providing very much in the way of practical guidance for the philosopher-scientist. Descartes, however, explicitly disavowed any intention of providing a full exposition of his method in the *Discourse*; the title 'Discourse on the Method' was chosen, as he explained to Mersenne, to make it clear that he did 'not intend to teach the method, but only to discuss it' (letter of 27 February 1637, AT I 349: CSMK 53). The *Discourse* was, in fact, intended merely as a general 'discursive' introduction to the three essays, the *Optics*, *Meteorology* and *Geometry*, chosen to illustrate the method; the first step towards understanding the Cartesian method is thus to examine the specialized treatises where he unfolds his mathematically-based conception of scientific knowledge (*see* GEOMETRY; LIGHT; COLOUR; MATHEMATICS; KNOWLEDGE). Two important general features of the method do, however, emerge from the account presented in the *Discourse*. First, in the continuation of the first of the four 'rules' of the method, quoted above, we find the recommendation 'to include nothing more in my judgements than what is presented to the mind so clearly and distinctly that I have no occasion to call it into doubt' (loc. cit.; for the central importance, in Descartes' account of knowledge, of restricting our judgements in this way *see* CLARITY AND DISTINCTNESS). Second, the remaining three rules all relate in one way or another to a further Cartesian notion which is just as fundamental as those of clarity and distinctness, namely that of order. As is made clear in the next paragraph following the introduction of the rules of method, Descartes' main inspiration here is the method of the geometers. Euclid began with simple, self-evident axioms, and proceeded by an unbroken chain of reasoning to the derivation of more complex results; it was Descartes' belief that the philosophy practised in his day was defective precisely because such methodical order was seldom observed, and hence, instead of a systematic attempt to uncover the truth, it all too often degenerated into sterile and irresolvable debates (cf. AT VI 8: CSM I 114–5). Inquiries into the nature of man, for example, typically began with the Aristotelian definition – 'man is a rational animal'; yet to begin in this way, as Descartes later observed in his dramatic dialogue *The Search for Truth*, is to be drawn into a maze from which there can be no escape:

'for two further questions at once arise – what is an animal, and what is rational? If, to explain the first, we reply that an animal is a "living and sentient being", and that living is an "animate body" and body a "corporeal substance", these questions, like the branches of a family tree, will rapidly multiply, and the result will be pure verbiage which will elucidate nothing' (AT X 516: CSM II 410). Descartes' insistence on order, on 'beginning with the simplest and most easily known objects', would, he hoped, lead to a wholly different style of scientific inquiry, one based on clear and self-evident first principles. The prescription is clear enough, but the identification of the required principles is far from unproblematic.

See also CERTAINTY; CIRCLE, CARTESIAN; INTUITION; KNOWLEDGE.

mind and body   Descartes uses the term 'mind' (French *esprit*, Latin *mens*) or 'soul' (French *âme*, Latin *anima*), to refer to the conscious, thinking self – 'this "I" by which I am what I am', as he puts it in the *Discourse* (AT VI 33: CSM I 127). Later, in the *Meditations*, he develops this conception more fully: 'What am I then?', he asks in the Second Meditation, and answers: 'I am in the strict sense only a thing that thinks (*res cogitans*), that is, I am a mind or intelligence, or intellect, or reason' (*mens, sive animus, sive intellectus, sive ratio*, AT VII 27: CSM II 18). Subsequently, the definition of 'thought' is widened to include volitional as well as intellectual activity: 'What am I then? A thing that thinks. What is that? A thing that doubts, understands, affirms, denies, is willing, is unwilling...' (AT VII 28: CSM II 19; in this passage, imagining and having sensory perceptions are also tacked on to the list of what a 'thinking thing' does, but these last two faculties later turn out, in the Sixth Meditation, to require treatment in a special category of their own; *see* IMAGINATION and SENSATION). The central fact to emerge, by the end of the *Meditations*, about the intellectual and volitional activities which Descartes classifies under the general label of 'thought', is that they belong to a substance which is entirely separate from the body. 'On the one hand, I have a clear and distinct idea of myself in so far as I am simply a thinking, non-extended thing; and on the other hand I have a clear and distinct idea of body in so far as this is simply an extended, non-thinking thing' (Sixth Meditation, AT VII 78: CSM II 54; *see* BODY and DUALISM).

Descartes' thesis of the incorporeality of the mind, its essential distinctness from the body, is among his most striking and controversial doctrines. Although he seems to have been drawn to the thesis for a variety of reasons (*see*, for example, LANGUAGE), his purely metaphysical arguments for that thesis are weak. In the first place, he suggests that his ability to doubt that he has a body, while being unable to doubt that he exists, shows that 'he is a substance whose whole essence or nature is to think, and which does not require any place or material thing in order to exist, and ... would not fail to be what it is, even if the body did not exist' (*Discourse*, Part IV, AT VI 33: CSM I 127). This argument is unsatisfactory, since my ability to imagine myself without a body may simply be due to ignorance of my own true nature; if I knew more, I might, for all the argument has shown, come to see that the supposition of continued existence without the body was incoherent. The Cartesian programme of systematic doubt, leading to the proposition COGITO ERGO SUM, does indeed seem to show that thinking cannot be 'separated' from me even by the most extreme application of that programme (AT VII 27: CSM II 18); but it does not show that my essence consists *only* in thinking where the word 'only' excludes everything else that could be said to belong to my nature (compare the objection made by a contemporary critic of the *Discourse*, which Descartes discusses in the Preface to the *Meditations*, AT VII 8: CSM II 7). Descartes himself acknowledged that the argument in the *Discourse* was inadequate, but all he can provide to supplement it in the *Meditations* is the claim that I have a 'clear and distinct' (and therefore divinely underwritten) conception of myself as a thinking thing, without extension, and of body as an extended thing without thought (Sixth Meditation, AT VII 78: CSM II 54). The problem with this, as Descartes' acute critic Antoine Arnauld pointed out, is that even if God underwrites our perceptions, the ability clearly to perceive X without Y does not entail that Y is in reality distinct from X. Someone ignorant of geometry might clearly perceive some of the essential properties of a right-angled triangle without perceiving that it necessarily has the property that the square drawn on its hypotenuse will equal the squares on its other sides; similarly, Descartes' reasoning from his clear perceptions about the nature of thought seems vulnerable to the possibility that a chain of connections, unperceived by him, would reveal that the body is, after all, essential for thought to occur (cf. Fourth Objections, AT VII 202–3: CSM II 142). Descartes has one final argument for the 'real distinction' between mind and body, namely that body, unlike thought, is always divisible (AT VII 86: CSM II 59); but the premise of the essential indivisibility of thought, even if accepted, does not entail the conclusion that the thing or substance which is doing the thinking is itself indivisible (nor is the essential DIVISIBILITY of matter itself entirely uncontroversial).

To meet the objection of Arnauld, referred to above, Descartes would, it seems, have to show not just that I have a clear conception of thinking substance apart from extended substance, but also that I have a clear conception of thinking substance as incompatible with, or logically excluding, extended substance (cf. Fourth Replies, AT VII 226: CSM II 159). This, however, is very difficult for him to show, for the reason that our nature as human beings does seem to involve an inextricable combination of both mental and physical attributes. Once again, it was Arnauld who challenged

Descartes on this point: would Descartes really want to 'go back to the Platonic view that nothing corporeal belongs to our essence, and that man is merely a rational soul and the body merely a vehicle for the soul – a view which gives rise to the definition of man as a "soul which makes use of a body"?' (AT VII 203: CSM II 143). Although Descartes was reluctant to put the matter this way, his position does seem to boil down to this, at any rate as far as pure intellection and volition are concerned; but when it comes to sensory attributes – seeing, hearing, feeling hungry, experiencing pain and the like – our connection with the body seems far more direct and intimate: we are, as Descartes himself acknowledged, 'not merely lodged in the body like a sailor in a ship, but very closely joined and as it were intermingled with it' (AT VII 81: CSM II 56; *see* ANGEL and HUMAN BEING). The relationship between the supposedly mutually exclusive substances, mind and body, is thus intensely problematic in Descartes; although incompatible, and of entirely distinct natures, they are 'joined and intermingled' – Descartes later uses the even stronger term 'united' – to form a sentient human creature.

The notion of the 'substantial union' between mind and body was developed further by Descartes in his correspondence with Princess Elizabeth, who asked him 'how the soul, being only a thinking substance, can determine the body to perform voluntary actions'; Descartes replied 'the question your Highness poses seems to me the one which can most properly be put to me in view of my published writings' (letter of 21 May 1643, AT II 664: CSMK 217). In a later letter he explained that his arguments hitherto had been largely concerned to establish the *distinction* between the soul and the body, but that, notwithstanding that distinction, each of us also has a notion of the *union* between soul and body 'which he invariably experiences within himself without philosophizing'. 'Everyone feels', Descartes went on, 'that he is a single person with both body and thought so related by nature that the thought can move the body and feel the things which happen to it' (letter of 28 June 1643, AT III 694: CSMK 228). The resulting paradox in the Cartesian system is that reason tells us one thing (the distinction), while experience tells us quite the opposite (the union), and yet both are correct. Descartes none the less continued to maintain that all the relevant facts could be accommodated within his classificatory schema: 'I recognize only two ultimate classes of things, first, *intellectual or thinking things*, and secondly, *material things, i.e. those which pertain to extended substance or body*. Perception, volition and all the modes both of perceiving and willing are referred to thinking substance, while to extended substance belong size, that is extension in length, breadth and depth, shape, motion, position, divisibility of component parts, and the like. But we also experience within ourselves certain other things which must *not be referred to mind alone or to body alone*. These arise ... from the *intimate union of our mind with the body*, and include, first, appetites like hunger and thirst, second, emotions or passions of the mind which do not consist of thought alone, such as anger, joy, sadness and love, and finally all sensations, such as those of pain, pleasure, light, colours, sound, smells, tastes, heat, hardness and other tactile qualities' (*Principles*, Part I, art. 48, emphasis supplied). The task of providing a full account of all the items within the third category, that relating to the substantial union of mind and body, is tackled in detail in Descartes' final major work, the *Passions of the Soul* (1649). But although that work provides a wealth of physiological and psychological detail on the circumstances in which the appetites, emotions and passions arise, there is little attempt to dissolve the fundamental philosophical difficulty of how two alien substances can unite to make such events possible.

In the *Passions*, Descartes frequently talks in a way which suggests both that the mind has causal powers *vis-à-vis* the body (e.g. it can cause the body to move), and that the body has causal powers with respect to the soul (e.g. passions and feelings are 'excited' by corporeal events in the blood and nervous system; compare also the account of memory in Part I, art. 42 (AT XI 360: CSM I 344). Descartes manages to supply a host of mechanisms whereby movements, once initiated in the PINEAL GLAND, can be transferred to other parts of the brain and body; but he does not seem to tackle the central issue of how an incorporeal soul can initiate such movements in the first place. And the same problem will apply when the causal flow is in the other direction. Descartes describes the physiological mechanisms whereby bodily stimuli of various kinds cause changes in the nervous system and brain which 'dispose' the soul to feel emotions like anger or fear (see, for example, *Passions*, Part I, art. 39). But he does not explain how mere brain events, however complex their physiological genesis, could have the power to arouse or excite events in the mental realm.

There is some evidence that Descartes simply did not accept that the idea of a causal transaction between alien substances was problematic. Compare the letter to Clerselier of 12 January 1646: 'the supposition that, if soul and body are two substances whose nature is different, this prevents them interacting, is one that is false and cannot in any way be proved' (AT IXA 213: CSM II 275; cf. letter to 'Hyperaspistes' of August 1641, AT III 424: CSMK 190). None the less, there are many other passages where Descartes seems to presuppose that causal transactions should be in some sense transparent to the human intellect (*see* CAUSE). Yet no such transparency could be available in the mind–body interactions described in the *Passions of the Soul*. Transparent connections can be unfolded so long as we remain within the realm of physiology, and trace how the stimulation of a sense-organ generates changes in the 'animal spirits', which in turn cause modifications in the movements of the pineal gland. But at the end of the story, there will be a mental event which simply 'arises' in the soul. Mind–body relations thus fall outside the scope of Descartes' 'normal' conception of science; the relevant events are not causal transactions in the strict sense, but more in the nature of divinely decreed correlations; for this 'occasionalist' theme in Descartes, *see* IMAGES.

It may be seen from all of the above that there are three main classes of problems which arise out of Descartes' account of mind and body. The first group concerns the validity of his arguments for the substantial distinction between mind and body; the second concerns the reconciling of that distinction, once established, with the thesis of the 'substantial union' of mind and body; and the third concerns the structure of the account Descartes provides of that union, and, in particular, the nature of the psychophysical transactions involved.

For an additional, and rather different set of problems, connected with the theological motivation for Descartes' account of the mind, *see* SOUL, IMMORTALITY OF.

mode Everything that can be attributed to body is for Descartes merely a 'mode' or modification of extension; thus to attribute a given shape to some object is simply to say that it is extended in a certain fashion (in length, breadth and depth). In the same way, the various modifications of consciousness which occur when we understand or will or imagine something are described by Descartes as 'modes' of thinking (see *Principles*, Part I, art. 53). The label 'mode', like the more familiar English term 'modification', presupposes, when applied to some object, that the object in question is subject to variation or change (e.g. from one thought to another, or from one shape to another); thus the celebrated piece of wax in the Second Meditation is perceived to be essentially just 'something extended, flexible and changeable' – capable of taking on any one of an indefinitely large number of different shapes (AT VII 31: CSM II 21). 'Hence', Descartes observed, 'we do not strictly speaking say that there are modes . . . in God, but simply attributes, since in the case of God, any variation is unintelligible' (*Principles*, Part I, art. 56).

Following the scholastics, Descartes distinguished a 'modal' distinction (a distinction either between a mode and the substance of which it is a mode, or between two modes of the same substance – *Principles*, Part I, art. 61) from a 'real' distinction (cf. DISTINCTION). Hence in *Principles*, Part I, art. 64, he writes that 'thought and extension may be taken as modes of a substance, in so far as one and the same mind is capable of having many different thoughts, and one and the same body, with its quantity unchanged, may be extended in many different ways (e.g. at one moment it may be greater in length and smaller in breadth or depth, and a little later, by contrast, it may be greater in breadth and smaller in length). The distinction between thought or extension and the substance will then be a modal one; and our understanding of them will be capable of being just as clear and distinct as our understanding of the substance itself, provided they are regarded not as substances, that is, things which are separate from other things, but simply as modes of things. . . . If we attempted to consider them apart from the substances in which they inhere, we would be regarding them as things which subsisted in their own right, and would thus be confusing the ideas of a mode and a substance' (AT VIIIA 31: CSM I 215–6).

See also SUBSTANCE.

morality   Although Descartes is not widely thought of as a moral philosopher, he unequivocally declared in the 1647 French preface to the *Principles of Philosophy* that the construction of a perfect moral system – *la plus parfaite morale* – was to be the crowning aim of his philosophy: 'by "morals" I understand the highest and most perfect moral system which presupposes a complete knowledge of the other sciences, and is the ultimate level of wisdom (*le dernier degré de la sagesse*)' (AT IXB 14: CSM I 186). Ten years earlier, in the *Discourse on the Method*, he had approached the subject in a far more tentative way, aiming to articulate only a 'provisional moral code', designed to provide temporary lodging during the reconstruction of the edifice of knowledge. The *code provisoire* consists of four maxims, the first of which is cautiously conservative in tone: 'to obey the laws and customs of my country, holding constantly to the religion in which by God's grace I had been instructed from my childhood, and governing myself in all other matters according to the most moderate and least extreme opinions – the opinions commonly accepted in practice by the most sensible of those I should have to live with' (AT VI 23: CSM I 122). The passive obedience to existing law which is advocated in the first part of this maxim corresponds to a consistently quietist streak in Descartes' character. He aimed to be a 'spectator rather than an actor in the comedy of life' (AT VI 28: CSM I 125), and seems to have been quite sincere in his readiness to leave the conduct of affairs of state to those who were called to high office by birth or circumstance. 'If I do not publish my views of morals', he later wrote to Chanut in 1647, 'it is because I believe it is the proper function of sovereigns, and those authorized by them, to concern themselves with regulating the behaviour of others' (letter of 20 November 1647, AT V 86–7: CSMK 326). A similar desire to avoid controversy characterizes Descartes' approach to 'the religion of his childhood' (for some of the special problems which arise in this area, however, *see* FAITH and THEOLOGY).

Descartes' second maxim is based on the need to continue functioning in ordinary life, despite the operation, in theoretical matters, of the Cartesian programme of systematic doubt. To avoid 'being indecisive in [his] actions while reason obliged [him] to be so in [his] judgements', he resolves 'to be as firm and decisive as possible in my actions, and to follow even the most doubtful opinions, once I had adopted them, with no less constancy than if they had been quite certain' (AT VI 24: CSM I 123). The background to this rather heavy-handed insistence that the method of doubt need not lead to practical indecision may be found in the sceptical movements of the early seventeenth century: the intellectual fashion for Pyrrhonian arguments (*see* DOUBT) had led many to fear, as Descartes puts it in a letter, 'that universal doubt may produce great indecision and even moral chaos' (letter of April 1638, AT II 35: CSMK 97). Descartes is extremely careful to dissociate himself from such extreme Pyrrhonism: 'while it continues, the doubt should be kept in check and employed solely in connection with the contemplation of the truth. As far as ordinary life is concerned, the chance for action would frequently pass us by if we waited till we could free ourselves from doubts, and so we are often compelled to accept what is merely probable' (*Principles of Philosophy*, Part I, art. 3).

The third and fourth maxims of Descartes' provisional code record his resolve 'always to try to master himself rather than fortune' and to choose a way of live devoted to 'cultivating reason' and continuing the path of self-instruction' (AT VI 25 and 27: CSM I 123–4). These maxims seem broader in scope than the first two, and appear to apply not just to the temporary need to carry on with ordinary life while philosophical speculation is in progress, but to the long-term project of securing a fulfilled and worthwhile existence. We see, in other words, the beginnings of Descartes' grand project for the 'perfect moral system' which was to be among the final fruits of his philosophy. The third maxim, which clearly bears witness to the Stoic ideas which influenced much of Descartes' moral thinking, tell us 'to aim to change our desires rather than the order of the world' and to 'become accustomed to believing that nothing lies in our power except our thoughts, so that after doing our best in dealing with things external to us, whatever we fail to achieve is absolutely impossible as far as we are concerned' (AT VI 25: CSM I 123). Unhappiness, on the Stoic view, consists of a tension between the inner world of our aspirations and the outer world of external circumstances; to live well is to live 'in accordance with nature', but since the external world is largely beyond our ability to alter, fulfilment consists in a state of inner detachment and acceptance of what cannot be altered. These themes are ones which Descartes was to return to in his correspondence with Elizabeth in the mid 1640s, where he examined the teachings of the Roman Stoic Seneca, whose *De Vita Beata* he had proposed to the Princess as a text for discussion. 'The things which can give us supreme contentment can be divided into two classes: those which depend on us, like virtue and wisdom, and those which do not, like honours and riches. . . . Everyone can make himself content without any external circumstance provided . . . first, he employs his mind as well as he can to discover what he should do in all the circumstances of life . . . second, he has a firm resolution to carry out whatever reason recommends . . . and third, he bears in mind that . . . all the good things one does not possess are equally outside one's power, and hence becomes accustomed not to desire them' (letter of 4 August 1645, AT IV 265: CSMK 257–8).

The reference in the passage just quoted to following the recommendations of reason is of some importance. The good life, as Descartes conceives it, is not merely a life of resigned acceptance, but a life guided by the inner light of the intellect. 'When virtue is unenlightened by the intellect', Descartes wrote to Elizabeth, 'it can be false . . . and in such a case the contentment which it brings us is not solid' (AT IV 267: CSMK 258). The science of morality, for Descartes, is an integral part of the 'tree of knowledge' (AT IXB 14: CSM I 186); the moral philosopher aims at a rational understanding of our own human nature and its limitations, so as to bring the practical benefit of solid and lasting contentment. The most important aspect of our nature, which it is the business of the moral philosopher to understand, has to do with the physiological basis and the psychological dynamics of the emotions that arise in the soul when it is affected by the body; this topic is the main subject of Descartes' final work, Les Passions de l'âme, and it is here that he comes closest to offering a set of practical prescriptions for the good life. The key to such a life turns out to be the use of reason in understanding how the body works, and devising techniques for the mastery of the passions (cf. AT XI 369–70: CSM I 348; see PASSIONS for further details, and also for some important qualifications regarding the Stoic orientation of Descartes' approach to morality).

motion Cartesian science aims to base an explanation of all physical phenomena on a conception of matter as extension, plus the assumption that the universe contains a fixed quantity of motion (measured as the product of extension times speed). Descartes tried to avoid providing a 'formal definition' of motion in the manner of the scholastics, since he believed that the idea of a body moving from place to place was in itself perfectly clear, and could only be made more obscure by further elaboration. 'Motion in the ordinary sense of the term', he wrote in the *Principles*, 'is simply the *action by which a body travels from one place to another*; by "motion" I mean local motion, for my thought encompasses no other kind, and hence I do not think that any other kind should be imagined to exist in nature' (Part II, art. 24; cf. Part I, art. 69). Commenting earlier on the traditional accounts based on Aristotle, he had scathingly observed that 'to render motion in some way intelligible, [the scholastics] have not yet been able to explain it more clearly than in these terms: *Motus est actus entis in potentia, prout in potentia est*. For me these words are so obscure that I am compelled to leave them in Latin, because I cannot interpret them – and in fact the sentence "Motion is the actuality of a potential being in so far as it is potential" is no clearer for being translated' (*The World*, ch. 6, AT XI 39: CSM I 94). The traditional definition (found in Aristotle's *Physics*, Book III, ch. 1) amounted, in Descartes' view, to a series of 'magic words which have a hidden meaning beyond the grasp of human intelligence', and simply 'generated difficulties where none exist', illustrating the folly of attempting to define what was already quite unproblematic (*Regulae*, Rule XII, AT X 426: CSM I 49).

By focusing on the supposedly simple concept of 'local' motion, or movement from place to place, Descartes aimed to avoid what he took to be the chimerical idea of absolute motion: 'the same thing can be said to be changing and not changing its place at the same time, and similarly the same thing can be said to be moving or not moving – for example a man sitting on board a ship which is leaving port considers himself to be moving relative to the shore which he regards as fixed, but does not think of himself as moving relative to the ship'; hence motion is simply 'the transfer of one piece of matter, or one body, from the vicinity of the other bodies which are in immediate contact with it, and which are regarded as being at rest, to the vicinity of other bodies' (*Principles*, Part II, arts 24 and 25). There is, however, a major problem in Descartes' account, namely that it presupposes our ability to identify different 'pieces of matter' which change location relative to one another; but the Cartesian universe, as Descartes frequently insists, is simply a homogeneous three-dimensional stuff – 'a real, perfectly solid body which uniformly fills the entire length, depth and breadth of space' (AT XI 33: CSM I 91). Even the talk of 'space' is in fact misleading, since Descartes denies any possibility of a VACUUM: 'there is no real difference between space and corporeal substance' (*Principles*, Part II, art. 11). Given these premises, it seems that the only way of individuating portions of matter is by reference to the fact that some particles are moving at a greater or lesser speed than others – and this indeed is how Descartes distinguishes his 'three elements' (*Principles*, Part III, art. 52). But now we seem to have an explanatory circle: motion is the shifting of parcel X relative to parcel Y, but parcels of matter can only be individuated by reference to their being in motion relative to each other.

Descartes might deny that the circle is a vicious one, since even in a homogeneous medium we can detect relative movements – for example, in the way in which a faster-moving current of water is sometimes visible in the middle of a slow-moving river. To differentiate portions of matter, he notes, we do not have to posit any substantial or qualitative differences in the stuff of which they are made: there is no 'glue' binding together the parts of bodies apart from the simple fact that they are moving or at rest relative to each other (*Principles*, Part II, art. 55). But the treatment of motion as simply a 'MODE' of extended stuff, as Descartes put it, still leaves the question of how a dynamic universe can be derived from the simple idea of extension in length, breadth and depth. The Cartesian answer to this is to invoke the active power of God, who, by his initial creative act and by his subsequent conserving power, 'created matter, along with its motion and rest, and now, merely by his regular concurrence, preserves the same amount of motion and rest in the material universe as he put there in the beginning' (*Principles*, Part II, art. 36).

For more on the operation of Descartes' laws of motion, *see* CONSERVATION; INERTIA and LAWS OF NATURE.

music For Descartes' interest in music, and its relation to his general conception of science, *see* Introduction, p. 7, above; *see also* COMPENDIUM MUSICAE.

N

native intelligence   One of Descartes' consistently held theses is that the innate powers of the human mind, provided they are guided aright, will lead us to certain knowledge of the truth far more effectively than all the inherited learning of past ages. His earliest major work, the *Regulae ad directionem ingenii* (*c.* 1628) embodies, in its very title, this notion of the proper guidance of the *ingenium* – the 'native intelligence' or innate power of reason which each of us possesses. The Latin term has the same root as the words *genus* ('race', 'stock', 'birth' or 'descent'), and *generare* ('to procreate'), and thus is strongly suggestive of an inborn faculty or natural human ability. In the *Discourse on the Method* (1637), the same theme is taken up. The 'method' is that of 'rightly conducting one's reason', and the book opens with the assertion that 'good sense' (*le bon sens*) is the 'best distributed thing in the world': 'the power of judging well, and of distinguishing the true from the false – which is what we properly call 'good sense' or 'reason' – is naturally equal in all men' (AT VI 1: CSM I 111). Finally, in the unfinished dialogue *The Search for Truth by Means of the Natural Light* (written either around the time of the *Meditations* or possibly in the last year of Descartes' life), we are told that the ordinary untutored 'Everyman' ('Polyander'), who is guided by his own unprejudiced judgement, has a far better chance of understanding the truth than the sophisticated scholar ('Epistemon'), steeped in the learning of classical antiquity (AT X 502–3: CSM II 403). 'A good man is not required to know Greek and Latin' (ibid.), for 'the natural light alone, without any help from religion or philosophy, determines what opinions a good man should hold on any matter that may occupy his thought, and penetrates into the secrets of the most recondite sciences' (AT X 495: CSM I 400).

For Descartes' theory of innate knoweldge, *see* INNATENESS.

natural light   *see* INTUITION

natures   *see* SIMPLE NATURES

O

Objections and Replies   The publication of the *Meditations* in 1641 was notable for the inclusion of six sets of Objections from various critics, together with Descartes' Replies. Descartes, through his friend and literary editor Mersenne, had arranged for the manuscript of the *Meditations* to be circulated before publication, hoping that 'people make as many objections as possible – and the strongest ones they can find – so that the truth will stand out all the better' (letter of 28 January 1641, AT III 297: CSMK 172). The First Set of Objections are by Johannes Caterus (Johan de Kater), a priest from Alkmaar; they contain a number of criticisms of Descartes' proofs of the existence of God. The Second Set, compiled by Mersenne himself, raise several important difficulties, including the problem of the Cartesian CIRCLE; Descartes' Replies include an axiomatic presentation of his arguments for God's existence, 'arranged in geometrical fashion' (AT VII 160ff: CSM II 113ff.). The Third Set of Objections are by the English philosopher Thomas Hobbes, who had fled to France for political reasons in 1640; Hobbes criticizes, among other things, Descartes' theory of the mind and his account of the idea of God. The Fourth, and philosophically most sophisticated, Set of Objections are by the theologian and logician Antoine Arnauld, still under thirty at the time. As well as raising a number of 'points which may cause difficulty to the theologians' (including how the Cartesian account of matter may threaten the doctrine of transubstantiation: *see* FAITH, RELIGIOUS), Arnauld also presents a telling critique of Descartes' account of the distinction between mind and body. The Fifth and longest Set of Objections are by the neo-Epicurean philosopher Pierre Gassendi, who raises a host of difficulties, some of great importance, others closer to quibbles, relating to almost every stage of the argument in the *Meditations*. The Sixth Set consist of a number of disparate points, again compiled by Mersenne; Descartes' Replies include an interesting discussion of the physiological and cognitive elements involved in vision (AT VII 437f: CSM II 295f).

The second edition of the *Meditations* (1642) included a lengthy Seventh Set of Objections by the Jesuit Pierre Bourdin, which were for the most part extremely hostile in tone, and often deliberately malicious. In addition to his detailed Replies, Descartes defended himself further in the LETTER TO DINET.

All the Objections and Replies are in Latin; the title page of the *Meditations* calls them *Variae Objectiones doctorum virorum cum Responsionibus Authoris* ('Various Objections of learned men, with the Replies of the Author'). When the later French edition of the *Meditations* appeared in 1647, the volume included a French translation of the first six sets of Objections and Replies by Descartes' disciple, Claude Clerselier. It also included an extended Letter to Clerselier (dated 12 January 1646, AT IXA 202ff: CSM II 269ff) in which Descartes continued the debate with Gassendi, begun in the Fifth Objections and Replies, and taken further by Gassendi, who had published a fresh set of 'Instances' or counter-objections, in 1644.

objective reality   The term 'objective' is regularly contrasted by Descartes with the term 'formal'. An IDEA, according to Descartes, can be considered either from the psychological point of view, as a certain modification of consciousness, or from the point of view of its representational content; Descartes calls the former aspect the 'formal reality' of an idea, and the latter its 'objective reality'. 'The nature of an idea is such that of itself it requires no formal reality, except what it derives from my thought; but in order for a given idea to contain such and such objective reality, it must surely derive it from some cause . . .' (Third Meditation, AT VII 41: CSM II 28–9).

The distinction between formal and objective reality is applied by Descartes not only to ideas, but to entities or objects. In this case, 'formal' reality will be actual, extramental existence, while 'objective reality' will be merely existence in the mind as an object of the understanding. '[By the sun in so far as it has objective being in the intellect] I mean . . . the sun itself existing in the intellect – not of course formally existing, as it does in the heavens, but objectively existing, i.e. in the way in which objects normally are in the intellect. Now this mode of being is of course much less perfect than that possessed by things which exist outside the intellect, but it is not therefore simply nothing' (First Replies, AT VII 102–3: CSM II 74–5). In the *Principles of Philosophy*, Descartes uses the example of a highly intricate machine to illustrate his notion of 'objective' or representative reality: 'If someone has within himself the idea of a highly intricate machine, it would be fair to ask what was the cause of his possession of the idea: did he somewhere see such a machine made by someone else; or did he make such a close study of mechanics, or is his own ingenuity so great, that he was able to think it up on his own, even though he never saw it anywhere? All the intricacy which is contained in the idea merely objectively – as in a picture – must be contained in its cause, whatever its cause turns out to be; and it must be contained not merely objectively or representatively, but in actual reality' (Part I, art. 17; *see* TRADEMARK ARGUMENT). Descartes' use of the term 'objective' (which is, of course, wholly different from modern usage) is borrowed from the scholastics. Thus Suárez writes: 'An "objective" conception is the thing or concept which is strictly and immediately represented by means of the conception; for example, when we conceive of a man, the mental act we perform in order to conceive of the man is called the "formal concept", while the man cognitively represented by means of that act is called the "objective conception"' (*Metaphysical Disputations*, 2, 1, 1; in Gilson, *Index*, no. 80).

ontological argument   In the Fifth Meditation, Descartes argues that 'existence can no more be separated from the essence of God than the fact that its three angles equal two right angles can be separated from the essence of a triangle. . . . It is a contradiction to think of God (that is a supremely perfect being) lacking existence (that is, lacking a perfection)' (AT VII 66: CSM II 46; cf. *Principles*, Part I, art. 14). The actual term 'ontological argument' is due to Kant, who isolated a special kind of proof for God's existence where 'abstraction is made from all experience' and the existence of a supreme being is 'inferred *a priori* from concepts alone' (*Critique of Pure Reason* [1781], A591/B619); while not anticipating the label 'ontological', Descartes himself does none the less clearly distinguish his own *a priori* proof in the Fifth Meditation from the quite different *a posteriori*, or causal argument in the Third Meditation (AT V 153: CSMK 337; for the latter proof, *see* TRADEMARK ARGUMENT).

A version of the ontological argument had been advanced many centuries before Descartes by Anselm of Canterbury (1033–1109), who had argued that a being 'than which nothing greater can be conceived' must necessarily exist, not merely in our thought, but in reality (*Proslogion*, ch. III). Thomas Aquinas, had, however, decisively rejected this reasoning as invalid (*Summa theologiae*, Part I, Qu. 2, art. 1), and Descartes' critics were able to deploy fairly standard Thomist objections to his approach in the Fifth Meditation. Descartes argues that the very essence of God implies his existence: 'I am not free to think of God without existence, that is a supremely perfect being without a supreme perfection, as I am free to think of a horse without wings' (AT VII 67: CSM II 46; *see* ESSENCE and EXISTENCE). Descartes' Thomist critics aptly pointed out that 'Even if it is granted that a supremely perfect being carries the implication of existence in virtue of its very title, it still does not follow that the existence in question is anything actual in the real world; all that follows is that the concept of existence is inseparably linked to the concept of a supreme being' (First Objections, AT VII 99: CSM II 72). In other words, the argument at best yields the hypothetical conclusion that *if* there is anything in the universe which meets the definition of a 'supremely perfect being', it would have to exist; but there is nothing to show that the antecedent of this conditional is in fact satisfied. Descartes' only reply to this is to claim that 'in the idea of a supremely perfect being the mind recognizes not merely the possible and contingent existence which belongs to the ideas of all the other things which it distinctly perceives, but utterly necessary and eternal existence' (*Principles*, Part I, art. 14). But although it may be inconsistent to suppose that a supreme being enjoys merely temporary existence, or that its existence depends on mere contingency, this fails to show, once again, that there is anything which qualifies for the title of a supreme being (so defined) in the first place.

For other criticisms of the argument, see Gassendi's comments in the Fifth Objections (AT VII 323ff: CSM II 224–7). For the later, and more sophisticated objections of Immanuel Kant, see Kant, *Critique of Pure Reason*, A598/ B626.

Optics The *Optics*, or, to translate the title more literally, the *Dioptrics* (*La Dioptrique*), was the first of the three specimen essays which Descartes published with the *Discourse* in 1637. The essay is divided into ten chapters, or 'Discourses', dealing respectively with (1) light, (2) refraction, (3) the eye, (4) the senses in general, (5) the images formed on the back of the eye, (6) vision, (7) the means of perfecting vision, (8) the shapes of transparent bodies which refract light, (9) the description of telescopes, and (10) the method of cutting lenses.

For the philosophical importance of the essay, and significance of the term 'Dioptrics', *see* LIGHT; *see also* IMAGES and MATHEMATICS.

P

pain Feelings of pain are, for Descartes, a prime example of those 'confused perceptions' which must be not be referred either to the mind alone, or to the body alone, but which arise from 'the close and intimate union of the mind with the body' (*Principles*, Part I, art. 48). The full list of such confused perceptions includes, first, appetites like hunger and thirst (cf. Sixth Meditation, AT VII 81: CSM II 56), second, emotions or passions 'such as those of anger, joy, sadness and love' (*Principles*, Part I, art. 48; *see* PASSIONS), and finally, 'all the sensations such as those of pain, pleasure, light, colours, sounds, smells, tastes, heat, hardness and other tactile qualities' (ibid.). One of the principal points Descartes is at pains to stress about such sensations is that there need be no resemblance between, on the one hand, the IDEAS that arise in the soul, and, on the other hand the events in the external world, and in the nervous system, that give rise to the relevant conscious experiences. (For the general outlines of the Cartesian account, *see* COLOUR and IMAGES. See also MIND AND BODY).

In the Sixth Meditation, Descartes points out that the sensation of pain is a valuable indicator, bestowed on us by 'nature', of what conduces to the health and welfare of the body (AT VII 76ff: CSM II 52ff.). But he also stresses that it is easy for us to be misled by such sensations, if we take them as 'reliable touchstones for immediate judgements about the essential nature of the bodies located outside us' (AT VII 83: CSM II 57–8). The need for caution in evaluating the data of sensation is a consistent theme in Descartes' philosophy, and it is a subject which he discusses in considerable detail in his early treatise, *Le Monde*: 'Everyone knows that the ideas of tickling and of pain, which are formed in our mind on the occasion of our being touched by external bodies, bear no resemblance to these bodies. Suppose we pass a feather gently over the lips of a child who is falling asleep, and he feels himself being tickled. Do you think the idea of tickling which he conceives resembles anything present in this feather? A soldier returns from battle; in the heat of combat he might have been wounded without being aware of it. But now, as he begins to cool off, he feels pain and believes himself wounded. We call a surgeon, who examines the soldier after we remove his armour, and we find in the end that what he was feeling was nothing but a buckle or strap caught under his armour, which was pressing on him and causing him discomfort. If his sense of touch, in making him feel this strap, had imprinted an image of it in his mind, there would have been no need for the surgeon to inform him of what he was feeling' (AT XI 6: CSM I 82; compare also the account of the feelings of warmth, and then of pain, produced by a fire, depending on the distance between object and perceiver, AT VII 83: CSM II 57). Examples of this sort were in fact fairly common in the seventeenth century (cf. Galileo, *Il Saggiatore*, 1623). Descartes draws three principal conclusions: first, that scholastic theories of sensory perception, which posited the transmission from object to observer of an INTENTIONAL FORM, have to be abandoned; second, that the nature of our sensory awareness has to be explained by reference to a divinely ordained institution whereby brain states give rise to wholly distinct conscious experiences in the soul (*see* GOD); and third, that 'the nature of matter, or body considered in general, consists not in its being something which is hard, or heavy or coloured, or which affects the senses in any way, but simply in its being something which is extended in length, breadth and depth' (*Principles*, Part I, art. 4; cf. EXTENSION).

passions In analysing the functions of the soul or thinking self, Descartes made a distinction between its actions and its passions. 'Those which I call its actions are all our volitions, for we experience them as proceeding directly from our soul, and seeming to depend on it alone. On the other hand, the various perceptions or modes of knowledge present in us may be called its "passions" in a general sense, for it is often not our soul which makes them such as they are, and the soul always receives them from the things that are represented by them' (*Passions of the Soul*, art. 17). Passions in the general sense of perceptions are then themselves divided: some (like the apprehension of some intellectual object) are, despite their passive or 'receptive' nature, directly initiated by the soul, when we direct our attention to the object in question (art. 20); others are more truly 'passions' in the strict etymological sense of things that 'happen to' the soul, being caused by the body without any involvement of the will.

Such mental happenings, caused by the body, are of three types: first, there are sensory perceptions referred to objects outside us ('as when we see the light of a torch, or hear the sound of a bell': art. 23); second, there are internal sensory impressions which we refer to our own bodies (such as hunger, thirst and pain: art. 24); and lastly, there are the perceptions we refer to the soul itself, such as 'feelings of joy, anger and the like' (art. 25). It is passions of this third type, which Descartes calls 'passions in the restricted sense', which are the main subject of *Passions de l'âme*: 'it is only this latter type which I have undertaken to explain here under the title "Passions of the Soul"' (ibid.).

Passions, in this restricted sense of emotions which arise in the soul when it is acted upon by the body, are divided by Descartes into six principal or 'primitive' kinds – wonder, love, hatred, desire, joy and sadness (art. 69). These categories are 'primitive' in the sense that all the other emotions are taken by Descartes to be analysable as modifications or combinations of the main six; thus anger is analysed as a violent kind of hatred combined with a desire involving self-love (art. 199). A proper understanding of the nature of the passions hinges, for Descartes, on a thorough investigation of physiology, since the passions are 'caused, maintained and strengthened' by disturbances in the heart, the blood and the nervous system (art. 46). The 'chief use of wisdom' thus lies in its teaching us how to be masters of the passions, as Descartes explains in the concluding sections of the *Passions of the Soul* (Part III, art. 212). Will alone is not sufficient, since we cannot directly control the relevant physiological changes in our bodies – any more than we can directly control any other events in the physical universe. But what we can do, by careful training, is to set up appropriate habits which should enable us, by the performance of actions that *are* within our power, to lessen or modify the effects of those changes. Just as animals, who lack reason, can be trained by careful repetition of the appropriate stimuli to behave in a controlled and orderly fashion, so we, who possess reason, can condition our physiological reflexes in such a way that the passions will be brought under the service of reason. 'Even those who have the weakest souls could acquire absolute mastery over all their passions, if only they employed sufficient ingenuity in training and guiding them' (art. 50).

Two aspects of Descartes' account of the passions are especially noteworthy. The first, already alluded to, is the extent to which the occurrence of the passions is, for Descartes, determined by ingrained patterns of physiological response. In art. 127 of the *Passions of the Soul*, Descartes refers to the work of the sixteenth-century scholar Vives, who had cited an example of a morbid condition in which laughter was aroused by certain foods (Vives, *De Anima et Vita* [1538], ch. 3). Descartes himself, in the correspondence, instances several cases of what we would now call 'conditioning', such as that of the dog that runs away on hearing the violin, if it has been previously 'whipped to the sound of music' (AT I 134: CSMK 20). A case from his own experience is cited in a letter to Chanut of 6 June 1647: 'The objects which strike our senses by means of the nerves move certain parts of our brain and there make certain folds ... the place where the folds were made has a tendency to be folded again in the same manner by another object resembling even incompletely the original object. For instance, when I was a child, I loved a girl of my own age who had a slight squint (*une fille de mon âge qui était un peu louche*). The impression made by sight in my brain when I looked at her cross eyes became connected to the simultaneous impression arousing in me the passion of love, that for a long time after when I saw cross-eyed persons, I

felt a special inclination to love them simply because they had this defect'
(AT V 54: CSMK 322. For 'folds in the brain', cf. *Conversation with Burman*,
AT V 150: CSMK 336). Because human beings are not pure disembodied
souls, but inextricably united with the body (*see* HUMAN BEING and MIND AND
BODY), our welfare is intimately bound up with these psycho-physical
patterns of response. But since we have the use of reason, enabling us to
establish the causes of such correlations, we have the power to modify the
conditioning process, and set up habits or dispositions which conduce to the
virtuous life. Drawing on the traditional Aristotelian account of virtue as a
ἕξις, a regular disposition of the soul (*Nicomachean Ethics*, Book II), Descartes plugs in his own conception of systematic scientific understanding,
to show how we can achieve genuine power even over those aspects of our
nature that are, initially, not under conscious control at all; thus the science
of morality is indeed one of the branches of that unified tree of knowledge of
which physics is the trunk (AT XIB 14: CSM I 186). For Descartes' use of
the term *habitude* ('disposition'), from the Latin *habitus* (the standard scholastic translation of Aristotle's ἕξις) *see Passions*, arts 54 and 161, and the letter to
Elizabeth of 15 September 1645, AT V 296: CSMK 267).

The second important feature of Descartes' account is that, despite his
debt to the Stoics (*see* MORALITY), his view of the passions diverges from the
typical Stoic position in being by no means entirely negative. The passions
are not simply a harmful aspect of our nature that is to be mastered and
suppressed; if properly channelled, they are the key to authentic human
flourishing. The final sections of the *Passions of the Soul* thus end on an
optimistic note, which holds out the hope, notwithstanding Descartes' official
dualistic view of the relation between mind and body, of a blueprint for
fulfilment that is specifically tailored to the needs of embodied creatures of
flesh and blood. 'The soul can have pleasures of its own. But the pleasures
common to it and the body depend entirely on the passions, so that persons
whom the passions can move most deeply are capable of enjoying the
sweetest pleasures of this life. It is true that they may also experience the
most bitterness when they do not know how to put these passions to good
use, and when fortune works against them. But the chief use of wisdom lies in
its teaching us to be the masters of our passions, and to control them with
such skill that the evils which they cause are quite bearable, and even
become a source of joy' (art. 212).

Passions of the Soul   Written in French, and published in Amsterdam and
Paris in 1649 under the title *Les Passions de l'âme*, this was the last philosophical work Descartes composed. In his correspondence with Princess Elizabeth
in the early 1640s, Descartes had been asked by the Princess to give an
account of 'the soul's actions and passions in the body'; Elizabeth had

professed herself unable to understand how 'an immaterial thing has the capacity to move and be moved by the body' (20 June 1643, AT III 685). In 1646, Descartes sent Elizabeth a small 'treatise on the passions' which he later expanded to form the final version of the book. The *Passions* is divided (like the *Principles of Philosophy*) into a large number of small articles; there are 212 in all. The first fifty articles, comprising Part I of the work, deal with 'The Passions in General'; Part II (articles 51–148) deals with 'The Number and Order of the Passions', and treats of the six 'primitive passions' (wonder, love, hatred, desire, joy and sadness); Part III is devoted to 'Specific Passions', and also contains Descartes' account of the virtue of GENEROSITY. The *Passions* is a long work, and is of considerable philosophical importance, both because of the light it sheds on Descartes' mature views concerning the relationship between MIND AND BODY (*see also* HUMAN BEING), and also because it provides (together with the letters to Elizabeth) the fullest exposition of Descartes' thoughts on how life should be lived (*see* MORALITY).

For more on the book's subject matter, *see* PASSIONS.

perception   Although the term 'perception', in its modern usage, generally refers to sensory processes like vision and hearing, Descartes reserves the verb 'to perceive' (Latin *percipere*) for the purely mental apprehension of the intellect, as in the famous rule 'whatever I clearly and distinctly perceive is true' (AT VII 35: CSM II 24). (For the nature of such perception, *see* INTUITION and CLARITY AND DISTINCTNESS.) When he wishes to refer to activities like seeing and hearing, Descartes employs the quite different Latin verb *sentire* ('to sense' or 'to have sensory awareness'; for this notion, *see* SENSATION).

perfection   'Whatever I clearly and distinctly perceive as being real and true, and implying any perfection, is wholly contained in my idea of God' (Third Meditation, AT VII 46: CSM II 32). The notion of God as the 'sum of all perfections' is crucial for Descartes' version of the ONTOLOGICAL ARGUMENT. The contrast between the infinite perfection of God and the imperfection of the human mind is crucial for Descartes' causal proof of God's existence from the idea of God (*see* TRADEMARK ARGUMENT). Finally, the notion of God as 'supremely perfect and therefore who cannot be a deceiver on pain of contradiction' (AT VII 62: CSM II 43) is crucial for Descartes' account of the reliability of the human mind, and the explanation of ERROR.

For the extent to which humans are capable of understanding the concept of supreme perfection, *see* GOD and INFINITE.

phantom limb   There are several places where Descartes discusses in some detail the phenomenon now known to medical science as the 'phantom limb'.

The most detailed account, apparently based on his own personal observation, comes in the letter to the Dutch physician Plempius, dated 3 October 1637: 'I once knew a girl who had a serious wound in her hand, and had her whole arm amputated because of creeping gangrene. Whenever the surgeons approached her, they blindfolded her eyes so that she would be more tractable, and the place where her arm had been was covered with bandages, so that for some weeks she did not know that she had lost it. Meanwhile, she complained of feeling various pains in her fingers, wrist and forearm; this was obviously due to the conditions of the nerves in her arm which formerly led to her brain from those parts of her body' (AT I 420: CSMK 64). Descartes drew two main conclusions from his study of this phenomenon. The first is that sensation occurs only in the brain (ibid.), or, as he put it rather more precisely in the Sixth Meditation 'the mind is not immediately affected by all parts of the body, but only by the brain, or perhaps just by one small part of the brain' (Sixth Meditation, AT VII 86: CSM II 59; *see* 'COMMON SENSE' and PINEAL GLAND). The second is that the false beliefs of phantom limb patients, and others who suffer similarly misleading sensory data, are an inevitable result of the completely uniform psycho-physical laws ordained by the creator for the health of the body: 'Notwithstanding the immense goodness of God, the nature of man as a combination of mind and body is such that it is bound to mislead him from time to time ... for there may be some occurrence not in the limb, but in one of the other areas through which the nerves travel in their route from the limb to the brain, or even in the brain itself. ... The deception of the senses is natural, since a given motion in the brain must always produce the same sensation in the mind, and the origin of the motion in question is much more often going to be something which is hurting the limb, rather than something existing elsewhere' (AT VII 88: CSM II 61; other cases discussed include the chronic sensation of thirst felt by the patient with dropsy).

For more on Descartes' theory of divinely decreed psycho-physical laws, *see* COLOUR.

philosophy   The term 'philosophy' was commonly used in the seventeenth century to refer to what we should nowadays call natural science, and Descartes often uses the term in this sense – e.g. when describing the curriculum he studied at La Flèche (*Discourse*, Part I, AT VI 8: CSM I 114–15). But more frequently, he employs the word in a wider sense, to embrace the whole of the 'tree of knowledge', encompassing the metaphysical roots, the trunk of physics, and the branches representing the specific sciences, reducible to three main studies – medicine, mechanics and morals (AT IXB 14: CSM I 186). It is the latter, in particular, which he has in mind when he promises to replace the 'speculative philosophy' purveyed by the scholastics with a 'practical philosophy (*philosophie pratique*) which will make us 'lords and masters of nature' (AT VI 62: CSM I 142). Descartes himself provides a splendid summary of his conception of philosophy as a reliable and all-embracing discipline in his Preface to the 1647 French edition of the *Principles of Philosophy*: 'The word "philosophy" means the study of wisdom, and by "wisdom" is meant not only prudence in everyday affairs, but also a perfect knowledge of all the things that mankind is capable of knowing, both for the conduct of life and the preservation of health [*see* MORALITY and MEDICINE] and the discovery of all manner of skills. In order for this kind of knowledge to be perfect, it must be deduced from first causes; thus in order to set about philosophizing – and it is this activity to which the term "to philosophize" strictly refers – we must start with the search for first causes or principles. These principles must satisfy two conditions. First, they must be so clear and evident that the human mind cannot doubt their truth when it attentively concentrates on them; and secondly the knowledge of other things must depend on them, in the sense that the principles must be capable of being known without knowledge of other matters, but not vice versa. Next, in deducing from these principles the knowledge of things which depend on them, we must try to ensure that everything in the entire chain of deductions which we draw is very manifest' (AT IXB 2: CSM I 179–80).

See also KNOWLEDGE; INTUITION and DEDUCTION. For Descartes' view of the relation between philosophy, so conceived, and the truths of religion, *see* THEOLOGY.

physics Although Descartes frequently insists that a sound physics must be based on reliable metaphysical foundations, there are strong grounds for believing that the driving force in Descartes' philosophy was his interest in physics. He is reported to have observed that 'one should not devote too much effort to metaphysical questions . . . lest they draw the mind away too far from physical studies and make it unfit to pursue them. . . . Yet it is just these physical studies which it is most desirable for people to pursue, since they would yield abundant benefits for life' (AT V 165: CSMK 346; cf. AT VI 61–2: CSM I 142–3). There is abundant evidence in the correspondence that Descartes attached enormous importance to the scientific work, eventually incorporated in *Le Monde*, which would 'explain the whole of nature, that is to say the whole of physics' (AT I 70: CSMK 7). And the great bulk of his magnum opus, the *Principles of Philosophy*, was devoted to the formulation of physical theories, Part I alone being reserved for 'those parts of metaphysics which need to be known for physics' (AT V 165: CSMK 347). When announcing his physical programme to the world, Descartes laid great stress on its mathematical basis (cf. AT V 160: CSMK 343); in practice, however, many of his physical explanations involve mechanical analogies rather than strictly quantitative laws (*see* MATHEMATICS; LAWS OF NATURE and MACHINE).

For some of the more important specific topics in Cartesian physics, *see* CONSERVATION; INERTIA; COSMOLOGY; CREATION; EXTENSION; MOTION; SPACE.

pineal gland   In Descartes' tortuous account of the relation between MIND AND BODY, the pineal gland functions rather like a 'fax machine to the soul', to use the pejorative, but not entirely unfair, tag of a modern anti-Cartesian philosopher of mind (cf. D. Dennett, *Consciousness Explained*). 'We need to recognize', Descartes wrote in the *Passions of the Soul*, 'that although the soul is joined to the whole body, there is a certain part of the body where it exercises its functions more particularly than in all the others.... On carefully examining the matter, I think I have established that this part is not the heart, or the whole of the brain, but the innermost part of the brain, which is a certain very small gland situated in the middle of the brain's substance and above the passage through which the spirits in the brain's anterior cavities communicate with those in the posterior cavities' (art. 31). Descartes' chief argument for fastening on this 'small gland' (the pineal gland or *conarion*) is that 'there must necessarily be one place where the two images coming through the two eyes, or the two impressions coming from a single object through the double organs of any other sense, can come together in a single image or impression before reaching the soul, so that they do not present to it two objects instead of one' (art. 32). The presupposition of this bizarre argument is that sensory awareness comes about by the soul 'inspecting' an image which is literally imprinted on the gland. For the 'homuncular' conception of the soul which is implied here, *see* 'COMMON' SENSE.

Descartes observed in correspondence that a further argument for selecting the pineal gland as the seat of the soul was that the physical organ where the soul exercised its functions must be 'very mobile, so as to receive all the impressions coming from the senses, but must be movable only by the spirits transmitting these impressions' (to Mersenne, 21 April 1641, AT III 362: CSMK 180; cf. letter of 24 December 1640, AT III 263: CSMK 162). The reason for the lightness and mobility of the gland is that Descartes wishes the 'seat of the soul' to be sensitive to minute fluctuations in the ANIMAL SPIRITS which function as neural transmitters in his theory of the nervous system. A further reason, never made fully explicit, connects with the problem of the transmission of information not from body to soul but vice versa: Descartes may have felt that a light and highly mobile organ was better suited to respond to the volitions of an incorporeal thinking substance. It scarcely needs saying that this bizarre notion would hardly provide a solution to the problem of psycho-physical causation; if it is difficult to see how my immaterial soul can make my legs and arms move, it is not in principle any easier to see how it can generate impulses in my pineal gland. Nevertheless, in the *Treatise on Man*, Descartes comes close to saying that the rational soul, stationed in the gland like a 'fountain keeper' surveying the flow of water in an artificial system of pipes and conduits, may be able to direct the flow of spirits to one limb or another: 'when a rational soul is present in the [bodily] machine, it will have its principal seat in the brain, and reside there like the fountain keeper who must be stationed at the tanks to which the fountain's pipes return, if he wants to produce, or prevent, or change, their movements in some way' (AT XI 131: CSM I 101; cf. *Passions*, art. 12). To the Cartesians who, later in the century, claimed that such action of the soul upon the pineal gland was not a problem, since only the *direction* of the animal spirits was altered, not the overall quantity of motion in the body, Leibniz aptly replied that a proper understanding of the principles of conservation showed that to ascribe to the soul power to change the direction of physical particles was 'no less inexplicable and contrary to the order of things' (*Considerations on Vital Principles* [1705], translated in Loemker, *Leibniz, Philosophical Papers and Letters*, p. 587).

preconceived opinions   Descartes employs this as a quasi-technical term (in Latin *praejudicia*, literally 'prejudices') to refer to the ballast of often ill-thought-out beliefs which all of us carry around with us before we begin to philosophize. 'Since we began life as infants, and made various judgements concerning the things that can be perceived by the senses before we had the use of reason, there are many preconceived opinions which keep us from the knowledge of the truth. . . . The only way of freeing ourselves from these opinions is to make the effort, once in the course of our life, to doubt everything which we find to contain even the smallest suspicion of uncertainty' (*Principles of Philosophy*, opening article). The two great generators of preconceived opinion are, for Descartes, first, the reliance on tradition and authority instead of the natural light within each of us (cf. *Search for Truth*, AT X 495ff: CSM II 400ff., and letter to Voetius of May 1643, AT VIIIB 26: CSMK 221), and second, the deliverances of the senses, which are often unreliable (cf. First Meditation, AT VII 18: CSM II 12). The clearing away of preconceived opinions is the first step in the Cartesian project for constructing a new edifice of reliable KNOWLEDGE.

Principles of Philosophy   This is the most comprehensive account of the Cartesian philosophical and scientific system, covering both the metaphysical foundations of the system (in Part I), the general principles of physics (Part II), and detailed accounts of a wide variety of terrestrial and celestial phenomena (in Parts III and IV). (For further details of the contents, see

Introduction, p. 8, above.) The *Principles* was first published in Latin in 1644, under the title *Principia Philosophiae*, and was dedicated to Princess Elizabeth of Bohemia. A French translation, made, with Descartes' approval, by the Abbé Picot, appeared in 1647 (*Les Principes de la Philosophie*); Descartes took the opportunity of the publication of the work in French to add a number of clarificatory points to the original text, and also provided an important introduction (also in French), which sets out his conception of philosophy as a unified system. It is here that we find the famous metaphor of philosophy as a tree, whose roots are metaphysics, the trunk physics, and the branches the other sciences 'which may be reduced to three principal ones, namely medicine, mechanics and morals' (AT IXB 14: CSM I 186).

Q

qualities, sensible 'If you find it strange that in explaining the elements I do not use the qualities called "heat", "cold", "moisture" and "dryness" – as the philosophers do – I shall say to you that these qualities themselves seem to me to need explanation. Indeed, unless I am mistaken, not only these four qualities but all the others as well, including even the forms of inanimate bodies, can be explained without the need to suppose anything in their matter other than the motion, size, shape and arrangement of its parts' (*Le Monde*, ch. 5, AT XI 25–6: CSM I 89). As may be seen from this passage, Descartes' programme for science aimed to dispense with qualitative notions, on the grounds that such notions were both obscure and explanatorily redundant; all the necessary work could be done by invoking only the precise, mathematically determinable properties of size, shape and motion. Although Descartes himself does not use the terms 'primary' and 'secondary' qualities, there are some respects in which his approach anticipates the views of Locke, according to which primary qualities (such as extension and motion) are really in objects, while secondary qualities (such as colour) are simply dispositions which objects have, in virtue of their primary qualities, to generate certain subjective sensations in our minds (cf. John Locke, *Essay on Human Understanding* [1689], Book II, ch. 8). Compare Descartes' *Principles*, Part IV, art. 198: 'the properties in external objects to which we apply the terms light, colour, smell, taste, sound, heat and cold – as well as the other tactile qualities . . . are, so far as we can see, simply various dispositions in the shapes, sizes, positions and movements of their parts which make them able to set up various kinds of motions in our nerves which are required to produce all the various sensations in our soul' (AT IXB 317: CSM I 285). The influence of Descartes' approach to sensible qualities may still be discerned today, in the debate over whether the 'qualitative' character of our experience can be accommodated within the objective or subject-neutral categories of physical science (cf. T. Nagel, *The View from Nowhere*).

For the relationship between the physiological and psychological elements in Descartes' account of sensible qualities, *see* COLOUR.

quantity Cartesian science is the science of quantity: 'I recognize no matter in corporeal things apart from what the geometers call quantity – i.e. that to which every kind of division, shape and motion is applicable' (*Principles*, Part II, art. 64; *see* GEOMETRY, MATHEMATICS, and LAWS OF NATURE). Descartes uses the term 'quantity' more or less interchangeably with 'extension' or 'extended substance', observing that 'the distinction between quantity and extended substance is purely a conceptual one, like that between number and the thing numbered' (*Principles*, Part II, art. 8; see also art. 9).

See also EXTENSION and SUBSTANCE.

R

rainbow Descartes wrote to Mersenne on 8 October 1629 that he had 'decided to write a little treatise on Meteorology, which will give the explanation of the colours of the rainbow – a topic which has given me more trouble than any other' (AT I 23: CSMK 6). The calculation and experimental confirmation of the angles of the bows of the rainbow appeared in Discourse Six of *Les Météores*, published in 1637. 'When I considered', Descartes writes, 'that the bow is capable of appearing not only in the sky, but also in the air near us, whenever there is a quantity of droplets of water illuminated by the sun, as we may observe in certain fountains, I was able to conclude without difficulty that the phenomenon arises merely from the way in which the rays of light act against the droplets, thus bending the light towards our eyes' (AT VI 325).

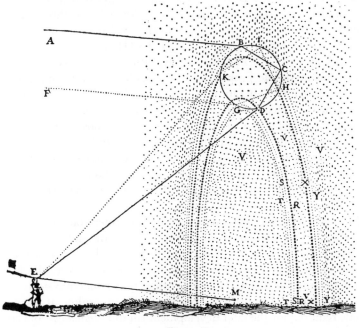

Figure 3

reality   For the distinction between 'formal' and 'objective' reality, *see* OBJECTIVE REALITY. Under Descartes' causal principle ('there must be at least as much reality in the cause as in the effect'; *see* CAUSE), whatever is represented 'objectively' in an idea must be present in its cause 'not merely objectively or representatively, but in actual reality, either formally or eminently' (*Principles*, Part I, art. 17); for this last distinction, *see* CAUSE, FORMAL VS. EMINENT.

refraction   *see* LIGHT

res cogitans* and *res extensa   These Latin phrases, meaning respectively 'thinking thing' and 'extended thing', are used by Descartes to refer to the mind and the body.
   See BODY; DUALISM and MIND AND BODY.

Rules for the Direction of our Native Intelligence   This work is often known as the *Regulae*, from its Latin title, *Regulae ad directionem ingenii*. It was Descartes' earliest major work, written in the mid to late 1620s, but never completed, and not published during the philosopher's lifetime. The manuscript was listed in the inventory of Descartes' papers made in Stockholm after his death, but the first published version of the Latin text did not come out until 1701 (though a Dutch translation had appeared in 1684).
   The plan of the *Regulae* was originally for there to be three parts, each containing twelve rules, but the whole of the final part is missing, and the second part is incomplete, ending at Rule XVIII (though the titles of rules XIX–XXI are given). The first twelve Rules are concerned with our apprehension of simple propositions, and with INTUITION and DEDUCTION, the two basic cognitive operations which yield reliable knowledge; the second dozen deal with 'perfectly understood problems' (i.e. those which are capable of an exact and definitive solution, being 'for the most part abstract and arising almost exclusively in arithmetic and geometry' – AT X 429: CSM I 51); the final dozen were to have dealt with 'imperfectly understood problems', where the aim may have been to show how the more complex problems of natural science could be subsumed under a mathematical model of problem-solving (*see* MATHEMATICS).
   The *Regulae*, despite its early date, and its unfinished state, is an extremely valuable source for Descartes' views on KNOWLEDGE and METHOD; it lays down, with remarkable clarity, what were to become the central planks of the Cartesian programme for philosophy and science. Moreover, although it is generally regarded as a methodological rather than a metaphysical work, the account it provides of the SIMPLE NATURES yields, in outline at least, all the materials required for the later development (in the *Meditations*) of Cartesian metaphysics.

S

sceptics Although Descartes was sometimes accused of being a sceptic, he emphatically distinguished his method of doubt in the First Meditation from the procedures of sceptical philosophers: 'When renouncing all my beliefs, I was careful to make an exception of all matters concerning faith and morals in general. Further, the [proposed] renunciation of beliefs applies only to those who have not yet perceived anything clearly and distinctly. The sceptics, for whom such renunciation is commonplace, have never, *qua* sceptics, perceived anything clearly; for the very fact that they had perceived something clearly would mean that they had ceased to be sceptics' (Seventh Replies, AT VII 476–7: CSM II 321). Descartes goes on to explain that his own systematic method of doubt should be understood as analogous to someone tipping out a basket of apples, 'in order to pick up and put back in the basket only those he saw to be sound' (AT VII 481: CSM II 324).

For more on Descartes and scepticism, *see* DOUBT.

scholastic philosophy In many respects, Descartes defined his philosophical outlook by contrasting it with the 'scholastic' philosophy which still dominated the schools and universities of the early and middle seventeenth century. Descartes refers to the prevailing system sometimes as the philosophy of 'the schools' (AT VI 62: CSM I 142), sometimes as the 'traditional philosophy' (AT VII 579: CSM II 390), and sometimes as 'peripatetic philosophy' (AT VII 580: CSM II 391). This last term is a synonym of 'Aristotelianism', being the label applied in classical antiquity to the followers of Aristotle; in the form in which it dominated the intellectual world of the Middle Ages, scholasticism was in fact a complex fusion of, on the one hand, the philosophical doctrines of Aristotle and, on the other hand, the demands of Christian theology (Thomas Aquinas, in his great syntheses, the *Summa theologiae* and the *Summa contra Gentiles*, being its most celebrated and comprehensive exponent).

Descartes had himself been educated in the scholastic tradition, and he asked Mersenne in September 1640, on the eve of the publication of his *Meditations*, to send him 'the names of the authors who have written textbooks in philosophy, specifying which are the most commonly used' (AT III 185:

CSMK 154); he later got hold of a copy of the *Summa philosophica quadripartita* of Eustachius a Sancto Paulo, a compendium of scholastic thought which he had studied in his youth, and which he planned to publish alongside his own *Principles of Philosophy*, to show how his own approach differed from that of the scholastics (AT III 233: CSMK 156–7). The plan was never put into effect, but the composition of the *Principles* (not a series of discursive reflections like the *Discourse* or *Meditations*, but a long string of short, expository articles) bears witness to Descartes' desire to provide a university course book which would replace the traditional scholastic texts.

Descartes' correspondence provides ample evidence of the hostility which his teachings aroused among the 'schoolmen' – particularly in the area of physics, where, he wrote to Huygens early in 1642, the scholastics were persecuting his ideas and trying to 'smother them at birth' (AT III 523: CSMK 210). Some of this hostility arose from the general apprehension felt in the seventeenth century that the teachings of the 'new' philosophers would subvert the authority of the Church (cf. COSMOLOGY, CREATION, FAITH). But there were also a number of important general ways in which Descartes' approach to philosophy-science diverged from that of his scholastic predecessors. First, he aimed to propound a unified scientific understanding of the universe, in contrast to the compartmentalized and piecemeal approach of the scholastics (cf. AT X 215: CSM I 3 and AT X 496–7: CSM II 400). Second, this science was to be based on mathematical principles, in contrast to the qualitative explanatory apparatus of his predecessors (*see* QUALITIES, SENSIBLE). Third, he wanted to develop a mechanistic model of explanation, avoiding wherever possible any reference to final causes and purposes; in this sense, Cartesian science was to stake its claim to a substantial degree of autonomy, in place of the traditional subordination of physics to theology (see *Principles*, Part I, art. 28 and Part III, art. 3, and cf. CAUSE, FINAL).

For discussion of particular areas where Descartes' views conflict with scholastic orthodoxy, *see* ANIMAL SPRITS; MATTER; IMAGES; for some points of contact, *see* CAUSE; ESSENCE; IDEA.

scientia   *see* KNOWLEDGE

Search for Truth   The full title is *The Search for Truth by means of the natural light* (*La Recherche de la Vérité par la lumière naturelle*). It is a dramatic dialogue, featuring three characters, Epistemon ('Knowledgeable'), a learned scholar well versed in traditional philosophy, Polyander ('Everyman'), the untutored person of ordinary good sense, and Eudoxus ('Famous' – but the Greek root also suggests someone of good judgement), who is the spokesman for Descartes' own views. The date of composition of the dialogue is very uncertain, but it covers the same themes as those presented in the *Meditations*,

and may possibly have been written during the early 1640s. The manuscript
of the work, which Descartes never completed, was found among his papers
in Stockholm after his death, but was subsequently lost; however, a Latin
translation of the work appeared in a collection of Descartes' posthumous
works (*Opuscula posthuma*) published in Amsterdam in 1701, and a manuscript copy of the first half of the original French text also survives.

The *Search for Truth* encapsulates Descartes' consistently held view that the
innate 'natural light' or 'light of reason', implanted within each of us, will
take us further on the road to knowledge than all the inherited wisdom of the
past (*see* INTUITION). The over-educated Epistemon, representing the typical
product of orthodox scholasticism, thus turns out to be far more resistant to
the Cartesian arguments than 'Polyander'; as Eudoxus says to Polyander at
the outset of the dialogue 'you are unprejudiced, and it will be far easier for
me to set you on the right track, since you are neutral, than to guide
Epistemon, who will often take up the opposite position' (AT X 502: CSM II
403; see AT X 521: CSM II 415). At the very start of the dialogue, indeed,
we have the resounding claim that 'the natural light alone, without any help
from religion or philosophy, determines what opinions a good man should
hold on any matter that may occupy his thought, and penetrates into the
secrets of the most recondite sciences' (AT X 495: CSM II 400). After a long
bout of preliminary sparring, the dialogue moves to the initial stages of the
Cartesian programme for metaphysics, whereupon Epistemon expresses
serious doubts about what has been achieved: 'after two hours of discussion,
I cannot see that we have made much progress, for all that Polyander has
learnt with the aid of this marvellous method you are making such a song
about is that he is doubting, he is thinking, and that he is a thinking thing.
Marvellous indeed! So many words for such a meagre result' (AT X 525:
CSM II 418). Eudoxus promises further progress, but at this point the
dialogue breaks off, unfinished.

sensation Descartes devotes a great deal of his attention to the analysis
and explanation of human sensory awareness, which involved both the
'external' faculties of sense-perception (such as vision and hearing) and also
'internal' sensations such as hunger and thirst. The Latin verb *sentire*, 'to
sense', or 'to feel' (corresponding to the French *sentir*) is generally his
preferred term for referring to such sensory awareness, which he contrasts
with 'perceiving' in the sense of having purely mental or intellectual awareness (Latin *percipere*; cf. PERCEPTION). When we are thirsty, to take one of
Descartes' examples, we do not merely have an intellectual *understanding* that
our body needs water; we experience a characteristic and intrusive sensation
of a distinctive kind – the mouth and the throat 'feel dry'. What kind of event
is this 'feeling'? According to the standard modern expositions of 'DUALISM',

to have a sensation like thirst is to be in a certain kind of *conscious* state; and hence, feeling thirsty is, for the dualist, assignable to the category of mind rather than body, since all consciousness belongs on the 'mental' side of the dualist's mind/body divide. But Descartes' own views about sensory experience are not quite as simple as this. Descartes does *not* say that sensations are mental events *simpliciter*; on the contrary, he explicitly says that 'I could clearly and distinctly understand the complete "me" without the faculty of sensation' (*sine [facultate sentiendi] totum me possum clare et distincte intelligere*; AT VII 78: CSM II 54; see AT VII 73: CSM II 51). Sensation, though it is an inescapable part of my daily experience, does not form an essential part of the *res cogitans* that is 'me'. Rather, Descartes explains, it is a 'confused' mode of awareness which 'arises from the union and as it were intermingling of the mind with the body' (Sixth Meditation, AT VII 81: CSM II 56). In the *Principles of Philosophy*, Descartes goes into rather more physiological detail: 'Sensory awareness comes about by means of nerves, which stretch like threads from the brain to all the limbs, and are joined together in such a way that hardly any part of the human body can be touched without producing movement in several of the nerve ends that are scattered around in that area. This movement is then transmitted to the other ends of the nerves which are all grouped together in the brain around the seat of the soul . . . . The result of these movements being set up in the nerves is that the soul or mind that is closely joined to the brain is affected in various ways, corresponding to the various different sorts of movements. And the various different states of mind or thoughts which are the immediate result of these movements are called sensory perceptions or in ordinary speech, sensations' (Part IV, art. 189).

See also HUMAN BEING; IMAGINATION; PINEAL GLAND.

simple natures   In the *Regulae*, Descartes advances what was to become a major theme of his philosophy – that there is a formal structure which all valid systems of knowledge manifest, and that this structure consists essentially in a hierarchical ordering: the objects of knowledge are to be arranged in such a way that we can concentrate to begin with on the items which are 'simplest and easiest to know', only afterwards proceeding to the more complex truths which are derived from these basic starting points. Thus at the end of Rule IV he observes: 'I have resolved in my search for knowledge of things to adhere unswervingly to a definite order, always starting from the simplest and easiest things and never going beyond them till there seems to be nothing further to be achieved where they are concerned' (AT X 379: CSM I 20; see Rule VI, which asserts that the 'main secret of the method' is to distinguish the simplest things from those that are complicated' (AT X 381: CSM I 21)). The human intellect, Descartes goes on to explain, has the power to 'intuit' these 'simple natures' or fundamental starting points for human knowledge: it simply 'sees' them with a simple and direct mental perception which allows for no possibility of error, since the simple natures are 'all self-evident and never contain any falsity' (Rule XII, AT X 420: CSM I 45; cf. INTUITION).

'We term "simple"', writes Descartes, 'only those things which we know so clearly and distinctly that they cannot be divided by the mind into others which are more distinctly known' (Rule XII, AT X 418: CSM I 44). Some of these simple natures are 'purely material'; these include shape extension and motion (and form the building blocks of Cartesian quantitative science). But others, Descartes asserts, are 'purely intellectual', and are 'recognized by the intellect by a sort of natural light, without the aid of any corporeal image'; it is the intellectual simple natures which enable us, for example, to recognize 'what knowledge or doubt or ignorance is' (ibid.). Finally, in addition to the material and intellectual simple natures, there are what Descartes calls the 'common' simple natures, which include the fundamental laws of logic (principles 'whose self-evidence is the basis for all the rational inferences we make', AT X 419: CSM I 45; in addition, the common simple natures include fundamental concepts like 'unity, existence and duration' which may be applied either to the material or to the intellectual simple natures). Using the basic rules of inference, we can make necessary connections and so link the simple natures together to build up a body of reliable conclusions. Descartes, though in the *Regulae* he goes into no details of how such reasonings are conducted, provides some striking examples which prefigure his later metaphysical inquiries: 'if Socrates says that he doubts everything, it necessarily follows that he understands at least that he is doubting'; or again, 'I understand, therefore I have a mind distinct from a body'; or again (most significant of all), '*sum, ergo Deus est*' – 'I am, therefore God exists' (AT X 421: CSM I 46).

What emerges from the *Regulae* is thus that the intellectual simple natures, together with the corporeal simple natures, comprise the two fundamental sets of building blocks for human knowledge (with the 'common' simple natures, or logical rules of inference, providing the cement which binds them together in the appropriate relations). 'The whole of human knowledge', Descartes declares in Rule XII, 'consists uniquely in our achieving a distinct perception of how all these simple natures contribute to the composition of other things' (AT X 427: CSM I 49). Although Descartes later abandoned the terminology of the simple natures, the programme for human knowledge which he lays out in the *Discourse, Meditations* and *Principles* none the less conforms, in many respects, to the conception outlined in the *Regulae*.

See also KNOWLEDGE.

soul, immortality of At no point in his life does Descartes seem to have entertained any serious doubts about the truth of the Christian doctrine of the immortality of the soul. For him, post-mortem survival meant the continued existence of the essential thinking self: 'this "I", that is to say the soul by which I am what I am, would not fail to be what it is even if the body did not exist' (AT VI 33: CSM I 127; when referring to the subject of consciousness, Descartes made no distinction between the terms 'mind' and 'soul': cf. Synopsis to *Meditations*, AT IXA 10; CSM II 10). In the dedicatory letter to the Theology Faculty of the Sorbonne, which was prefixed to the first edition of the *Meditations*, Descartes notes that the faithful are obliged to accept that 'the human soul does not die with the body' and suggests that a demonstration of this claim by 'natural reason' would serve the cause of religion and combat atheism (AT VII 2; CSM II 3). Over ten years earlier he had recorded his intention to combat those 'audacious and impudent persons who would fight against God', by establishing the 'existence of our souls when they are separate from the body'; this would be accomplished by demonstrating 'the independence of our souls from our bodies, from which their immortality follows' (letter to Mersenne of 25 November 1630, AT I 182: CSMK 29).

Descartes later admitted that he could not, in fact, provide a proof so strong as to eliminate the possibility, raised by Mersenne, that God might have endowed the soul with 'just so much strength and existence as to ensure that it came to an end with the body' (AT VII 128; CSM II 91). But he urged that we have 'no convincing evidence or precedent' to suggest that the annihilation of a substance like the mind can result from 'such a trivial cause' as bodily death, which is simply a matter of a 'division or change of shape' in the parts of the body (AT VII 153; CSM II 109). The point is expounded at length in the Synopsis to the *Meditations*: 'the human body, in so far as it differs from other bodies, is simply made of a certain configuration of limbs and other accidents of this sort; whereas the human mind is not made up of any accidents in this way, but is a pure substance. For even if all the accidents of the mind change, so that it has different objects of the understanding and different desires and sensations, it does not on that account become a different mind; whereas the human body loses its identity merely as a result of a change in the shape of some of its parts. And it follows from this that while the human body can very easily perish, the human mind is immortal by its very nature' (AT VII 14; CSM 1 10; cf. *Passions of the Soul*, arts 5 and 6).

This argument for immortality still needs the premise that a substance, once created by God, is 'by its nature incorruptible and cannot ever cease to exist unless reduced to nothingness by God's denying his concurrence to it' (Synopsis, loc. cit.). But whether a substance, once created, will continue to exist depends ultimately, Descartes reminds us, on the efficacious will of God, and we cannot know for certain what he has planned for the soul after death: 'I do not take upon myself to try to use the power of human reason to settle any of these matters which depend on the free will of God' (AT VII 153: CSM II 109). This caveat – together with his reluctance to encroach on the territory of THEOLOGY – may explain why Descartes was sometimes reluctant to assert he could prove the soul's immortality. The claim in the subtitle of the first (1641) edition of *Meditations* – *'in qua . . . animae immortalitas demonstratur'* ('in which . . . the immortality of the soul is demonstrated') – was dropped in the second edition of 1642 (cf. letter to Mersenne of 24 December 1640: AT III 266: CSMK 163). Compare also the distinctly resigned tone in the letter to Elizabeth of 3 November 1645: 'I confess that by natural reason alone we can make many favourable conjectures and have fine hopes, but we cannot have any certainty' (AT IV 333: CSMK 227).

space Since Descartes defines matter simply in terms of extension in length, breadth and depth, it follows that the distinction between a body and the space which it occupies is, for him, only a conceptual, not a real one: 'there is no real distinction between space . . . and the corporeal substance contained in it; the only difference lies in the way in which we are accustomed to conceive them' (*Principles*, Part II, art. 10). This proposition at first seems strongly counterintuitive: we can surely imagine a given body, such as a stone, being removed from a particular area so as to leave a space where the stone was (cf. art. 12). Descartes insists, however, that there can be so such thing as a truly 'empty' space: 'there is no difference between the extension of a space and the extension of a body. For a body's being extended in length, breadth and depth in itself warrants the conclusion that it is a substance, since it is a complete contradiction that a particular extension should belong to nothing, and the same conclusion must be drawn with respect to a space that is supposed to be a vacuum, namely that since there is extension in it, there must necessarily be substance in it as well' (art. 16). The idea of 'empty' space arises, in Descartes' view, from a prejudice derived from the senses; thus we call a jug 'empty' when all the water has been removed, and we do not detect anything else inside it, whereas in fact it is full of air (and the same applies, *mutatis mutandis*, in all other cases; arts 17 and 18).

Descartes' conception of space raises two principal problems. The first is that, in identifying it merely with 'extension in length, breadth and depth', he seems to be invoking the notion of mere 'dimensionality'; yet this pure geometrical concept seems to suggest something far more abstract than what is normally understood by real 'matter' or 'corporeal substance' (*see* EXTENSION). The second problem is that the denial of the possibility of empty space 'in the philosophical sense of a vacuum, i.e. that in which there is no substance whatsoever' (art. 16) seems strangely arbitrary and aprioristic; that is, it may follow from the way Descartes has defined his terms, but this does not seem enough to rule out the actual, empirical possibility that every bit of material stuff might be removed from a container, thus leaving nothing inside. Several of Descartes' correspondents challenged him on his views on this question: once the obscure Aristotelian thesis that 'nature abhors a vacuum' was abandoned (and Descartes makes it clear that he has no truck with this ancient notion, AT II 465: CSMK 131), then what is to stop us envisaging actual, or hypothetical cases where all the substance is removed from a given container? Descartes replied by simply repeating his definitional argument: 'If you wish to conceive that God removes all the air in a room without putting any other body in its place, you will have to conceive accordingly that the walls of the room touch each other; otherwise your thought will imply a contradiction' (letter to Mersenne of 9 January 1639, AT II 482: CSMK 132; cf. letter to More of 5 February 1649, AT V 272: CSMK 363).

substance A substance was defined by Aristotle as 'that which is neither said of a subject nor in a subject, e.g. an individual man or horse' (*Categories* 2a12). The contrast here is between *things* which exist independently (such as the individual horse) and *properties* or attributes (such as being fleet-footed) which can only be predicated of, or belong to, a subject. Taking up this notion of independent existence, Descartes makes the point that only God can be said to be utterly independent of 'any other thing whatsoever', and so only God qualifies as a substance in the strict sense (*Principles*, Part I, art. 51). Other things, however, are allowed by Descartes to qualify as substances in the secondary sense that they are independent of everything apart from God, or, as he puts it, they require only the CONCURRENCE of God in order to exist (art. 52).

Advancing his celebrated dualistic theory of substance (*see* DUALISM), Descartes lays it down that 'to each substance there belongs one principal attribute; in the case of mind, this is thought, and in the case of body it is extension' (*Principles*, Part I, art. 53); all the other features that can be predicated of minds and bodies are reducible to MODES of one or other of these attributes. Thus 'we can easily have two clear and distinct notions or ideas, one of created thinking substance, and the other of corporeal substance' (art. 54; to this list is added the 'clear and distinct idea of uncreated and independent thinking substance, that is of God'). The terminology of substances seemed problematical to some later philosophers; thus John Locke wrote that 'We have no clear idea at all, and therefore signify nothing by the word *Substance*, but only an uncertain supposition of we know not what *Idea*, which we take to be the *substratum* or support of those *Ideas* we do know' (*Essay concerning Human Understanding* [1689], I. iv. 18). But Descartes makes it quite clear that the term 'substance' does not refer to a mysterious 'substrate' hovering beneath the attributes of mind and body. The distinction between substance and attributes, he writes in *Principles*, Part I, art. 63, is a purely conceptual one: 'thought and extension can be regarded as constituting the natures of intelligent substance and corporeal substance, and then they must be considered as nothing else but thinking substance itself and extended substance itself. . . . We have some difficulty in abstracting the notion of substance from the notions of thought and extension, since the distinction between these notions and the notion of substance itself is merely a conceptual distinction' (*see* DISTINCTION).

It is interesting to note that the concept of substance does not have a great deal of work to do in Cartesian physics. The material universe, it is true, is described in terms of the classification *res extensa*, or extended substance, but the operation of the laws of nature is unfolded purely by reference to mathematical covering laws, describing the results of the interactions of moving particles of different sizes and shapes. Descartes' approach may thus be said to prefigure the modern conception of mathematically based science, in which the traditional terminology of substance and attribute is almost redundant. In Descartes' metaphysics, by contrast, the traditional apparatus plays a far more important role (*see* especially TRADEMARK ARGUMENT).

'subtle' matter   Descartes sometimes (e.g. at AT XI 255: CSM I 322) uses this term to refer to the matter which makes up the first of his three elements. It is distinguished, however, not by any special QUALITIES of the kind familiar from SCHOLASTIC PHILOSOPHY, but merely by the fact that the particles of which it is composed are extremely small and fast-moving. Cf. *Principles*, Part III, art. 52.

See also MATTER.

syllogism   The theory of the syllogism, as set out by Aristotle, was widely accepted in the seventeenth century as the basis for all valid reasoning. (The syllogism is a self-evidently valid pattern of argument, where a conclusion is derived from premises which logically entail it; thus, in the standard example, the conclusion 'Socrates is mortal' is derived from the major premise 'All men are mortal', conjoined with the minor premise 'Socrates is a man'.) Criticizing the traditional reliance on the syllogism Descartes observed in the *Discourse* that 'syllogisms are of less use for learning things than for explaining what one already knows, or for speaking without judgement of matters of which one is ignorant' (AT VI 17: CSM I 119). Elsewhere, however, Descartes explained that he had no wish to cast doubt on the validity of syllogistic reasoning as such, but, on the contrary, was perfectly prepared to use syllogisms himself when appropriate (AT VII 522: CSM II 355). He later remarked to Burman that the syllogism did indeed provide valid demonstrative proofs (AT V 175: CSMK 350) but that the methods needed for metaphysical discovery were very different from those needed for the exposition of what followed from already established results (AT V 153: CSMK 337–8; *see* ANALYSIS, METHOD OF).

For Descartes' discussion of whether his famous Cogito argument is syllogistic, *see* COGITO ERGO SUM.

T

theology The potential conflict between philosophy-science and theology often surfaces in Descartes' writings. In the final section of the *Discourse*, referring to the condemnation of Galileo for defending the heliocentric hypothesis, Descartes notes somewhat ruefully: 'I will not say that I accepted Galileo's theory, but only that before the condemnation I had noticed nothing in it that I could imagine to be prejudicial either to religion or to the state' (AT VI 60: CSM I 142). The strategy which he adopted for the rest of his life was to make a firm distinction between reason and faith; while vigorously defending those of his views that fell within the scope of natural philosophy, he firmly, and repeatedly, declined to take a stand on doctrinal topics such as the doctrine of creation in Genesis and the nature of man before the fall (see *Conversation with Burman*, AT V, 168, 178: CSMK 349, 353). Such questions were, Descartes in effect conceded, to be settled only by direct scriptural revelation. Questions about the existence of God, by contrast, or the nature of the human soul, were 'prime examples of subjects where demonstrative proofs ought to be sought with the aid of philosophy rather than theology' (Dedicatory Letter to the Sorbonne, AT VII 1: CSM II 3).

In the *Discourse*, Descartes writes that as a young man he 'revered our theology as much as anyone' but that he also had been taught that 'the way to heaven is open no less to the most ignorant than to the most learned' (AT VI 8: CSM I 144). That theology was not necessary for salvation reinforced Descartes' determination not to get embroiled in the heated theological debates which were such a prominent feature of the time in which he lived: 'it is more satisfactory to have a theology as simple as that of the country folk than one which is plagued with countless controversies, and thus corrupted, opening the way for disputes, quarrels and wars' (AT V 176: CSMK 351). In promoting his own philosophy, however, Descartes found it very difficult to avoid such controversies.

See FAITH.

thought Thought (Latin *cogitatio*, French *la pensée*) is the defining attribute of a mind or 'thinking substance'. Sometimes Descartes seems to use 'thought' in a narrowly intellectualistic sense, as when he defines 'thinking thing' as 'mind, intelligence, intellect or reason' (AT VII 27: CSM II 18); thus, the validity of the COGITO ERGO SUM argument may rest on the fact that to doubt that I am thinking is self-refuting, since doubt is an instance of thinking. But there is also ample evidence that Descartes used 'thought' in a much wider way to cover a whole range of mental activities: 'What is a thing that thinks? A thing that doubts, understands, affirms, denies, is willing, is unwilling, and also which imagines and has sensory perceptions' (AT VII 28: CSM II 19). This list includes not only intellectual activities (doubting, understanding), but also volitional activities ('is willing, is unwilling'; affirming and denying also involve the will, for Descartes – see JUDGEMENT). Descartes in fact distinguishes two principal modes of thought – an active mode (volition or willing) and a passive mode (intellection or understanding) (see PASSIONS). Finally, IMAGINATION and SENSATION are also classified as modes of thought, albeit of a special kind, since they involve the occurrence of physical as well as mental activity (see HUMAN BEING).

time   Just as Descartes regards matter as indefinitely divisible with respect to its extension (see DIVISIBILITY), so he regards time as indefinitely divisible with respect to its duration. In the Third Meditation, he also puts it forward as self-evident that all of the divisions of time are independent: 'a lifespan can be divided into countless parts, each completely independent of the others, so that it does not follow from the fact that I existed a little while ago that I must exist now, unless there were some cause which as it were creates me afresh at this moment, that is, which preserves me' (AT VII 49: CSM II 35). Gassendi criticized the principle of the independence of the moments of time as far from self-evident (Fifth Replies, AT VII 301: CSM II 209), but Descartes insists that 'if we consider the time or duration of the thing that endures, the individual moments can be separated from those immediately preceding them and succeeding them, which implies that the thing that endures may cease to be at any given moment' (AT VII 370: CSM II 255).

   See also CONCURRENCE; CONSERVATION.

'trademark' argument   This is the nickname now commonly given to Descartes' argument (developed most fully in the Third Meditation) that God's existence must be inferred to explain the presence, within the mind of the meditator, of the idea of God. The meditator reasons that the content of each idea found within him must have a cause; for nothing can come from nothing, yet 'if we suppose that an idea contains something which was not in its cause, it must have got this from nothing' (AT VII 41: CSM II 29). In most cases, the content of an idea presents no great explanatory problem: the content of many of my ideas, observes Descartes, could easily have been drawn from my own nature; other ideas (like those of unicorns) are simply fictitious, or made up – put together by my own imagination. But the idea that gives me my understanding of 'a supreme God, eternal, infinite, immutable, omniscient, omnipotent and the creator of all things' is different: 'all these attributes are such that the more carefully I concentrate on them, the less possible it seems that they could have originated from me alone.' So the idea of God must have, as its cause, a real being who truly possesses the attributes in question. In creating me, God must have 'placed this idea within me to be, as it were, the *mark of the craftsman stamped on the work*' (AT VII 40, 45, 51: CSM II 28, 31, 35; emphasis supplied).

Both in its logic and its terminology, Descartes' argument is heavily indebted to the work of his scholastic predecessors – as he indicates almost apologetically when he first introduces the argument in Part IV of the *Discourse* ('here, by your leave, I shall freely make use of some scholastic terminology' (AT VI 34; CSM I 128)). The premise that I have an idea of a perfect being is taken by Descartes as clearly following from his recognition of his own imperfection: 'How could I understand that I doubted or desired, that is, lacked something, unless there were in me some idea of a more perfect being which enabled me to recognize my own defects by comparison' (AT VII 45–6: CSM II 31). Here Descartes closely follows a fairly standard line of thought, which may be found, for example, in St Bonaventure's *Itinerarium Mentis in Deum* (1259): 'How could the intellect know that it was a defective and incomplete being unless it had some knowledge of a being free from every defect?' (ch. III, section 3, cited in Gilson, *Descartes: Discours de la méthode, texte et commentaire*, p. 316). In essence this is a variation on an earlier Augustinian argument (itself ultimately derived from Plato): the ability to make comparative judgements (x is better than y) could not exist unless we had within us a notion of perfect goodness, or God. (Cf. Augustine, *De Trinitate*, Book VIII, ch. 3, section 4, cited in Gilson, loc. cit. For the origins of the argument in Plato, where essentially the same reasoning is used to establish the existence of the form of the good, cf. *Phaedo* 74aff.)

In arguing that the idea of a perfect being must have been placed in his mind by an actually existing perfect being – God – Descartes relies on two principles well established in the philosophical theology of the Middle Ages and Renaissance. First, he presupposes what might be called the principle of the 'non-inferiority of the cause', i.e. the principle that the more perfect cannot be caused by the less perfect: 'I recognized very clearly that the ability to think of something more perfect than myself had to come from a nature that was in fact more perfect' (*Discourse*, Part IV, AT VI 34: CSM I 128). Descartes sometimes implies that this is just a variant on the simple and universally accepted axiom 'nothing comes from nothing': it is 'no less contradictory that the more perfect should result from the less perfect ...

than that something should proceed from nothing' (ibid.). But what Descartes in fact requires goes far beyond the 'common notion' that everything must have a cause. As Marin Mersenne later objected, we may readily accept that 'flies and other animals' must have *some* cause, without being forced to admit that this cause must be *more perfect* than them (AT VII 123: CSM II 88; for more on the principle of non-inferiority, *see* CAUSE). Second, Descartes' proof requires the even more problematic principle that the causal constraints operating in the real world are to be 'transferred' or carried over, so as to apply to the realm of our thought-contents. This principle of transfer mystified even those of Descartes' contemporaries who were thoroughly versed in the scholastic tradition. See the comments of the Thomist critics who wrote the First Objections: 'a cause imparts some real and actual influence; but what does not actually exist [an idea] cannot take on anything and so does not receive or require any actual causal influence' (AT VII 93: CSM II 67). Descartes insists, however, that the representational content of an idea is just as much in need of causal explanation as any other aspect of reality; for the background to this, *see* OBJECTIVE REALITY.

It should be noted, finally, that there are two distinct phases in Descartes' presentation of the 'trademark argument': in the first, Descartes reasons (as explained above) that our idea of God can only be accounted for by positing God as its cause (AT VII 41–7: CSM II 30–2); in the second, he says he 'would like to go further and inquire whether I myself, who have this idea, could exist if no such [perfect] being existed' (AT VII 48: CSM II 33). The second phase concludes: 'the mere fact that I exist and have within me an idea of a most perfect being, that is, God, provides a very clear proof that God exists' (AT VII 51: CSM II 35). Although the second phase of the argument presents certain interesting features of its own (cf. TIME), it seems to have been regarded by Descartes merely as an expository variation on the first (cf. First Replies, AT VII 105: CSM II 77). Both versions, at all events, hinge on the (supposed) need to explain how my (finite and imperfect) mind can have within it the idea of an infinite and perfect being.

See also GOD; INFINITE.

transubstantiation   *see* FAITH, RELIGIOUS

Treatise on Man   Published in 1664 under the title *L'Homme de René Descartes* (a Latin translation of the original French had appeared two years earlier), the so-called *Treatise on Man* in fact forms, together with *Le Monde* (*The World*), a single work. (*See* WORLD for date of composition and other details.) Although primarily devoted to the physiology of the human body, the *Treatise on Man* is also a valuable source for Descartes' views on the relationship between mind and body, and the nature of sensory experience.

See also ANIMAL SPIRITS; AUTOMATON; COLOUR; 'COMMON' SENSE; IMAGES; MEMORY and PINEAL GLAND.

Treatise on Mechanics   On 5 October 1637, Descartes sent to his friend Constantijn Huygens an 'account of the machines by which a small force can be used to lift heavy weights'. The 'account' was published after Descartes' death under the title *Traité de Mécanique* (1668). The short work provides a detailed account of a number of devices, including the pulley, the inclined plane, the wedge, the cog wheel, the screw and the lever (AT I 435ff: CSMK 66ff). The approach throughout is a quantitative one, and, typically of his general approach to science, Descartes always seeks, as far as possible, to apply rigorous arithmetical and geometrical techniques to the solution of the problems of mechanics.

U and V

union of mind and body   *see* HUMAN BEING

vacuum   *see* SPACE; ATOMS

virtue   *see* MORALITY; GENEROSITY

volition   *see* FREE WILL; JUDGEMENT; PASSIONS; THOUGHT

vortex   The solar system is, for Descartes, a plenum, with all the matter revolving about the sun. 'The celestial matter in which the planets are located turns continuously like a vortex with the sun at its centre.' Descartes was attracted to this account because it posited a simple, non-mysterious explanation for planetary motion, invoking the same kind of phenomenon as that to be observed when bits of flotsam are whirled about in the eddying 'vortices' of a river: 'we see the flotsam carried around with the whirlpool, and in some cases we see it also rotating about its own centre; further the bits which are nearer the centre of the whirlpool complete a revolution more quickly, and finally, though such flotsam always has a circular motion, it scarcely ever describes a perfect circle, but has some latitudinal and longitudinal deviations. We can without any difficulty imagine all this happening in the same way in the case of the planets' (*Principles*, Part III, art. 30).

See also ANALOGIES.

W

will   *see* ERROR; FREE WILL; JUDGEMENT

World, The   First published posthumously in Paris in 1664 under the title *Le Monde de M. Descartes ou le Traité de la Lumière* ('The World of Mr. Descartes, or the Treatise on Light'), *The World* was written by Descartes during the years 1629–33; on the eve of its planned publication, Descartes heard of the condemnation of Galileo by the Inquisition, and cautiously decided to withhold the work. He later wrote to Mersenne: 'All the things I explained in my treatise, which included the doctrine of the movement of the earth, were so interdependent that it is enough to discover that one of them is false to know that all the arguments I was using are unsound. Though I knew that they were based on very certain and evident proofs, I would not wish for anything in the world to maintain them against the authority of the Church … I desire to live in peace' (AT I 285: CSMK 42).

The World (which is, in fact, the first part of what was originally a continuous work, of which what is now known as the TREATISE ON MAN formed the concluding section) presents a general account of Descartes' principles of physics and cosmology, and then goes on to apply those principles to explain the formation of the sun, stars and planets, the earth and moon, and the nature of basic physical phenomena such as light and heat. After a (now lost) bridging section, the concluding portion (comprising the *Treatise on Man*) applies the same explanatory principles to human physiology. Although Descartes presents his account of the universe as 'a fable', unfolding the structure of an imaginary 'new world' (AT XI 31: CSM I 90), the reader is left in no doubt that the principles expounded are the ones which Descartes takes to be operating in the real world.

For some of the important scientific and philosophical issues raised in the treatise, *see* COSMOLOGY; CREATION; FAITH; LAWS OF NATURE; QUALITIES.

Bibliography

NOTE TO THE READER

The literature on Descartes is enormous, and the list that follows is necessarily highly selective. Entries are listed alphabetically in each of the four sections. (I have refrained from further subdivision into areas such as 'philosophy of mind', 'metaphysics', 'philosophy of science', etc.; such a procedure would be more misleading than helpful in the case of Descartes, since his system forms a unified structure in which different philosophical concerns constantly overlap.) Brief comments are added in square brackets in the case of some of the more important or widely available works cited.

1 TEXTS AND EDITIONS: DESCARTES

AT: Adam, C. and Tannery, P. (eds.), *Œuvres de Descartes* (revised edn., 12 vols., Paris: Vrin/CNRS, 1964–76). [This is the definitive Franco-Latin edition, containing all of Descartes' works, together with a wealth of textual and historical annotation.]

Alquié, F. (ed.), *Descartes, Œuvres philosophiques*, (3 vols, Paris: Garnier, 1963). [An extremely useful paperback edition arranged chronologically, and containing some valuable introductory material and notes.]

CSM: Cottingham, J., Stoothoff, R. and Murdoch, D. (eds.), *The Philosophical Writings of Descartes* (2 vols, Cambridge: Cambridge University Press, 1985); **CSMK**: Volume III of the preceding, by the same translators and Anthony Kenny (Cambridge: Cambridge University Press, 1991). [This is the new standard English translation of Descartes. CSM vols I and II supersede the earlier Cambridge edition of *The Philosophical Works of Descartes* by E. S. Haldane and G. R. T. Ross (1911); CSMK incorporates Anthony Kenny's translation of Descartes' *Philosophical Letters* (Oxford, 1970).]

Cottingham, J. G. (ed.), *Descartes' Conversation with Burman* (Oxford: Clarendon, 1976). [English translation with detailed notes and introduction. Large extracts from the translation are now included in CSMK (see above).]

Gilson, E., *Descartes, Discours de la méthode, texte et commentaire* (Paris: Vrin, 1925; 4th edn., 1967). [Contains an extremely detailed philosophical commentary on the *Discourse*.]

Hall, T. S. (ed.), *Descartes, Treatise on Man* (Cambridge, MA: Harvard University Press, 1972).

Mahoney, M. S. (trans.), *Descartes, The World* (New York: Abaris, 1979).

Marion, J.-L. (ed.), *Règles utiles et claires pour la direction de l'esprit* (The Hague: Martinus Nijhoff, 1977).

Miller, V. R. and R. P. (eds.), *Descartes, Principles of Philosophy* (Dordrecht: Reidel, 1983).

Olscamp, P. J. (trans.), *Discourse on Method, Optics, Geometry and Meteorology* (Indianapolis: Bobbs-Merrill, 1965).

Voss, S. H. (ed.), *René Descartes, The Passions of the Soul* (Indianapolis: Hackett, 1989).

2   TEXTS AND EDITIONS: OTHER PRE-TWENTIETH-CENTURY
WRITERS

Augustine, *De Trinitate*, in *Patrologiae Cursus Completus Series Completa*, ed. J. P. Migne (Paris, 1844–55).

Aquinas, St Thomas, *Summa theologiae*. Latin text with English translation (61 vols., Cambridge: Blackfriars, 1964–81).

Aristotle, *De Anima (On the Soul)*, trans. W. Lawson-Tancred (Penguin: Harmondsworth, 1986).

Aristotle, *Categoriae et Liber de interpretatione*, ed. L. Minio-Paluello (Oxford: Oxford University Press, 1974); trans. J. L. Ackrill, *Aristotle's Categories and De Interpretatione* (Oxford: Clarendon, 1963).

Bacon, Francis, *The Works of Francis Bacon*, ed. J. Spedding and R. E. Ellis, abridged J. M. Robinson (London: Routledge, 1905).

Baillet, A., *La Vie de M. Des-Cartes* (Paris: Horthemels, 1961; photographic reprint, Hildesheim: Olms, 1972).

Eustachius a Sancto Paulo, *Summa philosophica quadripartita* (Paris, 1609).

Galileo Galilei, *Dialogue concerning the two chief world systems* [1632], trans. S. Drake (Berkeley and Los Angeles: University of California Press, 1967).

—— *Le Opere*, ed. A. Favaro (Florence: Barbera, 1889–1901, reprinted 1968).

Hume, David, *A Treatise of Human Nature* [1739–40], ed. L. A. Selby-Bigge, rev. P. H. Niddich (Oxford: Clarendon, 1978).

—— *Inquiry into the Human Understanding* [1748], ed. L. A. Selby-Bigge, rev. P. H. Nidditch (Oxford: Clarendon, 1975).

Ignatius of Loyola *Exercitia spiritualia* [1548], trans. W. H. Longridge (London: R. Scott, 1919).

Kant, Immanuel, *Critique of Pure Reason* [1781], trans. N. Kemp Smith (New York: Macmillan, 1965).

Leibniz, Gottfried Wilhelm, *Philosophical Papers and Letters*, trans. L. E. Loemker, 2nd edn. (Dordrecht: Reidel, 1969).

Locke, John, *An Essay concerning Human Understanding* [1689], ed. P. H. Nidditch (Oxford: Oxford University Press, 1975).

Malebranche, Nicolas, *Œuvres complètes de Malebranche*, ed. A. Robinet (20 vols, Paris: Vrin, 1958–67).

Newton, I., *Mathematical Principles of Natural Philosophy and his system of the World* [1687], trans. A. Motte 1729; revised F. Cajori (Cambridge: Cambridge University Press, 1934).

Ockham, William of, *Quodlibeta septem* (Paris, 1487; Strasbourg 1491).

Plato, *Republic*, trans. H. P. D. Lee (Harmondsworth: Penguin, 1955).

Plotinus, *Enneads*, ed. A. H. Armstrong (Loeb Classical Library, London: Heinemann, 1966–84).

Sanches, Francisco, *Quod nihil scitur* [Lyons, 1581]. Latin text established, annotated and translated by Douglas Thompson, with introduction and notes by Elaine Limbrick (Cambridge: Cambridge University Press, 1988).

Sextus Empiricus, *Outlines of Pyrrhonism* (Loeb Classical Library, London: Heinemann, 1933).

Spinoza, *Ethics*, in *Opera*, ed. C. Gebhardt (Heidelberg: Winters, 1925, repr. 1972), trans. in *The Collected Works of Spinoza*, ed. E. Curley (Princeton: Princeton University Press, 1985).

Suárez, Francisco, *Disputationes metaphysicae* (Salmanticae, 1597).

3   GENERAL BOOKS ON DESCARTES AND EDITED COLLECTIONS

Butler, R. J. (ed.), *Cartesian Studies* (Oxford: Blackwell, 1972).

Gibson, A. Boyce, *The Philosophy of Descartes* (London: Methuen, 1932).

Cottingham, J., *Descartes* (Oxford: Basil Blackwell, 1986). [This aims to be an accessible introduction to all the main areas of Descartes' philosophy.]

—— *The Rationalists* (Oxford: Oxford University Press, 1988). [Covers Spinoza and Leibniz as well as Descartes.]

—— (ed.), *The Cambridge Companion to Descartes* (New York: Cambridge University Press, 1992). [A collection of essays covering the full range of Descartes' work.]

Doney, W. (ed.), *Descartes: A Collection of Critical Essays* (New York: Doubleday, 1967). [Contains some valuable articles.]

Grene, M., *Descartes* (Minneapolis: University of Minneapolis Press, 1985).

Hooker, M. (ed.), *Descartes, Critical and Interpretative Essays* (Baltimore: Johns Hopkins University Press, 1978).

Keeling, S. V., *Descartes* (London: Benn, 1934).

Kenny, A., *Descartes: A Study of his Philosophy* (New York: Random House, 1968). [A lucid and elegant study of the main elements of Descartes' thought.]

Lennon, T. M., Nicholas, J. M. and Davis, J. W. (eds.), *Problems of Cartesianism* (Kingston and Montreal: McGill/Queens University Press, 1982).

Moyal, J. D. (ed.), *René Descartes, Critical Assessments* (4 vols., London and New York: Routledge, 1991). [A large collection of some of the best work on Descartes in recent decades.]

Rodis-Lewis, G., *Descartes* (Paris: Libraire Générale Française, 1984).

Smith, N. Kemp, *New Studies in the Philosophy of Descartes* (London: Macmillan, 1966).

Sorell, T., *Descartes* (Oxford: Oxford University Press, 1987). [Brief general introduction in the Oxford Pastmaster series.]

Williams, B., *Descartes* (Harmondsworth: Penguin, 1978). [A subtle and stimulating study, which often relates Descartes' ideas to more recent philosophical concerns.]

Wilson, M. D., *Descartes* (London: Routledge, 1978). [Meticulous critical analysis of Descartes' principal arguments.]

4   MORE SPECIALIZED STUDIES AND OTHER WORKS

Alexander, P., *Ideas, Qualities and Corpuscles* (Cambridge: Cambridge University Press, 1985).

Alquié, F., *La Découverte métaphysique de l'homme chez Descartes* (Paris: Presses Universitaires de France, 1950; 2nd edn, 1987).

Balz, A., *Cartesian Studies* (New York: Columbia University Press, 1951).

Beck, L. J., *The Metaphysics of Descartes: A Study of the Meditations* (Oxford: Clarendon, 1965).

—— *The Method of Descartes: A Study of the Regulae* (Oxford: Clarendon, 1952).

Beyssade, J.-M., *La Philosophie première de Descartes* (Paris: Flammarion, 1979). [A lucid and rewarding study of Descartes' metaphysics.]

Chomsky, N., *Language and Mind* (New York: Harcourt, Brace and World, 1986).

Clarke, D., *Descartes' Philosophy of Science* (Manchester: Manchester University Press, 1982). [A valuable account of Descartes' conception of science.]

Curley, E., *Descartes against the Skeptics* (Oxford: Blackwell, 1978).

Dennett, D., *Consciousness Explained* (Harmondsworth: Allen Lane, 1992). [Attacks the legacy of Descartes in the philosophy of mind.]

Frankfurt, H. G., *Demons, Dreamers and Madmen* (Indianapolis: Bobbs-Merrill, 1970). [A stimulating account of some of the problems in the *Meditations*.]

Garber, D., *Descartes' Metaphysical Physics* (Chicago: University of Chicago Press, 1992). [Authoritative study of Cartesian science.]

Gaukroger, S., *Cartesian Logic* (Oxford: Clarendon, 1989). [Throws light on important aspects of Descartes' metaphysics, as well as his logic.]

—— (ed.), *Descartes, Philosophy, Mathematics and Physics* (Sussex: Harvester, 1980).

Gueroult, M., *Descartes selon l'ordre des raisons* (Paris: Montaigne, 1953). English translation by R. Ariew, *Descartes' Philosophy interpreted according to the order of Reasons* (Minneapolis: University of Minnesota Press, 1984). [A magisterial and enormously detailed account of the structure of Descartes' metaphysical arguments.]

Gilson, E., *Index Scolastico-Cartésien* (Paris: Alcan, 1913; 2nd edn., Paris: Vrin, 1979). [Invaluable sourcebook for medieval and scholastic influences on Descartes.]

Gouhier, H., *La Pensée réligieuse de Descartes* (Paris: Vrin, 1924).

Jolley, N., *The Light of the Soul: Theories of Ideas in Leibniz, Malebranche and Descartes* (Oxford: Oxford University Press, 1990).

Loeb, L. E., *From Descartes to Hume* (Ithaca, NY: Cornell University Press, 1981).

Marion, J.-L., *Sur la théologie blanche de Descartes* (Paris: Presses Universitaires de France, 1981). [A complex and original study of Cartesian metaphysics.]

Markie, P., *Descartes's Gambit* (Ithaca, NY: Cornell University Press, 1986). [A close study of Cartesian epistemology using the techniques of modern analytic philosophy.]

Nagel, T., *The View from Nowhere* (Oxford: Oxford University Press, 1986). [Highly influential recent book which sheds some light on the 'subjectivist' perspective that informs some of Descartes' philosophy.]

Nussbaum, M., *The Fragility of Goodness* (Cambridge: Cambridge University Press, 1986). [Important contribution to the recent revival of virtue theory in ethics; concerned with Classical writers, but throws indirect light on Cartesian ethics.]

Popkin, R., *The History of Scepticism from Erasmus to Descartes* (New York: Harper & Row, 1964). [Valuable sourcebook on the background to Cartesian epistemology.]

Rodis-Lewis, G., *L'Anthropologie Cartésienne* (Paris: Presses Universitaires de France, 1991).

Rorty, A. O. (ed.), *Essays on Descartes' Meditations* (Berkeley: University of California Press, 1986). [A useful collection of scholarly essays.]

Rosenfield, L. C., *From Beast-Machine to Man-Machine: The Theme of Animal Soul in French Letters from Descartes to La Mettrie* (New York: Oxford University Press, 1941).

Ryle, G., *The Concept of Mind* (London: Hutchinson, 1949). [Celebrated attack on the Cartesian view of the mind as 'ghost in the machine'.]

Sebba, G., *Bibliographica Cartesiana* (The Hague: Martinus Nijhoff, 1964). [A still useful reference work.]

Schmitt, C. B., *Aristotle and the Renaissance* (Cambridge, MA: Harvard University Press, 1983).

Schmitt, C. B., Skinner, Q. and Kessler, E., *Cambridge History of Renaissance Philosophy* (Cambridge: Cambridge Univeristy Press, 1988).

Scott, J. F., *The Scientific Work of René Descartes* (London: Taylor and Francis, 1952).

Watson, R. A., *The Breakdown of Cartesian Metaphysics* (Atlantic Highlands, NJ: Humanities Press International, 1987). [Examines the fate of the Cartesian system in the half-century following Descartes' death.]

Wittgenstein, Ludwig, *Philosophical Investigations*, trans. G. E. M. Anscombe (New York: Macmillan, 1952). [Contains implicit criticism of many of the presuppositions behind the Cartesian account of the mind.]

Index

Note to reader

Where words or phrases are printed in SMALL CAPITALS, this indicates that a corresponding entry will be found in the main body of the Dictionary.